The Last Train to Zona Verde

Paul Theroux's books include *Dark Star Safari*, *Ghost Train to the Eastern Star*, *Riding the Iron Rooster*, *The Great Railway Bazaar*, *The Elephanta Suite*, *A Dead Hand*, *The Tao of Travel* and *The Lower River*. *The Mosquito Coast* and *Dr Slaughter* have both been made into successful films. Paul Theroux divides his time between Cape Cod and the Hawaiian islands.

Books by Paul Theroux

FICTION

Waldo

Fong and the Indians

Girls at Play

Murder in Mount Holly

Jungle Lovers

Sinning with Annie

Saint Jack

The Black House

The Family Arsenal

The Consul's File

A Christmas Card

Picture Palace

London Snow

World's End

The Mosquito Coast

The London Embassy

Half Moon Street

O-Zone

My Secret History

Chicago Loop

Millroy the Magician

My Other Life

Kowloon Tong

Hotel Honolulu

The Stranger at the Palazzo d'Oro

Blinding Light

The Elephanta Suite

A Dead Hand

The Lower River

CRITICISM

V. S. Naipaul

NONFICTION

The Great Railway Bazaar

The Old Patagonian Express

The Kingdom by the Sea

Sailing Through China

Sunrise with Seamonsters

The Imperial Way

Riding the Iron Rooster

To the Ends of the Earth

The Happy Isles of Oceania

The Pillars of Hercules

Sir Vidia's Shadow

Fresh Air Fiend

Dark Star Safari

Ghost Train to the Eastern Star

The Tao of Travel

The Last Train to Zona Verde

The Last Train to Zona Verde

Overland from Cape Town to Angola

PAUL THEROUX

HAMISH HAMILTON
an imprint of
PENGUIN BOOKS

HAMISH HAMILTON

Published by the Penguin Group
Penguin Books Ltd, 80 Strand, London WC2R 0RL, England
Penguin Group (USA) Inc., 375 Hudson Street, New York, New York 10014, USA
Penguin Group (Canada), 90 Eglinton Avenue East, Suite 700, Toronto, Ontario, Canada M4P 2Y3
(a division of Pearson Penguin Canada Inc.)
Penguin Ireland, 25 St Stephen's Green, Dublin 2, Ireland (a division of Penguin Books Ltd)
Penguin Group (Australia), 707 Collins Street, Melbourne, Victoria 3008, Australia
(a division of Pearson Australia Group Pty Ltd)
Penguin Books India Pvt Ltd, 11 Community Centre, Panchsheel Park, New Delhi – 110 017, India
Penguin Group (NZ), 67 Apollo Drive, Rosedale, Auckland 0632, New Zealand
(a division of Pearson New Zealand Ltd)
Penguin Books (South Africa) (Pty) Ltd, Block D, Rosebank Office Park,
181 Jan Smuts Avenue, Parktown North, Gauteng 2193, South Africa

Penguin Books Ltd, Registered Offices: 80 Strand, London WC2R 0RL, England

www.penguin.com

First published in the United States of America by Houghton Mifflin Harcourt 2013
First published in Great Britain by Hamish Hamilton 2013
001

Copyright © Paul Theroux, 2013

The moral right of the author has been asserted

Maps by Jacques Chazaud

Printed in Great Britain by Clays Ltd, St Ives plc

A CIP catalogue record for this book is available from the British Library

HARDBACK ISBN: 978–0–241–14367–4
TRADE PAPERBACK ISBN: 978–0–241–14597–5

www.greenpenguin.co.uk

MIX
Paper from
responsible sources
FSC
www.fsc.org   FSC® C018179

Penguin Books is committed to a sustainable
future for our business, our readers and our planet.
This book is made from Forest Stewardship
Council™ certified paper.

ALWAYS LEARNING   **PEARSON**

To Albert and Freddy,
Sylvie and Enzo,
with love from Grandpa

When my father used to travel, he didn't fear the night. But had he all his toes?

— *Bakongo (Angola) proverb*

God almighty said to Moses, peace be upon him: Take an iron staff and wear iron sandals, and then tour the earth until the staff is broken and the shoes are worn out.

— *Muhammad bin al-Sarraj,* Uns al-Sari wa-al sarib (A Companion to Day and Night Travelers), *1630, translated by Nabil Matar*

Contents

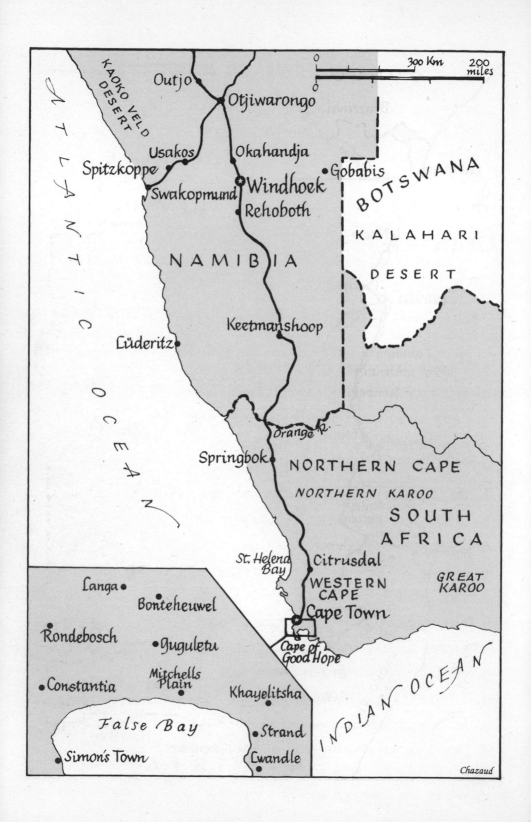

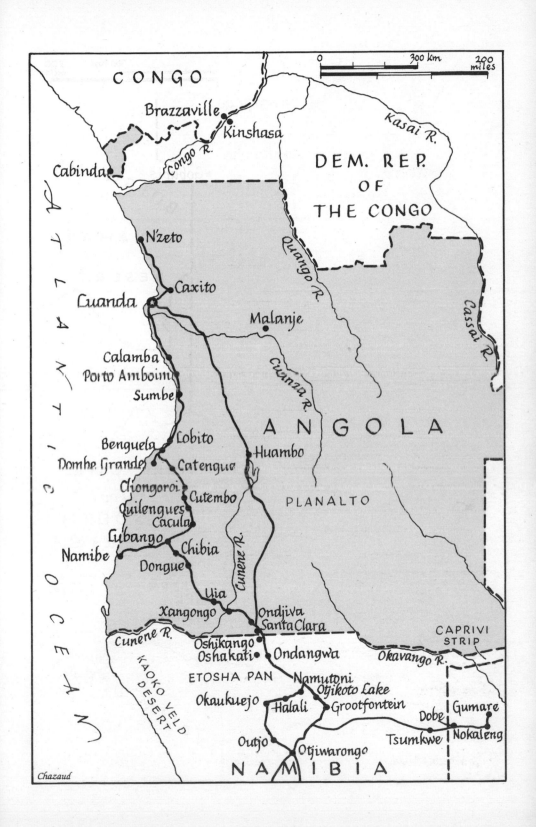

1

―― ―― ―― ――

Among the Unreal People

I N T H E H O T F L A T B U S H in far northeast Namibia I crossed a
bulging termite mound of smooth, ant-chewed sand, and with
just the slightest elevation of this swelling under my foot soles
the landscape opened in a majestic fan, like the fluttered pages of a
whole unread book.

I then resumed kicking behind a file of small-bodied, mostly naked men and women who were quick-stepping under a sky fretted
with golden fire through the dry scrub of what was once coarsely
known in Afrikaans as Boesmanland (Bushman Land) — pouch-
breasted women laughing among themselves, an infant with a head
like a fuzzy fruit bobbing in one woman's sling, men in leather
clouts clutching spears and bows, nine of us altogether — and I was
thinking, as I'd thought for years traveling the earth among human-
kind: The best of them are bare-assed.

Happy again, back in Africa, the kingdom of light, I was stamping out a new path, on foot in this ancient landscape, delighting in
"a palpable imaginable visitable past — in the nearer distances and

clearer mysteries." I was ducking among thornbushes with slender, golden-skinned people who were the earth's oldest folk, boasting a traceable lineage to the dark backward and abysm of time in the Upper Pleistocene, thirty-five thousand years or so ago, the proven ancestors of us all, the true aristocrats of the planet.

The snort of a startled animal out of sight stopped us. Then its hindquarters swishing through brush. Then the leaping clop of its hooves on loose stones.

"Kudu," one of the men whispered, bowing to listen to its departure without glancing aside, as though saying the familiar first name of someone he knew. He spoke again, and while I didn't understand, I listened as if to new music; his language was preposterous and euphonious.

That morning in Tsumkwe, the nearest town — but not a town, just a sun-scorched crossroads with many hovels and a few shade trees — I had heard on my shortwave radio: *World financial markets are in turmoil, facing the worst crisis since the Second World War. The Eurozone countries are approaching meltdown as Greece is expected to collapse into bankruptcy, its government having turned down a $45 billion loan to write down its debt.*

The people I was following were laughing. They were Khoisan-speaking, a subgroup of !Kung people who called themselves Ju/'hoansi — a clucking, hard-to-pronounce name meaning "Real People" or "Harmless People." Traditional hunter-gatherers, they had no history of using money. Even now, pushed to the margins of so-called Bushman Land (they knew this part of it as Nyae Nyae) — and irregularly settled, with some cattle and crops — these people seldom saw money and hardly used the decaying stuff. They still supplemented their diet by hunting and grubbing and foraging — and accepting pitiful handouts. They probably did not think about money, or if they did, they knew they would never have any. As the Greeks rioted, howling against their government, and Italians cried poverty in the streets of Rome, and the Portuguese and the Spanish stared hollow-eyed at bankruptcy, and the news was of failure, worthless currencies, and austerity measures, the Ju/'hoansi were indestructible in all their old ways, or seemed so to me in my ignorance.

The young woman in front of me dropped to her knees in the sand. She had the lovely, elfin, somewhat Asiatic face—but also suggesting the face of an extraterrestrial—that most San people possess. That is to say, pedomorphic, the innocent and fetching face of a child. She traced her fingers around a threadlike vine sprouting from the sand, crouched, leaned on one elbow, and began digging. With each scoop and handful of sand her eyes brightened, her breasts shook, and her nipples trembled against the earth, one of the minor titillations of this excursion. Within a minute she extracted a finger-shaped tuber from the dark, strangely moist hole she'd made and cradled it in her hand. As she flicked dust from the root, it paled beneath her fingertips. Smiling, she offered the first bite to me.

"*Nano,*" she said, and the word was translated as "potato."

It had the crunch, the mouthfeel, the sweetish earthen taste of raw carrot. I passed it back and it was shared equally, a nibble each, nine bites. In the forests, deserts, and hillsides across the world, foraging people like the Ju/'hoansi are scrupulous about sharing food; it is this sharing in their communal life that binds them together.

Ahead of us, kneeling on scattered nut shells and the leaf litter of a thornbush, two of the men, facing each other on the ground, were taking turns spinning a two-foot-long stick between their palms— chafing this spindle which, very shortly, raised a puff of smoke from the friction of its bottom end in a darkening piece of soft wood. The stick they call male; the dimpled wood block on the bottom, female. Sparks glowed from the hot drilled block, and one of the men coaxed more sparks, lifting the glowing, gently smoking wood, blowing on it with lips framed in a kissing expression. He scattered shells and dead leaves on it, then a handful of twigs. We had fire.

Strikes in Greece have cut off power in many cities, and the government is expected to default on its debt, plunging Europe into deepening uncertainty, putting the fate of the euro in doubt. The ripple effect could endanger the viability of American banks. Rock-throwing mobs protesting mounting austerity measures have begun looting shops in Athens . . .

It was like news from another planet, a dark, chaotic one, not this dazzling place of small mild people, smiling in the shadows of low bush, the women unearthing more roots with their digging sticks, one reclining in a patch of speckled shade, nursing her contentedly suckling baby.

They were spared the muddled and weirdly orphic metaphors of the failing market — *The subprime crisis was only the tip of the iceberg for an economic meltdown* and *Loans could not stop the hemorrhaging of stock prices* and *The red ink in Spain's regional governments surged 22 percent to almost $18 billion* and *New York City's economy faces an extreme downside risk from Europe's debt crisis, because its banks hold over $1 trillion of assets* — and the mocking realization that money was just colorful crumpled paper, hardly different from a candy wrapper, the market itself little more than a casino. *For the tenth straight day* . . . The panic, the anger, the impotence of the people confined in stagnating cities like caged monkeys. *Should Greece default on its debt, it will find itself in a death spiral.*

As the fire crackled, more roots were passed around.

"Look, Mister Bawl . . ."

One crouching man with homemade twine of split and twisted vines had fashioned a snare, pegging it to the spring of a bent-over branch, and with tiptoeing fingers on the sand he showed me how the snare snatched at the plodding feet of a unwary bird, a guinea hen perhaps — they were numerous here — one that they would pluck and roast on the fire. They indicated the poisonous plants and talked about the beetles they crushed and applied to their arrowheads to make them deadly, the leaves they used to ease their stomachs, the twigs for purifying a wound, for soothing a rash.

These Real People, the Ju/'hoansi, had been persecuted, harried, massacred, and driven off from the moment the first whites came ashore in Africa in 1652. The whites were Jan van Riebeeck, his wife and child, and his small party of Dutchmen, who named the land Groot Schur, Good Hope, where they settled to plant vegetables for a "refreshment station" to provision Dutch ships heading to East Asia.

Finicky on the subject of race, with the Dutch temperament for fine distinctions, they created a taxonomy to describe the indigenous people, designating the goat-herding Khoikhoi as "Hottentots" (mimicking the alveolar clicks in the way they spoke), the Bantu as "kaffirs" (unbelievers — the Dutch had gotten the word from the early Portuguese, who'd heard Arab traders use it), and the !Kung San as "Bushmen," for their preferred habitat. It was the pastoral Khoikhoi who named the San — their belittling word for "cattleless" (with the sense of being backward). All were pushed aside in the land grab by the Dutch, and though each group fought back, the so-called !Kung San fairly quickly withdrew, but not fast enough. They were hunted for sport into the late nineteenth century by the Boers. But these supposedly benighted people — self-sufficient foragers and hunters, city haters, apparently living outside the world economy — would, I believed, have the last laugh.

Even later, when these Ju/'hoansi I was visiting had plucked off their beads and laid down their bows and arrows and digging sticks, exchanging the pretty skins they wore for ragged Western clothes — torn trousers, faded T-shirts, rubber flip-flops, skirts and blouses; castoffs sent in bales from Europe and the United States — even then the curtain did not come down. The Ju/'hoansi still seemed ancient and indestructible and knowing, thoroughly habituated to their life in the bush, dealing with the outer world by quietly smiling at its foolishness and incompetence.

That is what I saw. Or was it an illusion? Perhaps what they were showing me was a persuasive reenactment of the old ways, like Mohawks in a modern pageant, wearing beaded deerskin jackets and paddling birch-bark canoes on the Hudson River. Anyone who took the Ju/'hoansi behavior as typical, as some anthropologists had written, was perpetuating a myth that had been affectionately invented, a travesty in the real sense of the word, a mere change of clothes, romanticizing a life that was antique and lost forever.

It is true that the Ju/'hoansi had been scattered and resettled, had been plagued by alcoholism, and many of them degraded by town life. But the Ju/'hoansi had kept some of their culture. Their language was intact; they still had their folktales and their cosmology; they had retained and passed on their strategies for bush survival. Many still tracked game, still hunted, though not with poison-tipped arrows; some still supplemented their diet with roots; and they could make a fire by rubbing sticks together. Their kinship system — family, relationships, dependencies — remained unbroken.

Clothed in rags rather than skins, they seemed no less the Real People. But perhaps I saw what I needed to see. Their traditional skills intact, their heads (I guessed) buzzed with the old ways. They even had their own peculiar manner of walking. Unlike the city dweller, that slouching, foot-dragging person grinning into the middle distance, the Ju/'hoansi were alert. They never sauntered or sloped; they moved fast but silently, bodies erect, listening as they flew along, treading lightly on the balls of their feet, balletic in their flight, in what was less like walking than dancing through the bush.

They were temperamentally suited to dealing with the stern austerity of the semidesert climate and had a sympathetic understanding of the animals they hunted. But they had never been a match for the people who persecuted them, including the !Kung San and the Herero people as well as the whites. Some !Kung San who had the misfortune to live near towns had been poisoned and neutralized with bubbly *oshikundu,* the home-brewed beer that Namibians made from fermented sorghum and sold in villages and shebeens. (*Shebeen,* an Irish word meaning "bad ale," was brought to southern Africa by migrants from Ireland and is used to describe the poorest drinking places.)

For their apparent gentleness, the complexity of their beliefs, and their ancient pedigree, foreign agencies and charities had taken a shine to the !Kung San. And so had anthropologists: the !Kung San were among the most intensively studied of Africa's peoples. But those who patronized them had much more to learn from these people than they could teach them. They were above all a peaceable, egalitarian people who had thrived because of their tradition of sharing and living communally. Historically, they had withdrawn deeper into the bush rather than face being exterminated in a futile war. They were notably patient and consequently a contented people. They were here before anyone else — catching game, making fire, digging roots — and I was convinced that they would be here after the rest of the world destroyed itself.

They had always lived at the margin. Could any outsider in a charity-minded, money-collecting, old-clothes-dispensing organization, and the benevolent well-wishers who gave them material support, show them a better way to live? Circumstances — politics mainly — determined that the Ju/'hoansi be confined to one place, and though they were by custom nomadic they'd had to acquire farming and animal-rearing skills. But if they were historically hunter-gatherers, with a connection to the land they regarded as the living mother, wouldn't they prevail that way?

Many Africans are people of regressed cultures, the scattered remnants of ancient realms that were demolished or subverted by slavers from Arabia and Europe — the kingdoms of Dahomey and the Congo, the vast fifteenth-century empire of southern Africa known as Monomatapa. Like the peasant folk of old Europe, a great number of Africans have lost or abandoned their traditional skills of thatching, iron-forging, wood-carving, food-gathering, farming, and the greatest skill of all, the mutual respect and fairness that help people rub along together in a congenial way. Within a few decades the majority of Africans will live in cities. Today, two hundred million people in sub-Saharan Africa live in slums, the highest number of slum dwellers in the world, according to UN-Habitat's "State of African Cities 2010 Report." And "slum" is a rather misleading word for these futureless places — as I was to see — of stupefying disorder.

At the town nearest to the tiny Ju/'hoansi village, the crossroads of Tsumkwe, about thirty miles down the road, there were some amenities: a shop that sold canned goods and bread and hard candy, a gas pump, and the semblance of a street market — a row of seven improvised stalls selling used clothes, meat, homemade beer, and, at the last stall, hair extensions. The stallholders yawned in the heat; business was poor.

For years I had longed to visit the !Kung San people and wander around the country. And I had another reason. For a previous book of mine, *Dark Star Safari*, I had traveled overland from Cairo to Cape Town down the right-hand side of Africa. This time, liking the symmetry of the enterprise, I wanted to resume my trip at Cape Town and, after seeing how that city had changed in ten years, travel north in a new direction, up the left-hand side until I found the end of the line, either on the road or in my mind.

But I had yet other reasons, just as pressing. The main one was physically to get away from people wasting my time with trivia. "I believe that the mind can be permanently profaned by the habit of attending to trivial things," Thoreau wrote in his essay "Life Without Principle," "so that all our thoughts shall be tinged with triviality."

In going away I wanted to frustrate the stalkers and pesterers, to be unobtainable and not to live at the beck and call of emailers and phoners and people saying "Hey, we're on deadline!" — other people's deadlines, not mine. To travel unconnected, away from anyone's gaze or reach, is bliss. I had earned this freedom: having recently finished a novel, and sick of sitting at my desk for a year and a half, I wanted to leave the house — and not just leave but go far away. "My purpose in making this wonderful journey is not to delude myself but to discover myself in the objects I see," Goethe wrote in his *Italian Journey.* "Nothing, above all, is comparable to the new life that a reflective person experiences when he observes a new country. Though I am still always myself, I believe I have been changed to the very marrow of my bones."

Africa drew me onward because it is still so empty, so apparently unfinished and full of possibilities, which is why it attracts meddlers and analysts and voyeurs and amateur philanthropists. Much of it is still wild, and even in its hunger it is hopeful, perhaps an effect of its desperation. "Give me a wildness whose glance no civilization can endure," Thoreau wrote in "Walking," "as if we lived on the marrow of koodoos devoured raw." Travel in Africa was also my way of opposing the increasing speed of technology — resisting it and dropping back, learning patience and studying the world that way.

Africa had changed, and, ten years on, so had I. The world had grown older too, and the nature of travel itself had continued to alter and accelerate. It is said that the known world has never been so well known or so easily within reach. In 2011, the year I was on the road, Namibia had a million foreign tourists, and South Africa had almost twice that number. But these visitors stayed on safe and well-trodden routes. Many places in South Africa rarely saw a tourist, and in Namibia tourists kept to the game parks and the coast, seldom daring the far north, the inhospitable borderland of Angola. As for the hardier travelers, the backpackers and wanderers, I had yet to meet one who had actually crossed the border into Angola.

While the known world is well traveled and distant places appear on the tourist itinerary (Bhutan, the Maldives, the Okavango Delta, Patagonia), there are places where no outsider goes. The rich travel to remote airstrips in Africa in chartered planes, with their own gourmet chefs and guides. The rest go on package tours or randomly backpack. Yet there are places that are slipping from view, inaccessible or too dangerous to travel to. Many bush tracks lead nowhere. And some countries are closed until further notice. Somalia, in a state of anarchy, is on no one's itinerary except that of arms dealers. Zimbabwe, a tyranny, is unwelcoming. And others — the Congo is a good example — have no roads to speak of. But even if roads existed, much of the Congo is a hostile no-go area of militias, local chiefs, and warlords, just as it was when Henry Morton Stanley traversed it on foot and by river.

In the course of my planning I kept reading that militant Islamists were busy killing unbelievers or raising hell in Niger and Chad, and in Nigeria the so-called Boko Haram gangs — Muslims who could not abide the sight of Westernized Nigerians — were killing any man who wore pants and a shirt, or a woman in a dress. These groups were looking for soft targets — backpackers, wanderers, people like you and me.

So I left on this trip with a sense of foreboding. A man who has been on the road for fifty years is an easy mark: alone, past retirement age, and conspicuous in a country like Namibia where the average life expectancy is forty-three. I consoled myself by thinking that the unlikely sight of an old man traveling alone in Africa meant that anyone who saw me would laugh me off as a crank. Dressed as I was in faded clothes, with a $20 wristwatch and cheap sunglasses, carrying a small, plastic $20 cell phone — how could I be worth mugging?

I also suspected that this trip would be in the nature of a farewell. For many older writers, and some not so old, a spell in Africa was a valedictory trip. The last serious journey Joseph Conrad embarked on, his twenty-eight days piloting a boat up and down the Congo River, formed the basis of the powerful novella *Heart of Darkness*, which he wrote eight years after returning from Africa, describing the book as "experience pushed a little (and only very little) beyond the actual facts of the case." After a lifetime of traveling, Evelyn Waugh spent the winter of 1959 in East and Central Africa and wrote an account of it in *A Tourist in Africa*. He died six years later. Both Laurens van der Post and Wilfred Thesiger spent their later years in African travel—van der Post in the Kalahari Desert, Thesiger in upcountry Kenya—and wrote about it. Hemingway's ultimate safari, his last serious journey, was to East Africa in 1953–54, and though he shot himself six years afterward, his fictionalized version of the safari, *True at First Light,* edited by his son Patrick, was published posthumously in 1999. After V. S. Naipaul published his *Masque of Africa*, a lengthy interrogation of "the nature of African belief" through six African countries, he made it plain that it would be his last travel book.

Africa can be fierce, and some of it frankly scary, but as Naipaul's experience showed, it can also be kind to an ailing and elderly traveler. You might expect people to say, "Go home, old man." But no —in general, Africa turns no one away.

And so this, the greenest continent, would seem the perfect landscape for a valedictory trip, a way of paying respects to the natural world and to the violated Eden of our origins. "All the hungers of life are blankly stated there," the English writer and traveler V. S. Pritchett wrote about Spain fifty years ago. But what he said could be an assessment of Africa too. "We see the primitive hungers we live by and yet, by a curious feat of stoicism, fatalism, and lethargy, the passions of human nature are sceptically contained." In Africa we see human history turned upside down, and it is possible in Africa to see where we have gone wrong.

"Africa gives one back the necessary feeling that the world is vast, prodigious and noble," wrote another traveler, and to this very region, Jon Manchip White, in *The Land God Made in Anger.* "In spite of what the pundits say, our planet is neither congested nor contemptible."

All solitary travel offers a sort of special license allowing you to be anyone you want to be. There are many endangered countries, or places whose futures are threatened. I think of the radioactive Ukraine, or anarchic Chechnya, or the overburdened Philippines, or tyrannized Belarus. Each of them could use a helping hand, but when the celebrity or ex-president or glamorous public figure wishes to make a charitable appearance it is nearly always in Africa, for the sake of the exotic—or is it the drama of high contrast in black and white, or its being hypnotically unintelligible? In Africa the traveler's license is unlimited, and Africa itself magnifies the experience in a way no other place can.

When I was following the spirited, fleet-footed Ju/'hoansi people through the low sunlit bush of Nyae Nyae, I knew I was where I wanted to be. And that kind of traveling was a way of recovering my youth, because as a twenty-two-year-old teacher at a small school in rural Africa I had spent some of the happiest years of my life —years of freedom and friendship and great hope.

If I had a sense of foreboding about this trip, it was because travel into the unknown can also be like dying. After the anguish of the goodbyes and the departure itself, you seem to diminish, growing smaller and smaller, vanishing into the distance. In time, no one misses you except in the casual, mildly mocking way of "Whatever happened to old so-and-so, who threatened to beetle off to Africa?" You're gone, no one can depend on you, and when you're only a dim memory, a bitterness creeps into the recollection, in the way that the dead are often resented for being dead. What good are you, unobtainable and so far away?

And that makes you two ghosts, because in the distant country, too, you're like a wraith, with your face pressed to the window of another culture, staring at other lives. And much of what you see, like the harmonious life in the bush, has another side.

It took me a while to understand that the window of Africa, like the window on a train rushing through the night, is a distorting mirror that partly reflects the viewer's own face. Among the Ju/'hoansi I was indeed witnessing a reenactment, and I came to realize that the folk who called themselves the Real People were, alas, unreal. The heroic pagan world of golden-skinned Ju/'hoansi was an illusion. I had hoped to find that rarity in the world, a country of uncontaminated delight, but what I found was a desperate people, sad static unhoping souls, not indestructible, as I'd thought, but badly in need of rescue.

2

═ ═ ═ ═

The Train from Khayelitsha

S OME WEEKS BEFORE MY VISIT to the Ju/'hoansi, who
sleep flat on the ground in their simple lean-to shelters, ever
wakeful because of the nighttime prowling of predators, I
woke from a sound sleep in a soft bed in a luxury hotel, between the
swooping green flanks of Table Mountain and the aqueous glitter
of Table Bay. This was in Cape Town, with its heights and cliffs, the
only city in Africa with a claim to grandeur.

Yawning toothily like a baboon, I switched on the TV and saw the
turmoil in Europe, the sort of improvidence and chaos that people
usually associate with Africa, and gave thanks that I was far away. I
would head north one of these days by road to Namibia, Botswana,
and Angola, and perhaps farther. No long-range plan was required.
I was alone, traveling light, and needed only a cheap one-way ticket.
A daily bus ran to Northern Cape province, to isolated Springbok,
and continued overnight past the Namibian border, which was the
east-west course of the Orange River.

An aging traveler now, I took my morning pills, two different
ones to keep gout away, a vitamin, and a dose of malaria suppres-

sant, and then dawdled, still groggy from jet lag. And remembering that I was on a journey, I dated and wrote the first line of my diary, about waking in a soft bed in a luxury hotel.

In such a pleasant place, no matter how far away, you never imagine you're too old to travel. I can do this till I die, you think as you summon room service for lotuses to eat ("On second thought, I will have the pepper-crusted Wagyu steak with the black truffle vinaigrette"). It's only when in a hovel in the bush, or being stared down by a hostile stinking crowd ("Meester! Meester!"), or eating a sinister stew of black meat or a cracked plate of cold, underdone, greasy, and eye-speckled potatoes, or banging in a jalopy for nine hours down a mountain road full of potholes — with violent death as close as that dark precipice to the right — that it occurs to me that someone else should be doing this, someone younger perhaps, hungrier, stronger, more desperate, crazier.

But there is such a thing as curiosity, dignified as a spirit of inquiry, and this nosiness has ruled my life as a traveler and a writer.

In much of Europe and North America a curious gaze is considered a hostile intrusion, and curious questions often arouse a vicious or unhelpful response. "You writing a book, pal? Well, leave this chapter out." But in Africa such close attention is taken for welcome concern, a form of friendliness, especially when customary pleasantries are exchanged and tribal niceties observed. What brought me back to this beautiful city, and this continent, was the wish to know more at first hand, that vitalizing itch that keeps all of us amazed and some of us on the road.

Over breakfast — salmon, scrambled eggs, fruit, guava juice, green tea, brown toast, and "Please pass the marmalade" — reading the *Cape Times*, I saw the headlines "Mountain Closed at Night" and "City Responds to Attacks." The reason for shutting down Table Mountain after dark was crime — muggers, thieves, or in South African slang, *tsotsis* and *skelms,* the local names for thugs. A number of nighttime strollers and people beaming in admiration at the city lights from their parked cars had been attacked, beaten senseless, and robbed. How it was possible to close such a mountain was anyone's guess. This enormous, dominant upswelling of rock, two miles wide on its plateau, constituted a ridge that extended forty miles to Cape Point.

But this was Africa, so subject to sudden change. Less than a month later, Table Mountain was named (along with Halong Bay in Vietnam, the Amazon rain forest, Iguaçu Falls, and three others) one of the Seven Natural Wonders of the World. Recognized across the globe as a marvel, Table Mountain was proudly reopened to the public.

That same day of my waking at the luxury hotel, I went for a walk. At Texies Fish and Chips on Adderley Street, in the Grand Parade near the train station, while I was eating my lunch of broiled kingklip and admiring the view, the apparent prosperity, the busy to-and-fro of shoppers, the scavenging pigeons pecking at crumbs tossed by passersby, I noticed some young men in the shadows of the arcade near where I sat at an outdoor table, returning my gaze. Seeing that I had had enough of my meal, one of them, a skinny teenage boy, came over and hesitatingly asked, "Can I finish?" I simply nodded, because he had taken me by surprise. He carried the remains of my food—the plate of greasy chips—a short distance away, scattering the pigeons, and wolfed them down.

Travel writing is sometimes no more than literary decor for a sort of mocking misanthropy or mythomania or concocted romance, but at that moment I felt only helpless pity. And I was to see this same desperate reflex a number of times during these African travels, the hungry lurking man or boy, waiting to take my leftovers, or someone else's, and eat them with his dirty fingers.

If I wondered why I had come back to Africa, I suppose I had to answer: to happen upon that, among other chance encounters. It was wrong for me to say that I was seeking something. I was not seeking anything. I was hurrying away from my routine and my responsibilities and my general disgust with fatuous talk, money talk, money stories, the donkey laughter at dinner parties. Disgust is like fuel. It took the curse off the zigzagging flight from New York to Dubai, and the next leg to Cape Town, twenty-two hours of flying, thirty hours of travel. But I was glad to get away. It was travel as rejection, as though in leaving I was saying to those fatuous people, *Take that.* And perhaps hoping they'd say afterward, *What happened? Where is he? Was it something I said?*

Most of all, I wanted to go back to Africa and pick up where I'd left off.

Ten years before, I was here and wandered through the slum of a squatter camp, called New Rest, on the desolate sand flats on the outskirts of Cape Town. On my return, the first place I wanted to go was this camp, to see what had become of its shacks, its outhouses, its bedraggled people who had settled in the wasteland beside the highway.

Was it still vexed, a slum made entirely of scrap lumber and ragged plastic, still shonky amid the windblown grit?

The majority of black South Africans live in the lower depths, not in picturesque hamlets or thatched huts on verdant hillsides. Three quarters of city-dwelling Africans live in the nastiest slums and squatter camps. But what happens to these places after a decade or so?

"Don't go to a squatter camp. Don't go to a black township. You'll get robbed or worse," a mixed-race clerk at Cape Town's central railway station had said to me one Sunday morning ten years ago, refusing to sell me a ticket to Khayelitsha.

I asked why. His adamant certainty captured my attention. He was not making a racial generalization. He would not sell me what he regarded as a ticket to violence. He explained that the train to Khayelitsha was routinely stoned, the windows broken, the passengers assaulted, by unemployed youths in the township and the nearby squatter camp.

The next day, provoked by his warning, I went to the New Rest squatter camp, and I wrote at the time of the 1,200 shacks that had been accumulating for a decade on the sandy infertile soil of Cape Flats, beside the busy road that led to the airport. Most of the 8,500 inhabitants lived in squalor. It was dire but not unspeakable. There was no running water; there were no lights or any trees. It was windy and bleak. Because it had been plopped down by squatters on forty acres of sand, there were no utilities, and as a consequence it stank and looked hideous. The houses were sheds made of ill-fitting boards, scrap lumber, bits of tin, and plastic sheeting. The gaps between the boards were blasted by the gritty wind. One man told me that he constantly had sand and dust in his bed.

Life could get no grimmer than this, I had thought then — the urban shantytown, without foliage, too sandy to grow anything but scrawny geraniums and stubbly cactuses; people having to draw water into plastic buckets from standpipes and burn candles in their huts; the huts cold in winter, sweltering in summer, very dirty, lying athwart a main highway and its noise. What could be worse? Call them "informal settlements," as some people did, and they would smell just as foul.

Yet for all this squalor the people at New Rest were upbeat and had a sense of purpose. One of the residents, the man who complained of sand in his bed, took me to the New Rest committee that met regularly in one of the shacks. The committee members told me that these squatters had come from the Eastern Cape, the old government-designated homelands of Transkei and Ciskei, as well as from the slums of East London, Port Elizabeth, and Grahamstown, industrial cities that were not faring well in South Africa's post-independence economy. The New Rest committee explained their aims: roads, piped water, electricity, and — in a process known as "in situ upgrade" — a permanent house to be built where each shack stood.

A master plan had been outlined and blueprinted by volunteer urban planners from the University of Cape Town. Every miserable shack, no matter how small, had been numbered and its plot recorded. A census had been taken. The idea of transforming a squatter camp into a viable township by upgrading existing dwellings — turning a slum into a subdivision — had been accomplished in Brazil and India, but not as yet in South Africa. The driving force behind this was the pride the people took in having found a safe place to live. The goodwill of foreigners had also helped: well-meaning visitors had contributed money to support the day care center, to purchase three brick-making machines, and to establish a trust fund to benefit the place. The fund was administered on a pro bono basis by a safari company and the New Rest/Kanana Community Development Trust, which promoted township tourism. Some children were sponsored by Americans and Europeans who sent money regularly to buy them clothes and for school fees. It was an improvisational, hand-to-mouth arrangement, but the element of self-help in it made me a well-wisher.

So what had happened since then?

On my second day in Cape Town, after another gourmet breakfast at my hotel, I took the thirty-minute drive down and around the mountain to the squatter camp. I had found a taxi driver who lived near New Rest, in an older settlement called Guguletu, where I also wanted to go, having visited it ten years before.

No visitor to Boston, where I was born, rises in a luxury hotel and, after a great breakfast, catches a taxi to tour, out of purely voyeuristic curiosity, the poorer parts of the city — the black section in Roxbury, where Malcolm X Boulevard enters Dudley Square; the poor districts of Charlestown and Chelsea; or the mean streets of Everett, with its corner shops, pool parlors, and three-decker wooden houses. Gawkers are not welcome in these places, but even if they were, no one would casually visit, because the poor sections of American cities are perceived as dangerous. So I was keenly aware of my privilege as a visitor to South Africa — that I was doing something I refrained from doing at home.

And it wasn't hard to accomplish this. In Cape Town, many poor townships, some of them nearly identical, make up the itinerary of the well-advertised sightseeing tours of the city.

"This is Imizamo Yethu," the guide says over the loudspeaker as the City Tours bus approaches a hillside of ramshackle houses and dirt roads. "This means 'Our Struggle.' It began as a squatter camp. It is now a township. It began in the 1980s when the pass laws ended. It grew in the nineties. You may get off here if you wish to be taken on a tour by a person who lives in the community. Another bus will follow in thirty minutes . . ."

My driver's name was Thandwe. Xhosa by tribe, he had come here as a small boy, twenty-seven years before, from Port Elizabeth in the Eastern Cape, to live with his uncle.

"I go home now and then," Thandwe said, "but this is where I intend to stay."

We were headed down the highway, the road most foreign visitors see, since it is the main road to Cape Town International Airport. I wanted — hoped — to find good news, to see something different.

"New Rest — it is there," Thandwe said, and indicated a settlement of tidy, russet-roofed houses that lay behind a high fence beside the road. They were not reconditioned huts or renovated hovels; they were new and solid-looking, and they stood very close together in what were obviously the footprints of the shacks and sheds that I had seen a decade before. This was the "in situ upgrade" that the urban planners had hoped for.

We turned off the highway onto the side road that led to New

Rest and cruised through this now much-improved township. Forty years ago this was a rural area with a spiritual aura and a ritual significance to the local Xhosa people. Initiates (*mkweta*) in circumcision ceremonies (*ukoluka*) were concealed in the bush here. When their penises were foreshortened with the blade of a spear (*mkonto*), the youths stayed as a group until their wounds healed. Ten years before, I had been told that in June and December, the newly circumcised boys were seen, "sometimes many of them, hiding in the bush on the far side."

That was no longer the case. Every bush had been cut down, houses stood where there had been scrubland, and there was not a tree standing. But I had seen a change, and I understood how it had evolved. First the new people from provincial villages created a squatter camp out of plastic sheeting, rags, and cut-down tree limbs; then the shelters were improved to hovels with old planks and scrap tin, to become the shantytown; in time came the addition of communal toilets and a standpipe for water; and at last, because of the tenacity of the people — the ones who on my previous visit had told me, "We are staying here. This is our home" — and the volunteer urban planners and well-wishers, it had been upgraded again. There was a government department, the Reconstruction and Development Program, dedicated to improving and rebuilding the squatter camps.

"It has shops now. The school is near," Thandwe said. "One of the reasons for these improvements was the World Cup."

After South Africa was named the host country for the 2010 FIFA World Cup, three enormous football stadiums were built in its major cities, and the seven existing stadiums were extensively renovated. New hotels were built, and public transport was improved, and with all this investment came a self-awareness that meant money would be spent on housing for the people who would be employed at the new facilities. The low-paid workers who maintain South Africa as an agreeable place that has solved the servant problem — the domestics, the gardeners, the mechanics, the scrubbers, the floor moppers, the bus drivers, the cabbies, the waiters, the nannies, the nurses, and the teachers — live largely in these townships. So improvements to their living conditions were essential to the running of the city.

Another day, another departure from my lovely hotel in the center of the city, another driver. This man was Phaks — pronounced "Pax." He had been recommended to me as an authority on township life and was himself a resident of the great sprawl of Khayelitsha, with its population of half a million and its more than 80 percent unemployment, the place with the worst reputation for crime, idleness, gambling, fighting, and binge drinking.

"But it's not all bad," Phaks said as he drove down the highway. He was fairly jolly but seemed to have unresolved matters weighing on his mind, and at times his expression darkened and he became aggrieved.

We swung past District Six, a lively area of Cape Town in the apartheid era that had defied the racism and thrived as a safe, multiracial inner-city neighborhood well known for its music, its food, its color and zest. In the late 1960s, wishing to reclaim the land and create a white area, the city government had forced its population of sixty thousand to leave and divided them by race, resettling them in specific townships — the whites to white areas, the blacks to Khayelitsha, the mixed-raced people ("coloreds") to Mitchells Plain and Bonteheuwel.

The idea was to create a whites-only neighborhood of new houses, to be called Zonnenbloom ("Sunflower"), but it hadn't worked. No one wanted to live there, and ten years ago it had sat empty, a barren field bordered by two old churches — all that remained of District Six were its churches.

But some houses had been built since I'd last seen it. In 2005 the

Reconstruction and Development Program had put up a number of new houses, and many of them — but not all — were occupied.

"They are for those who want to come back," Phaks said. "But some people are resisting."

"It's central, it's safe, the houses are new," I said. "Why would they not want to move back in?"

"They say it's not the same, so they stay away."

"What does 'not the same' mean?"

"It's not multiracial anymore. Just black."

Next he took me to Langa township, which was a bit nearer to Cape Town proper and, like many of the other townships, just off the main airport highway. Langa's distinction was that it was one of the first black townships. Phaks said that it had begun to be settled in 1900, but the local historian contradicted him and said it was 1927. Then Phaks said that the name Langa meant "Sun," and the local historian said that it was designated Langa after a famous nineteenth-century chief and anti-government activist, Langalibalele, who was exiled as an undesirable to a site near here.

The local historian, subcontracted by Phaks to join us, was a Xhosa man named Archie, who explained that this township was the consequence of the South African apartheid system, in particular the Group Areas Act, which compelled nonwhites to live in designated places. This hemming-in of nonwhites was enforced by the Pass Laws Act of 1952, which required all of them to carry an identity document known formally in Afrikaans as a *Bewysboek*, in English as "the Reference Book," and universally among the carriers as the *dompas*, or "stupid pass."

The *dompas* was, in effect, a passport, with as many pages as a normal passport. "The most despised symbol of apartheid," according to the South African parliamentarian and anti-apartheid campaigner Helen Suzman. "Within the pages of an individual's *dompas* were their fingerprints, photograph, personal details of employment, permission from the government to be in a particular part of the country, qualifications to work or seek work in the area, and an employer's reports on worker performance and behavior."

Protests against the pass laws—first by brave women in the early 1950s, then in the 1960s by men inspired by the women—led to suppression, outright massacre in Sharpeville, and more protests, which brought the apartheid struggle to the world's attention. South Africa now celebrates these protests with two national days, Women's Day and Human Rights Day. After thirty-four years of internal passports ruling the lives of South Africans of color, the pass laws were repealed in 1986.

With indignation bordering on rage, Archie was telling me about the hated pass laws and the Group Areas Act as we walked through the Langa streets, which were littered with garbage, old tires, and broken bottles. Even the recently planted flowers and patches of fenced-off grass had been trashed.

"Your Bill Gates helped us with the cultural center," Archie said, showing me around the Guga S'thebe Arts and Cultural Center, where in a back room three women were painting designs on ceramic pots and mugs, in an effort to teach skills and create employment. South African women seemed to have a spark, but more than 60 percent of the adult males in Langa were unemployed. The cultural center, brightly painted and with ceramic artwork on its façade, built for workshops and performances, was an imaginatively designed post-apartheid building, perhaps the only new one in the township. It had been deliberately constructed near the spot where in 1954 a demonstration by thousands of Langa residents had been held to protest the pass laws—a mass burning of the *dompas* —and a march to the center of Cape Town. Only ten years old, the center was already in a state of disrepair—unswept and seemingly neglected. On the township tour itinerary, it had more tourists visiting than local residents.

"How did Bill Gates help?"

"He gave us these computers."

Four unused computers, with grubby keyboards and blind screens, sat on desks.

"Unfortunately they have been out of service for a year."

What Archie did not say, and perhaps did not know, was that the Gates Foundation had given money to support an effort to increase awareness of HIV/AIDS. Langa had one of the highest rates of infection in South Africa. Saturday is "burial day" in Langa, and there were usually around forty burials each Saturday. In spite of efforts to educate Langa's people, the death rate from HIV/AIDS was rising.

"Come this way," Archie said.

When he kicked a beer can with the side of his foot, I used that as an opportunity to ask him why the carefully planted flower gardens in front of the cultural center were blighted, and the whole of this street and its sidewalk littered with beer cans and waste paper and blowing plastic.

"We don't know what to do with it. People throw it and it blows."

"Why not pick it up?"

"It is a problem."

"Archie, all it takes is a broom and a barrel."

"The municipality cares for it."

"If that's so, why is this crap still here?"

I deliberately put him on the spot because he was, so he said, the spokesman, and the cultural center was the primary destination of the township tour—as it happened, a busload of white visitors had arrived and were looking with that "where are we?" squint of tourists just off a bus. In a place where tens of thousands of people had no job and nothing at all to do—a number of people were conspicuously sitting around and talking, or gaping at the tourists—not one was picking up the masses of litter.

It is possible that Archie, still denouncing the injustice of the pass laws, did not see the disorder, and he seemed annoyed with me for mentioning it. As if to dazzle me — or perhaps to explain the dereliction — he began to declaim.

"There was a prophet here long ago! His name was Ntsikana — he made a prediction!"

"What was the prediction?"

"It was in the year 1600," Archie said, and in a solemn prophesying tone seemed to quote Ntsikana: "People will come from the sea." Archie raised one finger for emphasis. "These people will have a book and money." Archie wagged his finger. "Take the book but not the money!" Archie let his finger droop. "But they took both."

"They shouldn't have taken the money?"

Archie said, "That was the badness."

I remembered the name Ntsikana and later looked it up and found that there was a Xhosa prophet by that name, his life well documented. Indeed, he was a pioneer of "black theology," a self-created Christian (he'd had contact with missionaries, though he was never baptized and never studied with them) who had flourished in the late eighteenth to early nineteenth century. In 1815 Ntsikana had an epiphany, "an illumination of the soul," that confirmed in him a belief in monogamy, river baptism, and Sunday prayer to a sovereign God. He wrote hymns and composed poems. Because his conversion had occurred without any missionary intervention, so he said, his followers "claimed a pedigree for Xhosa Christianity independent of missionary influence."

"I am sent by God, but am only like a candle," Ntsikana said, using a felicitous image of illumination and finiteness. "I have not added anything to myself." Furiously proselytizing, he established rural congregations throughout the Eastern Cape. One day Ntsikana foretold the coming of a race of people to the shores of South Africa. He described them as people "[through] whose transparent ears the sun shines redly" and "whose hair is long as the tail-hairs of a zebra." Since he had previously seen whites, this prophecy proved accurate, and he apparently did warn his followers not to put much faith in the new people. Ntsikana died in 1821, and his grave, near Fort Beaufort in the Eastern Cape, is a place of pilgrimage.

Although Archie had a few details wrong, his sudden parable introduced me to this powerful sect, which still had many adherents. We were walking along the broken paving of littered roads that ran between a pair of two-story cinderblock buildings that had the prison starkness of much public housing. They had once been, Archie said, the hostels of migrant workers — all men — who were employed as field hands, common laborers, and domestics in Cape Town during the apartheid era. An effective way to control them was to house them in an isolated place, require them to carry the *dompas,* and separate them from their wives and children, who remained in distant villages.

Behind these beat-up hostels were small wooden shacks piled against each other. Ragged children, their noses running on this chilly morning, lurked in the doorways.

"More people," I said. "More shacks."

"Informal settlements," Archie said. The name always brought a grim smile to my lips because it conjured the image of people in bright bungalows, sprawled on sofas. "The name for them is *siyahlala.*"

I asked him to spell it, and I wrote it down.

"It is Xhosa," Archie said. "It means 'We are staying here.'"

He said five or six people lived in each shack, though there seemed hardly room for two. Scattered around the edge of the settlement, beyond the hostels, beyond the shacks, were shipping containers — great rusty steel boxes — and people were living in those, too, recent arrivals, Archie said. Some containers had been divided into two- or three-family dwellings, doors and windows blowtorched as crude openings in the sides. In front of several were stalls selling blackened sheep heads.

"We call them smileys." Archie explained that when the severed head was thrown on the hot grill, "the lips shrivel up in a smile." The locals ate them with "train smash," he went on, and laughed. "Tomato sauce."

As we strolled, teenagers stared at us from where they sat on benches or rubber tires. Some glowered from doorways, others glanced up from card games or from kicking a soccer ball, still others simply stood the way herons stand, motionless, on one leg, the other leg crooked behind it. All of the youths were idle, not a dozen or so, but scores of them, perhaps hundreds, apparently with nothing to do. A few of them began to follow Archie and me, but they quickly tired of this—maybe we were walking too fast for them. One of my rules in an apparently insecure place was to walk fast and look busy.

Archie said the hostels had been renovated in 2002, which perhaps meant that was when they had been painted the dull yellow I saw. He showed me inside one of them—a hive of dirty two-room apartments crammed with filthy mattresses.

"Six rooms here," he said at another of the hostels. The places were crammed with damp quilts, old clothes, broken shoes, and children's plastic toys, as well as CD players and radios.

"How many people live here?"

"Thirty-eight." He could see my incredulity. He said, "Some sleep on the dining table. And under it."

Misery acquaints us with strange bedfellows. The smell grew riper as we penetrated to the last narrow room, where there were two small beds. It housed a family he knew.

"Nine people in this room," he said.

I tried to imagine where they lay at night on the beds and on the floor of this room, which was no more than nine by five feet. He nodded, satisfied that he had startled me, because some of these township tours seemed designed to shock the visitor. But I also thought that there must be places like this in the United States, perhaps many, yet how would I ever know? There were no tours, no men like Phaks or Archie to guide anyone to them.

"And what is most disgusting is that they make use of one toilet," he said, meaning the thirty-eight occupants of the place.

"Where are the people now?"

"Outside," he said. "It is too small to live in by day."

This was also a habit of the village, where people spent the day in the open, under a tree or in the informal courtyard, and used their mud huts only for sleeping or for protection against nocturnal animals.

The next places Archie showed me were roomier, and one looked habitable. Certainly it was cleaner, a two-bedroom apartment in which one family lived. The watchful but polite matriarch nodded at me, and a small, stunned-looking boy peered from the side of a doorway. The rent was 500 rand a month, about $60.

More shacks stood nearby, of the meanest sort, just piled-up lumber and plastic sheeting, with low ceilings. It was hard to imagine anyone living in them.

"We call these *vezinyawo*, because they are so small," Archie said. He explained that the word meant "Your feet are showing" or "Your feet are outside," because one hut was not large enough to accommodate a whole supine human being.

Some streets adjacent to these shacks were lined with bright, compact bungalows, painted in pastel colors, surrounded by fences, with newish cars parked in the driveways. Other solid houses, some of them just completed, faced the main road, the highway to the airport, and these were the houses that foreign visitors would see as they passed by, perhaps saying, "Doesn't look that bad, Doris," never guessing at the shacks and doghouses beyond them that were out of sight. At one of them, a woman had set out on a wobbly table an array of beaded bracelets. She had made them with her own hands, she said. That expression made me look at her hands—the woman was wringing them in anxiety. She had nine children, and all of them lived in this shack. She looked pleadingly at me to buy, and I came away with my pockets bulging with beaded artifacts.

"And this is a shebeen," Archie said, parting the curtain that was hung on the doorway of a shack. The ceiling was so low I could not stand up straight, and the air was rank and doggy and warm with stink. When my eyes became accustomed to the darkness I saw six beer-swilling men inside, three on benches, three squatting on the floor, drunk and incapable at noon on a Monday. An old gaunt woman in an apron presided over the place, stirring a tureen of porridgy liquid.

One man grinned at me and drank from a large enamel cup, as a cat laps milk, and then he shook it, sloshing the creamy liquid inside.

"Have a drink," Archie said. I was certain he was testing me, showing me the worst of the township. I had tried to appear implacable, with my "How do you spell that?" and "Let's see another." But this was like a jail cell or the worst room of a madhouse. "This beer is made of maize and sorghum. It is called *umqombothi*."

"How do you spell that?"

A few days later, I heard this word again, in a lovely bouncy song about a proud woman who makes beer, "magic beer," performed by an energetic and melodious South African singer, Yvonne Chaka Chaka.

By then we had walked a mile or more and were still in Langa township. But Archie wanted me to see something else, something special, perhaps another shock.

"It is Mr. Ndaba," Archie said. "He is a traditional healer."

Mr. Ndaba lived in a room, another low ceiling — I had to stoop to enter, and to kneel to speak to him. The healer was seated on a stool, working his knife against something he held in his other hand.

I took a breath and retched. The room had the stinging smell of decay, a maggoty odor, and I soon saw why. Hanging from the walls and ceiling were old yellow monkey skulls and jawbones, the decaying pelts of small animals, fur, feathers, more bones, a dead pangolin, snake skins, porcupine quills, mummified birds, and in a corner a newly dead rat being chewed by a small mangy kitten.

"This is all medicine," Archie said. "He can cure AIDS."

"What's that?" I asked, pointing to the spotted pelt of a dead animal, possibly a civet cat.

"It is my hat," Mr. Ndaba said, and now I could see that he was eating. He spoke with his mouth full, and he was still stabbing and carving with his knife. The scrape of the blade was a dull sustained note. What he held was a lump of yellow bone and gray flabby flesh. He gouged some meat from it and raised the knife to his mouth.

"And what's that?"

"I am eating the head of a pig." As he hefted the thing in his hand, its ears wagged.

The pong of the rancid flesh hit me and I wanted to vomit.

"He is a healer," Archie said. "He can cure AIDS. He can make someone fall in love with you. He can cast away spirits. He can make you better. We call him an *igqirha*."

"How do you spell that?" I asked, ducking and leaving the hut.

As I left, Mr. Ndaba said goodbye in a kindly way. And I thought, How easy it is to mock the healer with a civet cat pelt on his head, surrounded by stinking bones and feathers and snake skins. But anyone who entered, wishing to be healed, trusting in the healer, would experience what scientists describe as a therapeutic encounter — the sense of well-being that you feel in the presence of a doctor you trust, one with a kindly, inquiring manner and with monkey skulls instead of diplomas on the wall. The stink itself, like the sight of a stethoscope, might create a placebo effect.

Still, in the intimacy of these shadowy huts I felt self-conscious, almost as if I didn't have a right to be there.

What is the point of these township tours? I heard whites in Cape

Town ask again and again, cringing in embarrassed disbelief. *Why do Africans advertise their squalor and sell tickets to their slums?*

It also struck me as odd that tourists were invited to see the townships and encouraged to examine the sad inner rooms, because they were just as dirty, disorderly, and crime-ridden as in the days of apartheid—perhaps more so. And the shocking thing was that when the residents moaned about the bad old days, all one could think of was how awful, how unfit for human habitation, they were now. Later in the day, in Guguletu, I saw a vanload of well-dressed Italian tourists drinking beer and mineral water at a grubby chicken restaurant—Italians who, without question, would not have dared enter the slums of Naples (depicted in the 2009 Italian film *Gomorrah* and based on a book of the same name by Roberto Saviano), which resembled Guguletu. There were also a few small restaurants in Guguletu that had been discovered by Cape Town foodies and cautiously visited not just for the meal but for the novelty of the filth and menace of their surroundings.

It seemed that curious visitors, of whom I was one, had created a whole itinerary, a voyeurism of poverty, and this exploitation—at bottom that's what it was—had produced a marketing opportunity: township dwellers, who never imagined their poverty to be of interest to anyone, had discovered that for wealthy visitors it had the merit of being fascinating, and the residents became explainers, historians, living victims, survivors, and sellers of locally made bead ornaments, toys, embroidered bags, and baskets, hawked in the stalls adjacent to the horrific houses. They had discovered that their misery was marketable. That was the point.

Look how the apartheid system forced us to live like dogs in a kennel! was the intended message. But the message that reached me was that the miserable former hostels for men were now filthy overcrowded rooms for whole hopeless families, most of them indigent and unemployed.

Phaks was waiting nearby. He said, "We go back?"

"There's one more place," I said. "Guguletu."

"Gugs," he said, using the local nickname, and off we rattled in his old van.

Ten years before, I had walked around Guguletu, noting how the township had achieved notoriety in 1993, when a twenty-six-year-old Californian, Amy Biehl, had been murdered there by a mob. A Stanford graduate, living in South Africa as a volunteer in voter registration for the following year's free election, she had driven three African friends home to the township as a favor. She had a ticket to California; she was to leave South Africa the next day. Seeing her white face, a large crowd of African boys screamed in eagerness, for this was a black township and she was white prey. The car was stoned, she was dragged from it, and though her friends pleaded with them to spare her ("She's a comrade!"), Amy was beaten to the ground, her head smashed with a brick, and she was stabbed in the heart. "Killed like an animal," I wrote in my notebook then.

Four suspects were named; they were tried and convicted of the murder, and the judge, noting that they "showed no remorse," sentenced them to eighteen years in prison. Three years later, these murderers appeared before the Truth and Reconciliation Commission. They had an explanation for the murder. "Their motive was political and not racial." They "regretted" what they had done. They newly claimed they had "remorse." They pleaded to be released under the general amnesty.

Everything they said seemed to me lame and baseless, yet they were freed because Amy's parents, Peter and Linda Biehl, had flown from California, attended their hearing, and listened to their testimony. They said that their daughter would have wanted a show of mercy, since she was "on the side of the people who killed her." The Biehls did not oppose the murderers' being released from prison.

So the killers waltzed away, and two of them, Ntombeko Peni and Easy Nofomela, were — astonishingly — given jobs by the Biehls, working as salaried employees for the Amy Biehl Foundation, a charity started by Amy's forgiving parents in their daughter's memory. Around the time I visited, the foundation had received almost $2 million from the U.S. Agency for International Development for being "dedicated to people who are oppressed."

In 2001, a small cross had been placed near the gas station where Amy had been murdered, and on a crude signboard behind the cross was daubed AMY BIHLS LAST HOME SECTION 3 GUGS — misspelled and so crude as to be insulting.

Now I said to Phaks, "Take me there."

The gas station was bigger and brighter than before. A new memorial, of black marble, much like a gravestone, had been placed on the roadside in front of it, on the fatal spot.

AMY BIEHL

26 APRIL 1967 — 25 AUGUST 1993

KILLED IN AN ACT OF POLITICAL VIOLENCE.

AMY WAS A FULBRIGHT SCHOLAR

AND TIRELESS HUMAN RIGHTS ACTIVIST.

"They killed her right there," I said. Phaks grunted, and we drove away. The wording bothered me. "What is 'an act of political violence'?"

"Those boys, they had a philosophy."

"What was it?"

"Africa for Africans — it was their thinking."

"That's not a philosophy. It's racism."

"But they were political."

"No. They killed her because she was white."

"They thought she was a settler."

He had told me that one of the chants at the time had been "One settler, one bullet."

"But South Africa was full of white people who were part of the struggle. They supported Mandela, they went to jail. Whites!"

"But those boys said they were sorry," Phaks said. "They apologized to the Truth and Reconciliation Commission. And her parents, they agreed."

"But what do you think her parents really felt?"

"I don't know. But you can see, they got their name there."

"And getting their name there makes up for the murder of their child?"

"It was political. The parents, they hired the boys to work for them," Phaks said, and now I could see he was rattled, because he was driving badly along the busy broken township roads, muttering at the traffic, the oncoming cars cutting him off.

"Phaks, do you have children?"

"Four."

"A daughter?"

He nodded — he knew what I was going to say.

"What would you do if someone beat your daughter to the ground and took a brick and smashed it against her head? Then stabbed her in the heart and left her to die?" He winced but remained silent. "Would you say, 'That's their philosophy. It's a political act'?"

"No."

"What would you think?"

"Myself, I wouldn't accept."

"What if they said sorry?"

Phaks was very upset now, so I shut up and let him drive, but he was still fretful from my badgering him and kept murmuring, "No, no. I can't. Never, never." *Nayvah, nayvah.*

The Amy Biehl Foundation had been founded to promote peace and mutual understanding. It had also been instrumental in improving the infrastructure of Guguletu — upgrading huts and bringing in utilities. Doing that was easier than peacemaking. According to data collected by the South African Institute of Race Relations, more than seven hundred people were murdered in Guguletu between 2005 and 2010. This amounted to one murder every two and a half days over those five years.

My challenging Phaks had had the effect of winding him up. Now he was contrary, as I had been, and he was batting the steering wheel with his palm, pointing out the graffiti, the litter, the men and boys idling at shop fronts and street corners, and perhaps with the memory of the boys who'd been released after murdering Amy Biehl he began to see insolence and misbehavior all over Guguletu.

"These kids don't behave," he said. "They are out of control. They show no respect — and you know why? Because they have too many rights. Everyone protects them! Even the government, even the barristers!"

"You mean they're not punished?"

"Not at all. When I was at school, if I did something wrong, I got a hiding. Then I came home, and when I told my father what had happened, he gave me a hiding!"

"Was that a good thing?"

"A very good thing. It has an impact, I tell you. It taught me a lesson. But this" — he gestured out the window; idle boys were everywhere, standing, sitting, eternally waiting — "this is really killing us."

"Not enough hidings," I said, to encourage him.

"Listen to me," Phaks said. "Here there is a constitution for children. Can you believe such a thing? If you take your belt and thrash the child, he can go to the police and lay a charge against you."

"So what's the answer?"

"A hiding is the answer," he said. "Take the rapist in Khayelitsha the other day. Did you hear about it? He was beaten. He was stripped naked. I tell you" — Phaks whipped his fingers — "he was really given a good hiding. He was bleeding. That was not the end of it. While he was lying there, three women stood over him and urinated on his body. Ha-ha!"

Phaks was in a good mood now, calmed with this peroration on rough justice. And he pointed out that in this part of Guguletu there were streets of new houses, like the streets earlier he had called "the Beverly Hills of Langa."

Improbable, this upgrade—it all seemed a neatened version of what I'd seen at New Rest, fixed and improved and hopeful, the transition from slum to township, the structures braced and thickened and made whole. And after this long day of townships was done, anyone would conclude—I certainly did—that a solution to the squatter camps had been found. Hovels were made into homes, and a kind of harmony was established.

This was how, throughout history, cities had been built, the slums made into habitable districts of the metropolis, the gentrification of Gin Lane, the bourgeoisification of the Bowery. I thought of old prints I'd seen of sheep cropping grass in Soho Square in London, of shepherds following their flocks through the weedy ruins of nineteenth-century Rome, of cows grazing on Boston Common.

But the day was not done. We left the bungalows of Guguletu and took a side road into what looked like a refugee camp: thrown-together shelters, sheds covered with tin, skeletal frames patched with plastic sheeting and piled with boulders and scrap wood to prevent the sheeting from blowing away, pigpens, doghouses, crude fences draped with threadbare laundry. The shacks stood close together, with only foot-wide passageways between their outside walls. Smoke rose from cooking fires, lantern light glowed in the growing dusk, and improvised power lines hung overhead, like the web of a drunken spider, spun higgledy-piggledy, the visible images of string theory mapped in the twilit sky—squatters tapping illegally into the national grid.

This settlement was new, housing the most recently arrived people, land snatchers and hut makers and desperadoes. Some had arrived yesterday, more would arrive tomorrow, the shacks stretching for another mile across the dusty wasteland.

What looked like a refugee camp *was* a refugee camp—for the poor fleeing the provinces, having renounced the countryside and the rural villages, just coming to squat at the edge of the golden city. They too wanted real homes, running water, and electricity. There was no end to this township: the hostels led to the shacks, the shacks to the hovels, the hovels to the roadside and the bungalows, and beyond the bungalows and the shebeens were the newcomers in the twig-and-plastic lean-tos, straggling across the flatland. No sooner had a solution been found than a new solution was needed. It was the African dilemma.

"People keep coming," Phaks said. "There are more townships you have not seen—Bonteheuwel . . ."

As he was listing them I saw, chatting by the roadside, in the vilest corner of the squatter camp, three teenage girls in white blouses, blue skirts, knee socks, and matching black shoes on their way home from school. They held satchels that bulged with books and homework. They stood out vividly because of the whiteness of their blouses in the failing light—harmonious and hopeful and a little surprising, like the sudden blown-open blossoms you see in a stricken ditch.

It was growing dark, and I had to return to town. Phaks said, "But I haven't shown you the last thing. It is a surprise."

We drove back to Khayelitsha. Phaks's surprise was a hotel, Vicki's Place, run by a cheerful woman who advertised her home as "the smallest hotel in Africa," just two rooms in a rickety two-story house. Many foreign journalists and travel writers had publicized Vicki's Place. Vicki had the newspaper and magazine clippings, all mentioning her good humor, her effort, her enterprise in this township.

Phaks had yet another surprise: his van wouldn't start. He sat wiggling the key in its slot, next to a fistful of wires he'd pulled out, hoping to find the problem.

"I'll take the train," I said.

"Bus is better."

Ten years before I had wanted to take the train but had been discouraged from doing so by the clerk in the ticket booth.

"I'm taking the train," I told Phaks.

He walked me through the back streets to the station and stayed with me and insisted on buying my ticket. When the train arrived we shook hands, we hugged, and he glumly said he'd have to return to his broken car.

"Keep your hand on your money," he said.

The train was fairly empty because it was headed to the city. Returning from Cape Town, it would be full. I looked for potential muggers and, scanning the passengers in the car, caught the eye of the woman in the seat across from me.

"Why are you here?" she asked.

"Just looking."

"Whites don't come here. White people don't live here," she said with almost boastful conviction.

"But I'm here," I said.

"Because you have that man to help you," she said. She must have seen Phaks at the ticket office. She looked defiant, almost contemptuous. "You wouldn't come here alone."

"What are those lights?" I asked her, to change the subject, and pointed to the slopes of Table Mountain.

"Rondebosch, Constantia." She had answered without looking up.

3

Cape Town: The Spirit of the Cape

NOTHING, APPARENTLY, IS HIDDEN in Cape Town: it is a city like an amphitheater. Its air breathing upon me sweetly, I sat in elegant, embowered, villa-rich Constantia, the district on the ridge I'd glimpsed the day before from the shacks of Khayelitsha. I was sipping a glass of sauvignon blanc in the majestic portico that was the tasting room of the main house at Constantia Glen Vineyard. From this vantage point I was able to see over the rim of my wine glass the poisonous cloud of dust that hung above the Cape Flats.

This visibility is one of the unusual features of Cape Town. The estates in its wealthiest enclaves, in the cliffy suburbs of the middle slopes of the mountain (Constantia, Rondebosch, Bishopscourt, Newlands), have views of the bleak horizontal profile of the suffering squatter camps and poor sprawling townships on the flatland below. The orderly green vineyards look down on brown muddled scrubland, and likewise, through the wide gaps in the plank walls or the rips in the blue plastic of the shacks in Khayelitsha it is possible to enjoy a panorama of university buildings and colonnades bulking on the heights of leafy Rondebosch.

Gated communities all over these highlands display signs warning any unwelcome intruder of 24/7 MONITORING AND ARMED RESPONSE, yet the poor have an unimpeded view of the rich, and vice versa. And each exposed person, squinting from this distance, looks passive and ubiquitous, like a sort of human vegetation.

The last time I'd been in Cape Town this winery did not exist — no vines, no casks, no activity except the mooing of cows. It had been a dairy farm, bought by an entrepreneur named Alexander Weibel, who'd had money and been interested in making wine. He plowed the hills and discovered that the land had clayey subsoil, had good water-holding capacity, and was rich in mica that would impart a "distinctive minerality," as he called it, to the white wine. He planted vines, fenced them, staked them, pruned them. He invested in winemaking equipment, and in 2007 he had his first harvest. His wine was acclaimed. All this within ten years.

"I know that's Khayelitsha," I said, looking down at the townships on the Flats.

"And that's Mitchells Plain," the helpful woman in the wine-tasting portico told me. "And Guguletu, and over there, past Langa, is Bonteheuwel. Coloreds live there."

Almost half the population of Cape Town was "colored." The word had not been abandoned, and neither had "coolie" (*koelie*), for Indian; though "Bantu," "Muntu," "native," "kaffir," and "Hottentot" were execrated and condemned. A supermarket manager, technically "colored," referred to one of his employees as a Hottentot while I was in Cape Town. (He pronounced the word the South African way, "Hot-not.") Someone overheard this and reported him to a superior. He was fired on the spot.

The township of Bonteheuwel was created when the old, lively, multiracial District Six, in central Cape Town, was bulldozed, and the different races were dispersed and resettled, each to a specific place with its own racial hue. That was how, with refugees and exiles, Bonteheuwel grew. It is known as much for the distinctiveness of its people as for the violence of its crime. Much of Bonteheuwel is controlled by street gangs, and unlike the rest of the townships with their random shootings and beatings, the Bonteheuwel gangs are organized, with menacing names, and engaged in endless drug and turf wars. What Bonteheuwel had in common with the other townships was that, with all its hardships and disorder, it was also a place with a life of its own, where music and art filled the clubs and galleries, and where residents set off in the morning to work in central Cape Town or to attend school.

It was from Bonteheuwel that twenty-two-year-old Donna-Lee de Kock traveled each morning with her mother to the Old Mutual Insurance building in Pinelands — a one-and-a-half-hour commute — to attend the Tertiary School in Business Administration. That's where I met Donna-Lee and her classmates. Ostensibly I was there to give a talk, but my deeper motive was to find out about the school and perhaps discover, after my time wandering around the townships, something promising.

This tertiary school, known by its acronym, TSiBA (the Xhosa word for "jump"), was good news. It was privately funded and nonprofit. I was particularly interested because the school had opened in 2005, since I had last been in South Africa. In the beginning 80 students were enrolled; there were now 320. No student was required to pay any tuition or fees, though it cost $10,000 a year to educate each one — for food, textbooks, transportation, computer, and writing materials. All the pupils were studying business administration or economics, and all were aiming to start businesses. The school's mission was to make something good happen. I liked its self-sufficiency, and its being a purely South African endeavor — not an institution imposed by a meddling Mrs. Jellyby, a foreign philanthropist, or a parachuting pop star. Nor was it connected to any government or politician.

Allowances were made for students from deprived educational backgrounds. If someone applied and was found to be worthy of consideration, but deficient in any academic area, a "bridging year" was provided to sharpen needed skills and bring him or her up to standard. The aim of the school was to provide a college education for young people who otherwise would not have access to it — those who were too poor or out of touch or badly prepared.

The school was founded by Leigh Meinert, a young woman from Cape Town who had degrees from universities in South Africa and Great Britain. Idealistic, white, from a winemaking family, she was committed to making a difference in South Africa. Her father, Martin Meinert, learned winemaking at his family's Devon Valley vineyard and also had a degree in viticulture and oenology from the University of Stellenbosch. With her father's encouragement, Leigh Meinert worked on a plan for higher education in South Africa that would reach out to ambitious, intelligent, but overlooked youths.

"I saw how insular my generation was, how little we knew about each other and how isolated we were from the richness of different cultures around us," Leigh Meinert had told a newspaper interviewer the year before I visited, summing up the situation she'd been born into in South Africa, at the time of Nelson Mandela's release from twenty-seven years in prison. "I wanted to do something to change that. Particularly at that exciting time, I wanted to be involved in building the nation, and to work specifically among people of my generation to integrate and build leadership."

These were rosy generalities, but she went to work to make them real. She had been developing the school for seven years and was still only in her early thirties. When I met her she was eight months pregnant, but she laughed at my suggestion that this might be a reason to slow down.

"Do you get any money from the government?" I asked.

"None at all — no government money!" And she laughed. "It's a free university. Maybe it's not a good idea to say that!"

"So how does this operate?"

"Old Mutual gives us space, and we get donations from companies, who also act as mentors. It's not complicated, though it took us a year just to plan it. It takes a lot of cooperation. And work."

"What happens to the graduates?"

"The companies that are our donors often hire them, or they might join other companies or start businesses of their own. The guiding philosophy is that after they get their degree they'll pay it forward. They'll give money or support or time — they'll give back. Because their own education was paid for by someone else."

This was a paraphrase of something she'd written and published: "Our students do not pay back their scholarships. The model, however, is designed to ensure that they pay forward through the transfer of the skills they have learned, through civic engagement and through social responsibility. We also endeavor to include them in the day-to-day running of the operation, which is not only in line with our endeavors to build leadership and entrepreneurship but also helps us keep the management team lean, flexible, young and innovative."

This seemed so hopeful, and consequently so unlikely, that I questioned it. "Do they actually come up with the money?"

"Yes, look!" she said. We were walking down a hallway as she gestured to the framed pictures on the wall. "These are some of them."

Each portrait was headed *A Pay It Forward Hero*, with details of the former student's academic history, present occupation, and how money or time was paid back to the school.

This seemed, in my experience in Africa, one of those rare, grassroots educational efforts that had actually succeeded. Here were clean classrooms, a library with books on the shelves, working computers, lights, running water, with spirited, serious, motivated students — and no foreign patronage. TSiBA had plans to move to a bigger building and was looking for more support.

The school certainly deserved it. The most sought-after postgraduate grant in South Africa was the Mandela-Rhodes Scholarship, which fully funded two years of study for "young Africans who exhibit academic prowess as well as broader leadership potential, an educational opportunity unique on the continent." Mandela himself, in inaugurating the jointly named scholarship in 2003, had said, "It speaks of a growing sense of global responsibility that in this second century of its operation the Rhodes Trust finds it appropriate to redirect some of its attention and resources back to the origins of [its] wealth."

Only thirty Mandela-Rhodes Scholarships were awarded in the whole of Africa each year. In the short time the school had been open, Leigh Meinert's students had bagged four of them.

Like other students at TSiBA, Donna-Lee de Kock, from the distant township of Bonteheuwel, was studying for a BA in business administration. Her mixed ancestry of African, Chinese, Indian, and white flickered in her features.

"I want to finish here and then go to a cosmetology school," she told me, "get a degree there, and then start my own business."

In the school library with about fifteen of the students, I asked them about their plans. Each one had the ambition of starting a business, and was specific about the time it would take, the study it required, the various steps. They were frank about the slowing economy, the high unemployment, and when I asked pointedly about government corruption, they merely smiled: they knew. They were unanimous on one point.

"We all have an aspiration to get out of the townships," one of them said.

Lingering in Cape Town, looking for more good news, I heard about an older migrant labor camp, called Lwandle, that had reinvented itself as a township and put itself on the map with its new museum. I got a ride there. Less than thirty miles from the center of Cape Town, Lwandle was another example of Cape Town proximity, the poor dusty township visible from the heights of the wealthy green city. In this case, miserable Lwandle in Somerset West was adjacent to the old lovely town of Stellenbosch, with its wineries and its university, under the steep and striated mountain ridge still known as Hottentots Holland.

The distinguishing feature of Lwandle was its high self-esteem, which was reflected in its self-promotion. Its showcase, the Lwandle Migrant Labor Museum, displayed its history over sixty years. The township had its own historian too, who greeted me and showed me around.

His name was Mr. Lunga Smile — as, he explained, in "smile for the camera" — and he had been educated at the local secondary school, Khanyolwetho High School. He was a cheery soul with a jumping, loose-limbed way of walking, like a man kicking a ball, and along with his outward energy was an eagerness to inform. He wore a warm plaid jacket and wool cap on this chilly overcast day, which gave an even greater bleakness to the wilderness of huts and hostels.

Like his counterpart Archie, the historian of Langa township across the Flats, Mr. Smile of Lwandle was able to convert his cheeriness into a sense of outrage when he pointed out the indignities suffered by township dwellers over the years.

"This was how the poor people lived before," he said. "Look at the bad construction. No running water. No heating."

To demonstrate the former hardships of the residents, one of the hostels, dating from 1958, had been preserved unchanged. It was a cinderblock one-story structure without heat or water, divided into different-sized cubicles, the smaller ones designated for sixteen people, the larger ones holding as many as thirty-eight.

"They were all men, working in the canning factories," Mr. Smile said.

It was the familiar story: men in search of work who had left their homes and families in the Eastern Cape to live in migrant labor hostels outside Cape Town. There, they were employed in the fertile Stellenbosch Valley by farmers as fruit and vegetable pickers and grape harvesters, and by the factories that processed and canned these products.

But the main employer, the Gant food and canning factory, had shut down in the 1980s, and with the vineyards more highly mechanized, fewer laborers were needed. I had come hoping to find good news, but I was discovering another paradox. The majority of the people in Lwandle were now unemployed, yet the resident population was increasing, and was idle. Lwandle and its nearby squatter camp were now home to eighty thousand people.

Mr. Smile led me through the old, cold, gritty building, with its dead air, its scorched walls, and its outside toilets with six bucket stalls.

"They had to empty the buckets by hand, carrying them over there," Mr. Smile said. "And a woman was not safe here. She could be assaulted when she was doing her business."

I clucked, made notes, and walked around the awful place, designated as Building 33, and Mr. Smile continued talking.

"This is where they lived—see, how close together!" He darted into a back room where some shelves represented beds. "They would say, 'My bed is my home.'"

I clucked some more, scribbled again, noting the dirty cement floors, the rooms like prison cells, the filthy ceilings, the windows so begrimed and unwashed I couldn't see through the glass.

"This is our heritage!"

Then I saw a hand-lettered cardboard sign and asked, "What's that?"

"It was put there by the people who lived here before."

"Before what?"

"Before it was made into a museum," Mr. Smile said. "They are objecting."

I copied the sign. It read: WE THE RESIDENTS OF ROOM 33 DESIDE TO WRITE THIS NOTICE DISAGREE WITH THE PEOPLE ABOUT THIS ROOM TO BE A MESSEUM. FIRSTLY GIVE US ACCOMMODATION BEFORE TO GET THIS ROOM. THANK YOU — FROM ROOM 33.

So the people who had been living in the hovel, who had been evicted in order to make the place a museum piece representing the worst example of a slum, wanted urgently to return and inhabit the hovel as they had always done; bad as it was, they were worse off where they lived now. They wanted their hovel back, even if it meant pigging it there.

"Where are they now?"

"Maybe a squatter camp," Mr. Smile said.

"So how is this better than it was before?"

"Now each person has his own space" — and by "space" he meant elbow room in the hovel — "rather than sharing it."

Former migrant labor hostels had been converted into dwellings for families, but they were just as crowded, dirty, and unheated. Small children, ragged and barefoot, chased each other on a chilly evening, running past a wall with a painting of Steve Biko, killed by police during the apartheid era, one of the martyrs of the freedom struggle. Not far from where we were talking, a woman was doing her laundry, slapping at wet clothes in a small public sink fixed to a standpipe by the dirt road.

The museum at Lwandle had been more successful than the cultural committee at Lwandle might have intended, since the whole of the township seemed to be preserved as a grubby reminder of the bad old days persisting into the present. The only difference was that instead of Lwandle serving as a camp for overworked men, it was now a camp of unemployed families, scraping by on handouts and menial labor.

The Migrant Labor Museum contained a display of photographs of residents of Lwandle, most of them women — "domestics," Mr. Smile said, explaining that they had been house servants for white families in Stellenbosch.

They were portraits of older women sitting in rough chairs in humble surroundings. One showed a stout woman in a voluminous dress. Her name was given, Nontuthzelo Christine Makhebane. A succinct caption in her own words summed up her melancholy existence here:

My home is where I was born. I am only staying here. My home is Ngqamakhwe. I only work here. But my future where I would die is Ngqamakhwe.

Ngqamakhwe, which I found on a map, was a tiny rural settlement halfway across the country, in the green bosom of the Eastern Cape.

"Why do these people come here if there's so little work?" I asked Mr. Smile.

"Because of drought in their village," he said. "Because of no food in the house. Because they have hopes."

And because, as Elias Canetti points out in *Crowds and Power*, people feel more secure in a crowd; so they flee the emptiness and insecurity of the countryside to seek consolation in an urban slum crowd, even a futureless and filthy one, like this in Lwandle.

In the thickening dusk and the dirty light, skinny children, some of them barefoot, were kicking a ball across a stony patch of ground and screaming at each other and then hooting at me as I passed.

Each evening in Cape Town, after traipsing through the townships, I returned to my luxury hotel. The difference in circumstances was emphatic, and the implications made me cringe. I was well aware that in the nineteenth century, wealthy, voyeuristic Londoners headed to the slums of the East End for the thrill of the gutter — the word "slumming" dates from 1884. During Prohibition, white New Yorkers looked for booze and exoticism in outings to the poorest parts of Harlem and the Bowery. Today, such social descents are a recognized branch of the travel industry; so-called slum tourism exists in India and South America and is a brisk business in South Africa.

Slum tourism perhaps originated when the first passionately nosy tourist met a hungry slum dweller who recognized a lawful opportunity and, instead of contemplating robbery, guided the tourist — for a fee — to see the people of the abyss. The poorest Africans began to realize that the very fact of their poverty engaged many foreign visitors who — associating poverty with danger and failure — could not possibly indulge themselves this way back home.

This sort of tourism has been denounced as "poverty porn" and exploitation, monetizing the misery of slum dwellers who had nothing else to offer. For some day-trippers, the experience was an extreme example of curiosity bordering on voyeurism, the leering intention of the alien tourist to feel the shiver of difference, the horror interest that was indistinguishable from slumming. But there were others — sympathetic, charity-minded outsiders — who were moved to contribute money as well as to gape, and having seen the slum they were contributing with a degree of understanding. As I had seen myself, early visitors and volunteers in the squatter camp of New Rest, with a genuine desire to help, had been instrumental in supporting a clinic and a nursery. And they had played a part in transforming the camp into a viable township.

Voyeurism is an element in much, perhaps most, of travel, but even so, I believed my visits were neither horror-driven nor high-minded. "When some people travel they merely contemplate what is before their eyes," the Taoist Lieh Tzu said. "When I travel, I contemplate the processes of mutability."

Of course I wanted to prettify my intentions — what traveler doesn't? — but I did think Lieh Tzu's point of view summed up how I felt: not slumming, not patronizing, but looking for changes. (And maybe a bit of voyeurism too; otherwise, why not stay home?) I wanted to see changes, and I had found many: the hovels-to-houses development at New Rest, the establishment of the Tertiary School in Business Administration in Pinelands, the diminishing of attacks with sticks and stones on Khayelitsha railway cars, and a general sense of uplift in the city. Seeing differences like that (the process of mutability) seems to me one of the purposes of travel, and often suggests how the world changes and gives glimpses of the future.

But after a day's immersion, I always went back to my hotel. My hotel was splendid — and slightly worrying for its splendor, because a hotel can be so much like home that it becomes a barrier to understanding the outside world and its discomforts. The pleasure of being at the hotel made me procrastinate; I knew that when I left it I would be traveling into the unknown — at least for me: I had never taken the road north out of Cape Town, toward Namibia, Botswana, Angola, and perhaps beyond. I had a map, and some money, and months ahead of me.

My hotel, the Taj Cape Town, had a spa where I sometimes got a massage ("Guest is God, sir, allow me to wash your feet"), and an Indian gourmet restaurant where I could be found most evenings tucking into my tandoori, my shirt front scattered with poppadom crumbs. Coffee and cream buns were served every afternoon in the lobby, where I sat in a leather armchair and read the latest installment in the *Cape Times* of the racist rants of one of South Africa's rising demagogues, Julius Malema, or wrote of my day's events in my notebook.

Capetonians tended to wince when I told them I was going to yet another township, much as a New Yorker might show bafflement — and rightly so — toward a visitor in Manhattan saying he'd spent the day in Brownsville, in Brooklyn, where there are eighteen low-income public housing projects, of somber and unprepossessing aspect. New Yorkers had now and then challenged me in this very way. Yet one of my most enlightening weeks in New York had been spent wandering in Brownsville and the South Bronx, gathering material for an essay ("Subterranean Gothic") about the far reaches of the New York subway system.

"Why do Africans invite people to see their misery?" a South African friend asked me. It was a frequent question. "And why do people go on these township tours?"

He happened to be a chef, a traveler, and a foodie. To introduce me to Cape Town's gourmet food scene, he had brought me to Aubergine Restaurant. I started my meal with crayfish bisque involtini with daikon and asparagus, and he ordered game-fish carpaccio, Namibian crab salad, and seared scallops accented by mizuna coulis. For my entrée I had seared ostrich fillet "accented with buffalo mozzarella and Cape gooseberries," and he chose rolled rabbit saddle with strips of crispy rabbit belly, flavored with lardo, served on a haricot vert purée. He went on badgering me about slum tourism while I listed for him the miseries I had seen in the townships, which for me was every bit as arresting and unusual as the seared ostrich fillet with gooseberries, and much more enlightening.

"This 2005 Boekenhoutskloof from Franschhoek is an excellent pairing with the ostrich."

"Yes, just a touch more, thanks. What was I saying?"

"You were going on about the squatter camps."

I thought then, and I still believe, that the only way to understand a city is to see its periphery, because that's where the workers generally live, the people who are employed to maintain it — who were probably the ones sweeping the crumbs off this table at the Aubergine and others in the back prepping the food. A city cannot function without such people. That was as true of New York as of Cape Town: city workers never lived downtown, but rather on the fringes, in the townships, and commuted by train or minibus to their jobs. The woman who made my bed at the Taj — a venerable building, once a bank, which shimmered near the park and botanical garden known as the Company Gardens — this smiling, wheezing soul who always asked in a welcoming way if I was enjoying myself, clocked off each day to return to her humble home in a dusty township on the Cape Flats.

My foodie friend said I should take a tour around the mountain to see the tidy seaside communities. I did that the next day, with Claire Jones driving and narrating. Claire had come out from England as a small girl long ago. She'd thought of leaving during the oppressive years of apartheid, but had stayed and been exhilarated by the political changes, the release of Mandela, the new prosperity, the World Cup.

"It's my home. I travel, of course, all the time. But I always come back. I don't want to live anywhere else."

She took me down the west-facing coast and the high cliffs ("and those rocks are the Twelve Apostles, but don't count them, there's more than twelve") to Sea Point, Bantry Bay, Clifton, and Hout Bay ("they used to issue passports here, as a joke"), then over to Scarborough, where on a bench a huge nanny in a pinafore and floppy sun hat held a tiny white girl in her vast soft lap. We then went over the ridge — glimpses of knuckle-walking baboons — to Simons Town (and a new category of tourist: chattering, well-heeled tourists from the People's Republic of China); to Boulders Beach to look at the jackass penguins I'd seen ten years before — but many more of them now, and better protected; and up the shore of False Bay to Fish Hoek and Glencairn and Kalk Bay, where the fishermen were just purring into the harbor, in their beamy wooden open-decked boats, with crates of freshly caught kingklip — all-Xhosa crews, all raised as fishermen, their blackness set off by yellow oilskins.

It was a simple jaunt. I was sightseeing, an aimless, usually goofy activity I generally disparage for its self-indulgence, but the sights were beautiful, the food was excellent, the weather was perfect—it was all so undemandingly pleasant there was nothing to write about; and I had the feeling that once I left, I would be on a bumpy road, headed through dust into uncertainty.

And something else held me back too: a nagging thought that kept me idling, in a way cowering, in the comforts of Cape Town. It was the morbid belief that I might not return, not just to Cape Town, but home; that I was setting off to suffer and die.

As a young man, I never entertained this idea of death in travel. I had set off for Africa almost fifty years ago with the notion that my life had at last begun, that I was free in this great green continent, liberated from my family and its paternalism just at the time many African countries had liberated themselves from the paternalistic hand of colonialism. And when Africans told me how they had been repressed, confined, belittled, exploited, and infantilized by their colonial overlords, be it Britain, Belgium, Portugal, or France, I thought of my fierce mother saying, "It's your own damn fault" and "You're not going anywhere—you have no gumption," and my father saying, "Get a job—money doesn't grow on trees" and "Why are you so defiant?" and "Why do you write trash?"

So Africa had been deliverance for me, a liberating embrace and an opportunity. Many people feel that same relief, happiness, and sense of possibility on first arriving in Africa. Africans themselves inspire it. And in Africa I had at last something to write. At that time, the early and mid-1960s, many parts of the continent, remote and seldom visited, beckoned to me. I became a teacher in a small school in Malawi and then a professor at Makerere University in Uganda. On vacations, I traveled to the Congo, Nigeria, Ghana, and Kenya, up and down Malawi, and to the Lower Shire River, a marshy tributary of the Zambezi. I got married in Uganda, and my first child was born there. Africa gave me everything. I never thought of death: Africa had given me life.

But my good luck in travel had held for so long that it was bound to give out at some point, and surely soon. Africa had changed. Countries I had loved to visit had imploded or failed, and the people themselves often said, pleadingly, "We are hopeless, sir," as they extended their hands, appealing for money. I would soon leave for the malarial part of Africa, the pushing-and-shoving part, where life was precarious, where there wasn't enough food or water, where buses gasped down the bad roads, and where people had been so thoroughly abandoned by their governments, so left to their own resources, they were possessed by their own fears for survival. Why should any of them care about an aging white man asking nosy questions and scribbling the answers in his notebook?

In a life of travel, I had been in awful places and taken foolish risks, and I had survived. I always thought of myself as the Fortunate Traveler. But at some point even the luckiest person, full of hope, opens a door and finds a skeletal reflection on the other side. And so the traveler each morning in the mirror, like Webster in Eliot's poem, becomes much possessed by death, and sees the skull beneath the skin, the hollow eye sockets, the lipless grin.

In my last few days in Cape Town, I prowled the markets and shops. Many of them sold industrial curios for tourists, fake masks and beads and baskets, though a few small shops had the genuine article: old carvings and village implements — stools, trophy staffs, digging sticks, ritual objects. I love old wooden objects that have been handled and used: the stool that has been polished by a skidding bottom, the symmetrical neck rest that has supported the drowsing head of its owner for many years, the wooden bowl with its pumpkin-colored patina, the ivory bracelet darkened by the wearer's wrist, the fetish object glowing with the nervous chafing of superstitious fingers. I found a Yaka fetish, a staring, open-mouthed cubist figure with a long neck and nothing else, carved out of black wood, small enough to hold in my hand. It seemed to be a frightener. The Yaka people straddle the border of the Congo and Angola, most of them near the Kwango River at the edge of the top most part of Angola, where I was headed. It became my personal fetish and protector.

And I bought a detailed map and a bus ticket.

The last item on my Cape Town wish list was a boat ride. I longed to get a view of the city from the sea. I had never been on a boat off-shore. My modest request was converted by some well-wishers into a picnic on a fifty-six-foot motor yacht, *The Spirit of the Cape.* The name was appropriate: it was the spirit of the Cape that I wanted to feel. We set off from a mooring next to the Cape Grace Hotel and sailed past the docks and the pedestrian swing-bridge into Table Bay, six of us on board, good companions, great food, the lovely sea, and looming above us the mountain that had been first glimpsed by the Portuguese explorer Bartolomeu Dias in 1488; he called it Cabo das Tormentas for the torments of its storms and rough seas.

On this blindingly bright day, a cold wind gusting in from the south, we sailed about three miles offshore and then coasted south, past Table Mountain, monumental in the sunlight, the numerous Apostles arrayed in rock near the summit, the city scattered across their granite robes. Anyone knowing its history, especially its re-cent history, could be confident that Cape Town was a city with a future, one that inspired the notion that all things are possible. Robben Island, just offshore, was no longer a penal colony, and its most famous prisoner had guided the country to freedom and was still alive and smiling, affectionately known to all by his clan name, Madiba.

The plateau to the south was a national park, where troops of chacma baboons frowned and skittered amid the low-growing, sweet-smelling bushes that Afrikaners called *fynbos.* The land looked blessed, the uttermost end of the earth, a paradise — as it was when its only inhabitants were hunter-gatherers who called them-selves the Real People. As a passage to the East Indies, it had been renamed Good Hope.

On *The Spirit of the Cape* we drank beer and ate cold pink prawns and slices of pizza. We talked about travel, and I learned from my fellow picnickers that the Cape is the home of *The Flying Dutchman,* the ghost ship that sails endlessly and is a lesson to all travelers, especially to those who overreach themselves. And—since the legend was based on an actual overzealous captain—to travelers who don't know when to stop.

"So, Paul, where are you headed?"

I began fumblingly to describe my itinerary. Several of the men had been to Namibia, but none to Tsumkwe in the remote northeast, home of the Ju/'hoansi people, where I hoped to go. None of the men had seen Angola, though they knew ex-soldiers who'd been —the South African army had fought there, laid land mines there, and bombed the towns, fighting against Namibian guerrillas as well as supporting one of the factions in the twenty-seven-year Angolan civil war. But these days Angola was pretty much terra incognita, noted for its oil reserves, its many unexploded land mines, and its isolation.

"Are you sure you want to go there?"

I said, "Oh, yes. I'm looking forward to it."

"The roads are supposed to be really awful."

I said, "I'm not in a hurry."

"Probably no roads at all in some of the places."

It would have been pretentious to say "I follow no path, the path follows me," but it was, pompously, how I felt.

I said, "There's always a way if you're not in a hurry."

"You can see it all here," the captain said. He switched on the GPS, and soon in lighted segments the west coast of southern Africa appeared on the screen. He dialed it larger and scrolled up.

"There's the northern part, Namaqualand and the interior," he said, his fingers spider-walking on the screen. "That smooth part of the coast—there are diamond mines all over it. That hook is Luderitz, where Namibia starts. There's Walvis Bay—lots of shipping there. And Swakopmund, and the Skeleton Coast."

"See that line?" one of the others said. "That's the Kunene River, the border of Angola. I've been up there in a helicopter with safari clients, but not over it. No one goes across except the Himba."

The Himba people were seminomadic herders, venerators of fire, famously traditional and handsome in beads and shell ornaments, red clay clotting the women's long braids.

As *The Spirit of the Cape* turned near an old, partly submerged wreck at Clifton, and rode the swell back to the harbor, the captain helpfully traced the meandering line with his fingertip, indicating the watercourse border that divided Namibia from Angola. But the map had so little detail, its simple topography glowing on the screen in the wheelhouse, it seemed to depict a land unknown and undiscovered.

4

The Night Bus to Windhoek

L IKE A SHEEPISH BOY, round-shouldered and self-conscious, slumping in his father's expensive car and going off
to school, I said, "Yusuf, please drop me here," as the powerful black Mercedes approached the bus station. The station entrance was indistinct in the early morning mist. I preferred to be
anonymous. Well, who wouldn't? No one is more conspicuous than
a person sliding out of a big limo to climb onto a beat-up bus. But
the hotel concierge had insisted, wishing to give me a good send-
off, and it seemed churlish to refuse. At a discreet distance – Yusuf
heeding my request – I jumped out before he could open my door.
He was smiling, chuckling softly, as he shook my hand and gave me
the morning paper, a neatly folded *Cape Argus*.

"Good journey, sir." *Jinny.*

"You're smiling because I'm taking the bus," I said, breathing diesel fumes from the idling buses.

"Not at all, sir."

"Why, then?"

"Because you have bought a one-way ticket only, sir." *Tucket.*

Yes, I did not know how far I'd get, or whether I was coming back this way. It was a leap in the dark, northerly, in the direction of the Congo.

The whole color spectrum of South African racial identities was represented at the station, preparing to board the bus: black, Indian, Cape Malay, "colored," Chinese, and some beefy Boers, all of us headed to Springbok and the border, and perhaps across it. No formalities except a perfunctory ritual with the driver, who held a clipboard and checked my name. It was casual and orderly, with no security, no delay; as soon as we were on the bus, we were driven out of the city, toward Namibia and *l'Afrique profonde,* into the gut of the greenest continent.

I sat by the window reading the *Cape Argus,* relishing the prospect of the long trip and catching up on the news. All week, in and out of the townships, I had been following the progress of a public battle between disciplinarians in the ruling party, the African National Congress, and Julius Malema, the boisterous president of its Youth League, who rejoiced in his own mayhem. Malema was always in the news for his offensive pronouncements: his shouted threats to whites and Indians, his demands that the mines should be nationalized, that Botswana must be invaded and its government overthrown, that the white-owned farms in South Africa be overrun and seized—handed wholesale to black South Africans—as had happened disastrously in Zimbabwe, a ruined country on the brink of bankruptcy that Malema admired and frequently visited.

Though he was depicted in the press as a buffoon, and had three convictions in South African courts for uttering hate speech, Malema was a possible future leader of South Africa. Indeed, he was a leader now, though a divisive one. Only thirty years old, but wealthy, dangerous, and vindictive, he was just reckless enough to seek the highest office. The current president, Jacob Zuma, who, as his mentor, seemed an older, cannier version of this arrogant bully, had begun to fear him. Like Zuma, Malema had—so newspaper investigations reported—enriched himself through shady deals and backhanders in state contracts. As a result, he owned a newly built mansion in a posh suburb of Johannesburg.

Malema had presided over the Youth League since 2008, and pictures of him, fist upraised, ranting at a microphone, from year to year showed him sequentially swelling, an intense black wire of a man transformed, growing fatter and balder until his big smooth head was almost without features, like an overinflated balloon with eyes swollen to wicked slits, a face that did not achieve any expression except when, with popping eyes and bared teeth, he succeeded in inspiring fear by spreading racist menace.

Popular among the black urban poor for his unapologetic insults, his bellowed speeches were widely quoted. So were his unruly press conferences, where he went out of his way to humiliate journalists and anyone else who disagreed with him, especially members of the foreign press. His abuse was memorable for being blunt: "stupid," "imperialist," "little tea girl," "go away!" It seemed that no one in the government knew what to do with him, and that malicious thought gave him pleasure, because the more he was censured, the greater was his defiance.

Those noisy obedient souls who were his following had the leisure to show up any time, anywhere they were summoned, to cheer him, wave signs, and jump up and down—his audience's peculiar display of approval was energetic jumping, giving a Malema rally the look of an enormous aerobics class. These jumpers were nearly all young, unemployed males from the townships—hardly reassuring to Malema's opponents (of whom there were many) since the largest proportion of out-of-work South Africans lived in the townships. They were the many millions with nothing to do and nowhere to go, for whom Malema offered a diabolical sort of hope in the politics of racial incitement.

Demagoguery in Africa, as far as speechifying was concerned, had never mattered much. Though spitting and screaming speeches were fairly common among up-and-coming party hacks, a gift for oratory was not crucial to an African politician aiming to be a tyrant. The traditional chiefs and kings did not engage in public speaking, but merely whispered their wishes to their right-hand man — the *porte-parole* in West African kingship, the "chief's messenger" in East and Central Africa — the mouthpiece who conveyed the words that had to be obeyed.

Though the sympathies and howls of the rabble, the poor, the mob, might be helpful, they were seldom decisive factors in promoting a man to power, unless the mob was also well armed. In every African tyranny it was the army's loyalty to the leader and its impartial cruelty that made the difference. Once a leader established himself as a dictator, he controlled his country through the army and the police, supplemented by the thuggery of self-appointed intimidators in the ruling party's youth league. Speechmaking was irrelevant; if you had armed men on your side, no further persuasion was needed. An African dictator could be a mute and merciless enforcer and spend many decades in power without ever being seen in public.

But, oddly and perhaps unique to Africa, music always mattered to the political process. Never mind the speeches — who had the patience to listen to the lies? Along with the gun, music was the most persuasive influence in African political life, as it was in African culture; politics was dominated by rousing songs. This had always been the case. In the early 1960s in Nyasaland (soon to be Malawi) the defining song was "Zonse Zimene za Kamuzu Banda" — "Everything Belongs to Kamuzu Banda," both a hymn and a prediction, in praise of the incoming prime minister, sung in villages, at political meetings, and by the students at my little school. Banda took power, suppressed and jailed the opposition, and went on to rule (the music still playing) for the next thirty-four years.

South Africa's President Jacob Zuma had his personal anthem, which he sang and danced to in public at every opportunity. It was a song from the struggle, about his machine gun.

> *Umshini wami, umshini wami (My machine gun, my*
>   *machine gun)*
> *We Baba (O Father)*
> *Awulethu, umshini wami (Please bring me my machine gun)*

An inconvenient fact is that South Africa was not liberated by all-out war and certainly not by machine-gun-toting guerrillas. There was no Gettysburg in South Africa, only the waste ground of Sharpeville, which was the site of a one-sided massacre of sixty-nine unarmed protesters. Mandela was not sprung from Robben Island by an indignant mob in a mass, Bastille-storming movement of prisoner liberation. Toward the end of his sentence, Mandela was secretly transferred to a serene, bucolic, country-house setting in the winelands where, with the connivance of the white government, he quietly awaited elections and the transfer of power.

Violent protest, sabotage, and armed struggle had been factors, but not decisive ones, in South African independence, which was gained through stubbornness, labor unrest, paralyzing strikes, public disorder, backroom negotiations, economic sanctions, and especially foreign pressure. The South African army was well armed and overwhelming. Independence was not taken but given, and was long overdue, in the drip-drip-drip of history's inevitability. Zuma's machine-gun anthem, and his war dance to its tune, was merely grimly comic posturing, but it had symbolic value to a populace that still felt aggrieved.

Julius Malema — uneducated, corrupt, canny, crazy-acting, and power mad — much resembled Zuma. He was one of Zuma's supporters and had a personal anthem too, called "Shoot the Boer." Like Zuma, he sang it with exaggerated gusto, hamming it up. You might be excused for thinking — if you didn't know the meaning of the words — that this was exuberant clowning, like a turn in a minstrel show, mimicking an "end man" in blackface, shuffling and playing for laughs; the only prop lacking was a banjo or a tambourine.

But he was serious. A huge headline in the *Cape Argus* I was reading on the bus concerned Malema, denouncing the man for defiantly leading his followers in singing his signature hate song because it seemed he would not stop singing it. "Shoot the Boer" was perfect for a black South African politician on the make — tuneful, with few words, easy to remember, anti-white, and an incitement to murder.

This song, too, had come out of the struggle, but the country had moved on, as it had moved on from *Bring me my machine gun.* Yet there were a great many people in South Africa who liked the message of murder and revenge, because many had yet to find any work, any wealth, any place for themselves, and they were envious of the visibly rich and enraged over them. These disaffected people were the township toughs who stoned trains, hijacked cars, and terrorized neighborhoods with brazen robberies that sent crime statistics soaring. With an annual homicide rate of 32,000, and rapes amounting to more than 70,000, South Africa led the world in 2011 in reported rapes and murders.

Given that "Shoot the Boer" advocated the killing of white farmers, it was another dire statistic that, since apartheid was banned in 1994, more than 3,000 white farmers had been murdered by black assassins. Most of the victims had been ambushed on isolated farms in the veldt. The anthem's lyrics in Zulu were brutally simple:

> *Ayasab' amagwala (The cowards are scared)*
> *Dubula dubula (Shoot shoot)*
> *Ayeah*
> *Dubula dubula (Shoot shoot)*
> *Ayasab' amagwala (The cowards are scared)*
> *Dubula dubula (Shoot shoot)*

Awu yoh
Dubula dubula (Shoot shoot)
Aw dubul'ibhunu (Shoot the Boer)
Dubula dubula (Shoot shoot)

Except for the misguided folk who sang this with Malema at his political rallies, the song was condemned in newspaper editorials and by many citizens as hate speech, calling it an embarrassment and a backward step for the country.*

But wait: one voice was raised in defense of Julius Malema, fat and sassy in his canary-yellow baseball cap and canary-yellow T-shirt, his fist raised, shouting "Shoot the Boer — shoot, shoot." This supporting voice was the confident brogue of the Irish singer Paul Hewson, known to the world as the ubiquitous meddler Bono, the frontman of U2. He loved the song. The multimillionaire rocker, on his band's "360-Degree Tour" in South Africa in 2011, had squinted through his expensive sunglasses, tipped his cowboy hat in respect, and asserted that "Shoot the Boer" had fondly put him in mind of the protest songs sung by the Irish Republican Army.

"When I was a kid and I'd sing songs," Bono reminisced to the *Sunday Times* in Johannesburg, "I remember my uncles singing . . . rebel songs about the early days of the IRA."

He treated the reporter to a ditty about an Irishman carrying a gun, and added, alluding to "Shoot the Boer," "It's fair to say it's folk music."

So willing was Bono to ingratiate himself — and, in his haste or ignorance, oblivious of the grotesque murder statistics and the horror of people who feared for their lives — that he went out of his way in his approval of the racist song, bolstering his argument with

---

* For his hate speech and for "sowing divisions," Julius Malema was removed from his Youth League post and expelled from the African National Congress in April 2012. Later that year he reemerged, using the killings by police of striking miners to position himself as a leader once again, with his stated theme: "The government has turned against its people."

the observation that "Shoot the Boer" was a thoroughly Irish senti-ment. Maybe so; though many disagreed, Irish and South Africans alike. His comments caused howls of rage by people in South Africa who noted the paradox that, just the year before, in April 2010, Bono (sharing the stage with former president Bill Clinton) had been honored by the Atlantic Council, which conferred on him the Distinguished Humanitarian Leadership Award.

And here I was, reading this in a bus headed north through the high veldt, with a man who might well have been a Zulu in the seat in front of me, an elderly black woman behind me, and two men who were undoubtedly Boer farmers conversing in Afrikaans in the seat across the aisle.

Into the heartland we went, down the main streets of small towns that were lined by the arcades and porticoes of hardware stores and old shops, past the immense farms and spectacular landscapes of the Northern Cape — a great relief, and uplifting after my experi-ence of the dense dogtowns and squatter camps and townships and the fortified suburbs.

Many of the South Africans I'd met had wanted to be reassured. How are we doing? they'd asked, but obliquely. How did South Africa compare to the country I had seen on my trip ten years be-fore and written about in *Dark Star Safari*? I could honestly say it was brighter and better, more confident and prosperous, though none of it was due to any political initiative. The South African people had made the difference, and would continue to do so, no thanks to a government that embarrassed and insulted them with lavish personal spending, selfishness, corruption, outrageous pro-nouncements, hollow promises, and blatant lies.

The new prosperity was evident as we traveled up the N1 highway past Century City, which was still being developed when I was last in South Africa and had grown to an enormous complex of houses, high-rises, and "the largest shopping mall in Africa," Canal Walk, with hundreds of stores, resembling its sister stereotype, the residential community and shopping center in Florida or California, after which it had been modeled. And serving the same purpose: the middle-class flight from the city, seeking space and security. Well-funded and well-swept Century City was the opposite in every respect of the improvisational townships ten miles to the south of it.

Past a power station, a prison, and Corpus Christi Church (REFUEL HERE AND CONNECT WITH GOD confidently lettered on its sign out front), we swung north on a new road, passing more suburbs — and I noted that the more expensive-looking the home, the higher the perimeter fence or brick wall. In a republic of open country, one that celebrated the freedom of African space, every substantial dwelling was surrounded by walls, every house a fortress.

Up a road lined with gum trees through Durbanville, we passed the first heights of the green bosomy veldt, the gentle Tygerberg Hills, covered with grapevines in orderly rows. They were the extensive plantings of D'Aria Vineyards, composed of two wine farms, Doordekraal and Springfield. The first vintage of this winery was a sauvignon blanc, produced and offered for sale in 2005.

This fact I found out in the next town, Malmesbury, where the bus stopped for half an hour and I was able to talk to one of the Boers in the seat opposite.

His name was Hansie, a miner, headed to Springbok, but he had come this way often, noting the settlement and expansion of Durbanville and the nearby farming towns. This vineyard was no more than ten years old.

"There was nothing here before, just veldt and some old farms," Hansie said. "Now's it's a working wine farm."

He asked me where I was from. I told him.

"You could have stayed at D'Aria instead of the city — it takes guests as well. Nice and quiet."

Over the past decade he had seen the towns here grow, settled by Capetonians looking for a serene life in the hills. The place we had stopped, Malmesbury, was an example, a market town in an old farming district, surrounded by wheat fields, on Hansie's route to Springbok. This town, too, had grown.

"Lots of new people here," he said. "Lots of new shops. It's coming up. And, ach, only thirty kilometers from Cape Town."

Thitty kilometers, he said, and added that we were in Swartland, so called because of the *bleck* soil.

I wanted to ask Hansie about Julius Malema but did not have the heart to speak the name of a man who was obviously his nemesis. South Africans are not unusual in being sensitive about reminders of their history, but their recent past was so full of ambiguities none could say what the future might hold for them.

"Catch you later," he said, releasing me so that he could, as he said, "buy an ass cream cone."

Remembering I had no food or drink with me, I went into a large supermarket just off the main road which loomed like a warehouse and was stacked with merchandise, toppling crates and irregular piles of canned goods in ripped-open cardboard boxes.

The owners were Chinese, and their English was almost non-existent. All I wanted were some bottles of water, which I couldn't find until the woman at the register, with helpful ducklike nods and nasal yips, guided me from where she stood behind the counter. She and the man piling cans were perhaps some of the new people. They were the first of many immigrants from the People's Republic that I was to meet on this trip, and though most of them were doing business in remote and unpromising places, they seemed content, absorbed, unflappable, even grateful, their feet squarely on the ground.

After Malmesbury, the countryside widened into an immensity of low hills and surrounding black ridges. As Hansie had said, the darkness of the soil had earned the region the name Swartland. It was only in such a rural place that South Africa made sense. This was its heartland, its food supply, gentle, settled, serene. I described in my diary the sunlit landscape, cattle browsing in the meadows, the distant farmhouses, the empty roads, the peacefulness.

I held that happy memory in my head, thinking of Malmesbury as a blissful realm, mentioning it later to my friends in Cape Town. And they referred me to a headline in the local newspaper, "Couple Attacked on Malmesbury Farm":

> A couple was attacked with an axe and steel pipe at their house outside of Malmesbury in the Western Cape this morning, police said.
>
> Captain FC van Wyk said three men forced open the back door of the farmhouse around 3 am.
>
> "They demanded money and other valuable items from the 30-year-old victim and his 26-year-old fiancée," Van Wyk said.
>
> "The intruders overpowered and assaulted the couple with an axe and a steel pipe. The man suffered multiple injuries to his back, chest, arms, and legs."
>
> The men ransacked the house and fled with wine and a DVD hi-fi system.

This assault immediately found its way to the Afrikaner Genocide Archives website, which was dense with accounts of attacks on farmers and other rural crimes, and gave more details about the incident in Malmesbury. The victims were Pieter Loubser and not his fiancée but his wife, Brenda, members of the Wes-Kaap Simmentaler cattle breeders' club. The Loubsers ran a dairy farm — their milk, sold locally and in Cape Town, was one of the cheaper food items to be found in the townships. The other facts tallied: an early morning break-in by three men, an ax attack in the bedroom, the demand for money, the theft of valuables, the serious injuries. And another detail, something new: "Other news sources also say that Brenda was very brutally sexually assaulted."

This account concluded: "Farm attacks place the food security of this country in great danger. Irresponsible behaviour and statements by radical young black politicians are directly responsible for this—despite the fact that they themselves fatten themselves with food produced by those same farmers which are so badly maligned by these leaders."

So anyone who believed, with Bono, that Malema's song "Shoot the Boer" was no more than a harmless bit of folklore, and encouraged it to be sung like an Irish ditty, seemed to me an accessory to such assaults. It was obviously an incitement and made life hell for the people who lived on isolated farms. But by the time this crime took place, Bono and U2 were far away, singing somewhere else in the world, perhaps being awarded another prize for being humanitarians, leaving the local farmers here to face the music.

Back on the bus, we continued through farmland, past Mooreesberg and Piketberg, Swartland leading into deeper valleys until the rocky hills swelled to jagged mountains—no trees at all, only strange piled-up rocks like giant cairns, scattered with low scrub and the sweet-smelling *fynbos* that reminded me of the maquis of Corsica, whole hillsides of herbs among sharp cliffs and slopes of smashed rock—the roughest clusters of granite softened by sprouted wildflowers.

Descending to the town of Citrusdal, I was reminded of a young woman at a winery in Constantia whose grandparents farmed here, and I remembered the name Citrusdal for being so specific.

"Granny doesn't speak a word of English," she had told me. "Only Afrikaans. And she never leaves the farm. She's only been to Cape Town a few times in her life. They think I'm so odd to be here. I'm 'the grape girl'!"

Orange groves, mile after mile of their dense boughs and deep green leaves, covered the sunny valleys of Citrusdal. If I'd been in my own car, I would have stopped and stayed the night in this pretty town, among the fragrant trees, at the edge of the Cedarberg Wilderness, so beautiful that my Afrikaner writer friend the late Etienne Leroux, author of *Seven Days at the Silbersteins* and other novels, chose this wilderness as his burial place. It was easy enough to get to, only two or three hours from Cape Town, but for all its proximity a great empty landscape that had once belonged to the San people, who had left their vivid cave paintings behind.

The road was perfectly smooth, looping around the hills, just two lanes of it, the main thoroughfare headed up the left side of Africa. To keep order — and order was the priority — it had been essential for the old white-dominated South African government to create a world-class road system: the army needed it to move with speed and efficiency, to control the population and to fight the long and bloody insurgency in the territory of South-West Africa and beyond. This highway built for jeeps and troop trucks, as well as for moving produce in the bad times, was now a road for sightseers and travelers to Namibia.

In the window seat just ahead of Hansie, an older woman sat reading an article in *Weslander,* an Afrikaans newspaper, with the headline "Hoërskool Brand!," showing a photo of a school in flames. Squat and plump, with a shelving belly and short white hair, she had the Roman emperor look of Gertrude Stein. On her wide lap she had a brown bag of sandwiches, which she ate as she read the paper, looking content.

We had by now passed the larger groves of fruit trees and the wine farms, and the land looked as though all the topsoil had been blasted from it, leaving only low scrub, prickly bush, and bare rock. But even in this seemingly unpromising place to farm I saw irrigated valleys of grapes and citrus. This was at Clanwilliam and Vanrhynsdorp, the place names suggesting the different nationalities of those who had settled here.

Dorp was the right designation for the roadside settlements, the blunt and slightly comical Afrikaans word meaning "village" or "small town." We pulled in at one, another pit stop at the edge of the much drier veldt, where there were no farms at all, the rubbly semidesert looking like New Mexico or Arizona.

I struck up a conversation with a woman here, in her early thirties perhaps, simply to ask why she was taking the bus and how far she was going. It turned out she was going all the way to Namibia too. Her name was Anke, and she was of mixed race, perhaps part German, part African or Malay.

"I'm visiting my grandparents in Windhoek," she said, "just for a break. I need a break."

She lived in Cape Town and had a business there, making children's furniture, and though business had been slow, she said it was picking up.

"Why are you taking the bus?" I asked.

"I always take the bus. I wouldn't dream of going any other way." She had the fluttery Afrikaans way of making the word "dream" into a stammer of two syllables, as if whispering ecstasies. "I love looking at the hills and the farms. It's nice and relaxing on the bus."

I agreed, and this rolling road was the only way of seeing how one country slid slowly into another.

Anke had been cheerful, yet in the next couple of hours a great sunlit sadness descended as the land flattened, the trees vanished, the mountains slipped down, and all the miles to the horizon filled with only reddened grass and low blue tufts of bush. The sheer size of the landscape was daunting, its dryness like desert, and some of the soil held the hard glitter of salt. Nothing grew higher than ten inches or so.

In Cape Town, my bedside reading had been *Voices,* a memoir by Frederic Prokosch, a somewhat forgotten American writer of the middle decades of the twentieth century who had spent much of his life as an expatriate in Europe. His novel *The Asiatics* had been a bestseller in 1935 because it seemed such an elegant and accurate depiction of a young man's travels through China and India. But the travel in it, so evocative and convincing, had all been invented — Prokosch had hardly stirred from his home in New Haven when he wrote the book, and his later life was marked by a succession of hoaxes. *The Asiatics* was much admired by the traveler Bruce Chatwin, who habitually fictionalized his travel writings, punching up mild episodes and giving them drama, turning a few days in a place into a long and knowledgeable residence. Prokosch's many encounters with great writers in *Voices* also seemed like hoaxes, and the world-weariness itself was an affectation.

"Yes, there are still those endless jungles and deserts down in Africa," a European socialite tells the author. "But what do we care about Africa? Nothing that matters happens in Africa."

This was still the ignorant opinion of many people in Europe and the United States. I had copied it into my notebook and given *Voices* away, but I was reminded of "nothing happens" in this long stretch of emptiness that was taking us up the winding, narrow road to Springbok.

We were in the Namaqualand interior, in a stony immensity of low hills and gullies, a desolate grandeur I associated with dinosaur bones. The patches of white I took to be rocks were sheep, in the far distance as small, immobile, round, and mute as stones.

I was thinking — and wrote this in the notebook that bounced on my knee — how I often questioned what I was doing when I happened to be so far away in a parched climate like this. Way past retirement age and alone, I rode among bald hills and scrub, headed to Namibia. If it seemed purely self-indulgent to be here, what perverse aspect of my personality was I indulging?

I argued myself into thinking that physical experience is the only true reality. I didn't want to be told about this, nor did I wish to read about this at second hand. I didn't want to look at pictures or study it on a small computer screen. I didn't want to be lectured about it. I wanted to be traveling in the middle of it, and for it to be washing over me, as it was today, in the emphatic weather, very hot, the glissades of light and heat that gave it a visible lifelessness — now very bright, and all the vitality burned away.

Under the aqueous, utterly cloudless, late afternoon sky and the setting sun lay a landscape of broken and piled-up stones, tortured into sharp valleys and flinty cliffs. The place looked ancient and as if no one had ever lived here, and it matched the profile of an old woman on the bus who stared at the African stones like Karen Blixen, and had the same iguana face.

Sundown at Springbok was an unexpected and eerie arrival at a twilit town surrounded by rock, with smallish, stucco-walled houses embedded in the slopes of a valley of broken granite. As a settlement it seemed an absurdity. What was the point of such a place, glowing in the middle of the descending darkness, not another town for miles?

The answer was that copper had been found near here, the first mineshafts sunk in the seventeenth century by the earliest Dutch settlers. Copper and zinc were still mined in the area, but Springbok was best known today for the profusion of wildflowers that appeared in August and September, the South African spring. The darker history was that of the massacre of the Nama people — the Namaqua — by the Germans who'd come south from Windhoek, heavily armed. The indigenous Nama had lived hereabouts since the dawn of humanity and had flourished because of their proximity to the Orange River. But the discovery of copper and diamonds by the Dutch, and farther north the German imperative to have a whole colony to itself, meant that the native population had to be dealt with mercilessly. In a war that took place between 1904 and 1907, most of the Nama and Herero people were exterminated and the rest driven away or enslaved.

This is the brutal sort of history that produces shock in the tourist, but since it has its parallels all over the Americas, where genocide and slavery were routine, it is sanctimonious to tut-tut.

Anyone in Springbok could point out that the Wampanoag Indians captured in King Philip's War by the embattled Pilgrim fathers were sent wholesale on ships and worked to death as slaves on Caribbean sugar plantations. The curious experience of African history is that it so often throws up images of one's own country's past. But in South Africa it is all so awful and so recent it is a happier diversion to concentrate on the wildflowers.

Half a dozen people on the bus got out at Springbok and, relieved to be home, reassured by their arrival, overcoming their shyness, called out "Safe travels!" to the rest of us.

Darkness fell. We had come almost four hundred miles and were near the border of Namibia. Later, in the glare of lights on tall poles, we pulled into a gas station, and while the other passengers scrambled for food—platters of fried potatoes served up by smiling women dressed like nurses in white smocks and white caps—I looked for someone to talk to. I found a man at the edge of the lights, which was the edge of the desert. He wore a wool hat and thicknesses of ragged clothes. He turned, surprised, because he happened to be shouting at his dog, a poor, beaten-looking mutt that seemed submissive and confused.

"Where are we?"

Instead of answering, the man shouted at me and walked away, his dog following.

"Steinkopf," a bystander said.

Farther down the road, not long after that, we came to a high chainlink fence surmounted by razor wire and looking like the perimeter of a prison. Making it more prisonlike were watchtowers and dazzling lights and men in uniform with wicked rifles slung under their arms. The border.

Some people collect antiques or stamps or Beatles memorabilia. I collect border crossings, and the best of them are the ones where I've had to walk from Cambodia to Vietnam, from the United States to Mexico, from Pakistan to India, from Turkey to the Republic of

Georgia. To me a frontier represents the life of most people. "I became a foreigner," V. S. Pritchett said of being a traveler. "For myself that's what a writer is — a man living on the other side of a frontier." It's a thrill to go on foot from one country to another, a mere pedestrian exchanging countries, treading the theoretical inked line that is shown on maps.

Often a frontier is a river — the Mekong, the Rio Grande, the Zambezi; or a mountain range — the Pyrenees, the Ruwenzoris; or a sudden alteration in topography, a bewildering landscape transformation — hilly Vermont flattening into Quebec. But just as often — perhaps most of the time — a border is irrational yet unremarkable, a seamlessness that goes by the name of No Man's Land, a width of earth bounded by fences. You can hardly tell one country from the other. Often there is no visible difference, as any migrant who crosses the Sonoran Desert from Mexico to Arizona can testify — wasteland straddles the frontier; if there is any drama, it is imposed by the authorities, heightened by the presence of police or the Border Patrol. Otherwise, the border is a contrived and arbitrary dotted line, a political conceit dividing communities and people, creating difference and disharmony. I suppose the act of walking across a border is my way of undoing difference and seeking harmony, even if it is only in my head. It is nearly always a happy act, even in the darkness of night, slowed by officialdom and inspections.

There's an equality in pedestrian border crossings, too: no first class, no fast lane, no preferential treatment. You line up at the office, get your passport stamped, your bags searched, and off you go, perhaps to find a ride on the other side or to reboard the bus. The bus doesn't leave until everyone is processed, and while waiting the travelers shuffle their feet and become restlessly talkative.

My map gave this limit of South Africa as Vioolsdrift.

"*Viool* means 'violin,'" a woman told me. We had gotten off the bus and were going through immigration. "It's a funny name for a place."

Drift means "ford," as in fording a river. The Orange River was the border, but "violin"? One story had it that a Nama man, named Jan Viool after his fiddling, lived here and gave the place its pretty name.

The woman I was speaking to, one of the passengers, was elderly but uncomplaining, standing in the chilly night carrying a small bag. She had a complex ancestry: "I'm German and Malay and Herero, and some Khoisan, and others."

Her name was Johanna, and she was going home to Windhoek. This was the best way, through the Northern Cape. "Beautiful countryside," she said, "especially when there's flowers." She loved to travel, even on this old bus.

"I've been to Britain. It was nice. But my cousin lives in Croydon, a sort of suburb. I didn't like it at all. Too many people. Not like this." Johanna gestured to the emptiness, the surrounding darkness, the immensity of night sky, the glitter of stars. "I went to Malaysia once, just to see it."

"Did people ask you where you came from?"

"Ach, yes. Some of them asked, 'Are you an Australian aborigine?'" And she laughed. "I told them 'Namibia,' but they had no idea what I was talking about. They didn't know this country. Never heard of it."

Her friend Edith was with her, the woman I'd spotted who looked like a Roman emperor with her scraped-down Gertrude Stein hair. But now I could see that she had a distinct and rather handsome hue that marked her as mixed race. She was bound for Rehoboth, on the road to Windhoek.

"They say the most dreadful things about us," Edith said. "They" I took to mean the world at large. "But you know, we have everything here, plenty of food and lots of space. I reckon we're luckier than most people, but no one knows us, no one really gives a toss."

"You've traveled the world too?"

"A bit. Enough to know that I don't want to live anywhere else."

She regarded the night sky. "And it's peaceful here now. Not like what it was. We had a war, you know. Shooting. Bombs."

"It's so much better now," Johanna said.

"Except there's no work for the young people," Edith said, and turned because someone had shouted — the bus driver, calling to us. Edith shuffled toward the bus, muttering, "Mustn't get left behind."

The Namibian side was Noordoewer ("North Bank" in Afrikaans). Another stroll, more formalities, a new country. It was getting late, and when we set off on the bus again I slept, not waking until the stop in Keetmanshoop, where I saw Edith again, hugging herself against the chill.

"How are we doing?" I asked.

"Very well. Only five hundred kilometers to go."

Johanna screeched. Edith laughed. Other passengers were yawning and stamping the fatigue out of their feet. No one minded the distance. Off we went into the darkness, deeper into Namibia, across the desert.

5

Night Train from Swakopmund

N A DAZZLING HIGH-DESERT early morning, I stepped off the bus into thin air, in the center of Windhoek, a city of wide streets with the kind of old-fashioned wooden arcades jutting over sidewalks that you see in cowboy movies. It was a Sunday. The dignity and somnolence of a Sunday, gone in most countries, was observed in Windhoek, and that made my arrival simpler. Among families in formal churchgoing clothes — men in suits, women in frilly dresses or long-sleeved robes, all smiling as though newly baptized — I walked toward a hotel a few blocks away. And I saw that rarest of workers in Africa, a street sweeper — two of them, actually — one chucking at the granite gutters with his yard-wide broom, the other scooping with his shovel, succeeding in their labors. The clean streets added a touch of surrealism to this African capital.

Stopping to look and to catch my breath, I became self-conscious in my way of gaping at the city. It had become my habit on this trip, a sudden pondering of a landscape or a particular face — faces can seem topographical too, like lumpy landscapes. More than merely observing, I was studying the features and shadows, trying to seize them somehow, thinking that I might not see them again because I probably would never return. I couldn't recall ever having had this feeling before in my traveling life; even in the worst places I believed I might be back to search for changes. There was a finality in my way of looking now, a gaze with more remembering in it.

> *Look thy last on all things lovely,*
> *Every hour . . .*

Someone who seems doddery is perhaps not doddery at all but only an older person absorbed in squinting concentration, as though on an ultimate trip, memorizing a scene, grateful for being alive to see it. Knowing that a return to Africa for me was probably out of the question — how much more can these bones take? — made me want to be scrupulously truthful. None of it was trivial, all of it was meaningful; everything I saw mattered much more. And a great deal that I witnessed in Namibia was a revelation.

Most people come to Africa to see large or outlandish animals in the wild, while some others — "the new gang — the gang of virtue" — make the visit to tell Africans how to improve their lives. And many people do both — animal watching in the early morning, busybodying in the afternoon.

Lots of African countries offer this opportunity — Kenya (game parks and slums), Uganda (gorillas and tyrants), Tanzania (colorful Masai herders and urban shantytowns), Malawi (lakeshore luxury and one million AIDS orphans). And there are other tourism-and-busybody opportunities, notably in South Africa, where you can travel without much trouble from a game drive on a wilderness safari to a township tour and see — by the way — that both experiences (game viewing, slumming) have a certain pathos, even an aesthetic, in common.

One of the features of tourism through the centuries, from the Grand Tour onward, is that not far from the five-star hotels there is starvation and squalor. In most destinations you can't be a tourist without turning your back on human desperation or holding your nose. India is the enduring example: glory in the background, misery in the foreground, no vision of gold without a whiff of excrement. But we are in Africa now, a continent plagued with foreign advisers. I have stayed in African hotels, usually the more expensive ones, where virtually every other guest was a highly paid advice giver.

You can hardly meet a visitor to Africa who doesn't have an opinion on how the continent should be fixed. The well-publicized high-profile do-gooders provide a gilt-edged mirror in which many of these flamboyant ambitions are reflected, through a glass, darkly.

Four examples, wearing theatrical makeup, come to mind. The modestly gifted, semieducated, but hugely popular movie star, whose provable skills are purely thespian, decides to become an ambassadorial presence in the Sudanese territorial struggle. The aging, dissolute singer visits Malawi, adopts both a posture of piety and a child or two, and leaves with the promise of a new school. The TV talk-show billionaire hobnobs with a head of state and founds a luxurious academy for girls in Johannesburg. The married, scandal-plagued pair of superstars find seclusion from their fans in Namibia, the wife giving birth in a private hospital, and thereafter providing the maternity ward with a large endowment.

In each case, the donors are from faraway America, professional performers, novices in Africa, and they seem weirdly euphoric — wild-eyed and deafened by the power their money has given them — for money can't buy belief or obedience in Hollywood the way it can in Africa. These stars act out their concern in public, their patronage rising to the level of a performance, like giant infants fluttering money into a beggar's outstretched hands and pretending to ignore the applause. It is as though they have set out to prove that a person in such a shallow and puppetlike profession is capable of a conscience.

Does this improvisational charity do any good? History suggests no, that the countries are worse off for it. Many African economists, including Dambisa Moyo, from Zambia, and the Kenyan James Shikwati, have convincingly argued that most aid is harmful. In her book analyzing foreign aid to Africa, *Dead Aid,* Moyo declares that the $1 trillion that African countries have received since the late 1940s has discouraged investment, instilled a culture of dependency, and created corruption, all of which have impeded growth and retarded the nations' economies.

This is also the view of the Sudanese telecom billionaire Mohamed Ibrahim, who was quoted in the *Wall Street Journal* in 2012 as saying, "It's my conviction that Africa doesn't need aid." In his view, corrupt governments are the problem. "Without good governance there's no way forward." Ibrahim is a generous philanthropist in Africa but refuses to give money to any badly governed country. A great deal of aid is plainly political, and much is pure theater, something that comes naturally to the performers and public figures who involve themselves in these efforts at African improvement, which, when you look closely, are often efforts to improve the irregularities in their own public image.

Still, a lack of human charity is an appalling defect, so I am not condemning the actions of these people, only questioning them and finding them mostly misguided. And the ambiguous, self-indulgent, or egomaniacal fame hogger, speaking with the tongues of men and of angels, is never more of a clanging cymbal than when playing a starring role as a philanthropist. No one is a bossier moralizer than a decadent celebrity.

Poor Africa, the stage on which so many outsiders dramatize their lives, test their theories, and reinvent themselves. And there are tens of thousands of others, well-intentioned organizations and generous donors who are also engaged in the business of aid. Namibia is a wonderful place to observe this parade.

Namibia — vast country, small population, and mostly arid stony desert — receives the attention of many charity-minded Americans. There is only one city in the land, and it is hardly a city — Windhoek, the capital, has a quarter of a million people. It is the same size as Newark, New Jersey, and I can well believe that many visitors from Newark to Windhoek make the journey with the idea of telling the locals how to live their lives.

In fact, Newark and Windhoek face some similar problems. Both cities struggle to maintain literacy programs and alleviate poverty and unemployment. One difference is that the high school graduation rate is higher in Windhoek than in Newark, where it is a mere 29 percent (so said New Jersey's Governor Chris Christie in a speech at Harvard Business School in 2011). The neighborhoods of Windhoek are dangerous, yes, and though there are fewer homicides than in Newark, there are twice as many robberies and three times the number of burglaries. Windhoekians are, however, demonstrably more polite. Windhoek has a balmier climate than Newark, and has access to diamond mines. It is not far from an unspoiled coast, and herds of lions and elephants roam nearby. Windhoek's streets are cleaner than Newark's too.

This is not Newark bashing. The streets of Windhoek are swept more often than those in many U.S. cities. Arriving by bus early that morning for the first time, I stood on a wide street, impressed by Windhoek's cleanliness, orderliness, and look of well-being. I sensed its pride, even a sort of civic smugness.

Instead of giving advice on community development, it would make more sense for outsiders to inquire how this order came to Windhoek, and to Namibia at large, especially given the country's colonial history, which is shamefully rich in massacres and oppression, and its war of independence, which started in 1966 and went on for twenty-four years — Namibian guerrillas pitted against the well-armed South African army, mostly in wicked skirmishes in the bush. After the whirlwind of all this trouble came years of peace and order.

The high literacy rate (above 90 percent) accounts for the fact that there are five daily newspapers in Windhoek, not including one in German, the *Allgemeine Zeitung,* known in Namibia as the *AZ.*

"Actually, it is written in Southwest German, the language spoken by German-speakers in Namibia," a former editor explained to the Deutsche Welle website on the paper's ninetieth anniversary. The editor, a Namibian-born German, gave the Southwest German word *rivir* as an example. "It doesn't mean river and it doesn't mean *Fluss,*" the German word for river. "It means a dry river," or wadi.

Deutsch-Südwestafrika, like many African colonies, started as a small private trading post, until the foreign population grew, flexed its muscles, and began grabbing more land, which needed protection. The modest trading operation of 1883 turned into a German colony, and flourished, but after the defeat of Germany in World War I, the whole territory was turned over to the South Africans, who ran it as their colony, imposing their biases, their racial laws, their army and police, and their own settlers. Yet there had been trekkers from South Africa in this area for a century or more, and in the most remote pans and valleys of Namibia the graves of Boer trekkers bake in the sun. I was to see one cluster of seven tombstones in Etosha, northern Namibia, near an elephant wallow in the middle of nowhere, and another in Humpata, in south-central Angola.

Race-conscious white South Africans had an obsession for categorizing people. But it proved to be a dilemma, because in South-West Africa people came in every shade from white to black, with all the coffee and tea tones in between. Take Edith, for example, the mixed-race woman I had met on the bus. Proud of her Namibian

heritage, she was on her way to Rehoboth, with its Baster population. The Basters traced their ancestry to the early Dutch in this territory whose mingling with indigenous Nama people had produced
a distinct community that proudly called themselves Basters — from
the Dutch for "bastard" — a word and a designation they still rejoice
in. *The South African Guidebook* for 1923: "The Bastards are descen-
dants of a cross of Cape European farmers and Hottentots. They
number between three and four thousand and live in the Rehoboth
District. The Bastards are ruled by a chief with the title of 'Captain.'"

It was not until I arrived in Namibia that I made onward plans,
but even so, these plans were vague. I had volunteered to speak at
a UNESCO-sponsored event in Tsumkwe, in the far northeast, for
the experience of meeting the local people, and I wanted to see the
coast, but otherwise I simply had no plans other than to travel overland in a northerly direction, into Angola.

I found it easy to find my way in Namibia, which was crisscrossed
by well-trodden paths, filled with busloads of tourists from Europe.
Many of them were Germans, making a sentimental journey to
their former colony and agreeably surprised to find *Gemütlichkeit*,
German hotels, German restaurants, and about forty thousand per-
manent-resident Germans (twice the pre-independence number).
Thousands more Germans lived seasonally in the seaside town of
Swakopmund, a sunny refuge from the German winter.

Though Namibia is twice the size of California, it has a population of only two million people — one of the smallest populations
of any African country — and most of them live in Windhoek or
in the far north, above the so-called Veterinary Fence that bisects
the country (a protection against the spread of hoof-and-mouth
disease). Namibia is a land of extremes: ultrarich in minerals that
range from uranium, which the United States buys in increasing
quantities, to lead, zinc, tin, silver, tungsten, and gem diamonds.

Most Namibians are farmers, but poor ones. While Namibia has one of the highest literacy rates and per capita incomes in Africa, it ranks near the bottom in land and income distribution.

"Tourists say they're disappointed — it's not Africa," a man named Karl said to me. I had bumped into him at Windhoek's main rail station, where he was picking up parcels that had been sent from the coast by the mail train. By "not Africa" he meant the place was too orderly, not obviously poor or tyrannized. "But this is the way all of Africa could be."

We talked a little while. Karl had been born into a farming family in the small cattle-raising town of Gobabis, in eastern Namibia at the edge of the Kalahari Desert. The English traveler Francis Galton had described this remote place. One of the earliest explorers in that part of the country, Galton was also the first European to write about the animals in Etosha, in his *Narrative of an Explorer in Tropical South Africa* (1853). I asked Karl, who was about seventy, what life had been like growing up in his hometown.

"Very quiet," he said. "And it's still quiet."

He had gone to boarding school in Cape Town, he said, a long journey by train. "My brother and I took the narrow-gauge line from Gobabis to Windhoek, changed to the broad-gauge line into South Africa, to Upington, changed again at De Aar on the high veldt, and finally got to Cape Town — four days in the train."

His parents, his grandparents, all had been farmers. The somnolence and early rising of rural life: nothing changed for years, and even this elegant, white-plastered railway station in Windhoek had been in use for a century, as an important stop on the Trans-Namib Railway and in Karl's life.

"No tourists came here, and the country didn't change much until they found uranium," Karl said. "Then they needed people to work in the mines, and we got people from other countries. And some from Europe overwintering."

The first uranium deposits had been found in the 1920s, larger seams were discovered in the 1960s, and bigger finds were made in the seventies. New mines were opening as late as 2007. Mining by cartels accounts for two thirds of Namibia's income but employs less than 10 percent of the workforce.

With Karl's help, because no one was on duty at the station, I discovered that there was only a night train to the coast, leaving in the dark, arriving at dawn. So taking it I would see nothing but the interior of the train, my disappointed face reflected in the coach window.

Pondering the night train versus the day bus to Swakopmund, I walked back along Bahnhof Street and around the small city center, breathless in this mile-high place. Windhoek looked the way Harare, in Zimbabwe, had once looked: a colonial capital and market town with streets wide enough to allow an ox wagon to make a U-turn. Harare was now a desperate ruin on the verge of bankruptcy, but Windhoek had grown larger without having lost its character, was well kept, proud, as solid as ever, and invested in. The uniformity of the fat squat German architecture — churches and municipal buildings and bungalows — was unmistakable and looked bombproof, built to last, as though on a street in Berlin instead of in this distant plateau in the Namib Desert. "This uniformity derives from the sense of fitness and superiority of the German outlook," Jon Manchip White wrote in his 1971 account of his journey through this country, *The Land God Made in Anger.* White, who traveled the area in the early 1960s, provides marvelous summaries of the history and culture, though he sometimes overeggs his descriptions, even of mild, dull Windhoek, asserting that the city gives the traveler "a sense of necromancy . . . The African mystery is omnipresent. The deserts press round him as pitilessly as the jungle at Kinshasa."

No "African mystery" now; only brisk, self-important Namibians busily talking on cell phones. I wandered into a shop and asked a man where I might buy a phone. He said they were easy to find and inexpensive, and he gave me the name of an electronics store where I could sign up for one.

The store was on a side street, a rack of sample cell phones in a display case, and at the counter a woman was waiting on a customer. In the corner, at the edge of the counter, a small boy sat on a stool, his arms folded.

Seeing me, the woman clerk said, "Go there," and gestured to the child.

I smiled and hesitated, and the boy said nothing. Then I saw that the child, about the size of an eight-year-old, was actually a grown man, with San features and bat ears and tiny hands.

I said hello.

"I am Jakob," he said.

He was polite and patient. He'd seen me hesitate, on the point of ignoring him, taking him for a child. But here he was in a responsible job, explaining what I would have to do to get a cell phone that worked in the country. And though the phone he showed me seemed very cheap, I decided to buy it some other time.

I thanked Jakob and went away, wondering what miseries he had suffered. There were people of small stature all over Central Africa, in the Congo and in southern Angola and northern Namibia, who called themselves the Twa, or Batwa ("Twa People"). I knew of scattered groups of them in Uganda, where their villages were close to the Congo border. They gathered on the road to Bundibugyo, waving at passing cars. When a car slowed down, they called out, "Me pygmy. Take picture," and demanded money. The Twa, who are part-time hunter-gatherers, tend to live near other peoples in a semidependent way, trading and negotiating, but have their own customs — one of which allows a woman whose husband has committed adultery to strangle the woman who presumes to be her rival. (The man is not punished.)

Jakob could have been a Twa, but I didn't raise the delicate subject because the one trait that unites the Twa is that they are despised by whomever they live among. And even if Jakob had not been a Twa, he would probably have been identified as one of these pygmoid people who live at the margins of the country.

I spent my time in Windhoek outfitting myself with supplies. Since I was headed to the bush after my trip to the coast, I needed more Malanil, a daily dose against malaria. This being southern Africa, I could buy the drug cheaply without a prescription, as I could my gout medicine and certain antibiotics. I found a Namibian pharmacist who helpfully described dosages. I bought batteries, insect repellent, a hat, spare socks, an elephant-hide belt, and a padlock for my bag.

Windhoek was so rich in safari gear I could have outfitted myself for an ambitious hunting expedition — safaris do not get more elaborate or bloodier than in Namibia. The abundant waterholes and low bush make it a prime destination for shooting animals, not just the Big Five (elephant, lion, leopard, buffalo, rhino) but the great horned plains game too, like kudu, oryx, and eland. These animals are gunned down on concessions in the bush operated by safari companies, which also take care of stuffing and mounting the dead beast — the object of the whole ridiculous charade being the trophy.

There were hunters at my hotel, easily identifiable by their funny hats, new khaki clothes, and rifle cases — like oversized Boy Scouts — and by the way they walked in small groups, warily, keeping to themselves except when they were traipsing after their local guide. The guide was the key man in the whole enterprise. He was the arranger, the facilitator, the hirer of cooks and trackers and camp staff, the man who would drive them to the hunting concession or game ranch and bring them to within easy shooting distance of the animals, for which they'd bought licenses to kill. It was safari tourism, trophy hunting for dummies.

At the hotel, assuming I was someone he'd met the day before, a Namibian man—a Herero, he told me later—invited me to a party to watch the Rugby World Cup final, France against New Zealand.

The rugby party was a raucous, boozy crowd, screaming at a wide-screen TV in one of the hotel lounges. The Namibians cheered for the New Zealand team, known as the All Blacks; the whites cheered for France; and when New Zealand won by one point there was an eruption of hilarity rather than pandemonium.

The Namibians were not uniformly black, nor were the whites uniformly white. They were so mixed, from such obviously different racial groups, that they were unclassifiable, and because of such differences they could not make any racial assumptions. This made them easygoing, nonconfrontational, somewhat friendly, and mild-tempered.

I sat drinking beer, watching the brutal back-and-forth of the rugby match, and fell into conversation with the man in the next chair, who said he was from Huambo, in central Angola. He was an Ovimbundu, uprooted by the long Angolan civil war, and he went home only now and then. He praised his country: "It is more lively than Namibia. The people are so happy." His name was Neto.

"I'm thinking of going to Angola by road."

He smiled at me, as though at a child's innocent misstatement. "No. The road is bad. There are many flights from Windhoek."

"But I want to go over the border and see the south of Angola."

"There is nothing but bad roads."

When was the last time he'd been there?

"Many years ago."

"Maybe the roads have been fixed."

He considered this, tapping his teeth, distracted by a run in the rugby match. "Maybe. But anyway, Luanda is better. Much bigger than Windhoek."

I saw that I would get nowhere with him on the subject of overland travel to his country, and mentioned that I planned to go the next day to Swakopmund.

"Small, but it's okay."

I said I'd opted for the bus over the train, at least for the way down to the coast.

"That's better," he said, and though he was as black as anyone I was to meet in Namibia, he added, "Only black people take the train."

Under a cloudless sky, the bus, with its load of Namibians and foreigners, left tidy Windhoek and passed through freshly painted provincial towns along the way — orderly Okandjia, tiny house-proud Karibib, and dignified Usakos, with stucco houses in pink and yellow pastels and thick-steepled Lutheran churches, the settlements surrounded by hot bright dust. I remembered what Karl had said about visitors being disappointed because none of this seemed like Africa. But I liked its unexpectedness; it was all new to me, and so well built and maintained. Descending to the coast, we rode along level savanna, through grassland and an immensity of gravel, then across pale stony desert.

The mountains in the distance, some as sharp as blades, were the Erongoberg, according to my map, and the pyramidal peak beyond the strange colonial town of Usakos might have been Spitzkoppe, a place I wanted to go for its rock paintings.

A big, dark chacma baboon crept through tall grass and appeared between withered clumps at the roadside. He hesitated, flinging his arms in confusion, opening his jaws wide and looking fierce. On back roads and riverbanks in Africa, I have had various encounters with troops of baboons and found them fearless and unreasonable, with terrifying teeth. Even the wisest book on the subject of baboons, *The Soul of the Ape,* by the South African naturalist Eugene Marais, does not reassure me.

I mentioned this to the man in the seat next to me—Cleo, a Namibian. He said, "They can be troublesome. They steal fruit from the farms."

I looked into the enormous empty spaces of Erongo, the broken rock and rubble that stretched for miles, and wondered aloud what other animals might be there.

"There are ostriches. There are jackals," Cleo said. "Even leopards you can find them."

Swakopmund was a small Germanic seaside town of right angles on a grid of streets, bright but chilly from a brisk wind off the Atlantic. The old railway station, dating from 1901, had been turned into an elegant hotel, but otherwise there were no big hotels, only small inns and guesthouses. The many villas and well-built houses were where many Europeans—mostly Germans—spent the winter. I met a man from Hannover who had spent every winter for the past thirty years in Swakopmund. Some of those years would have been a time of civil war and turmoil in Namibia, yet he had found his annual sunshine and beer and schnitzel. He said he would have bought a house and retired here except his wife couldn't stand it. His name was Friedrich, and parting from me he said, as a farewell, "As Germany is to Europe, Namibia is to Africa. Hard-working. Wealthy. Sensible. It is heaven!"

He recommended the Hansa Hotel, so I stayed there. It was small and hospitable and served good food. The other guests were from Germany and Holland, with a few Italians and Africans, all tourists, because there was no business in Swakopmund except tourism. The uranium mines were distant, as were the diggings for gems—tourmalines, garnets—which were mined somewhere in the desert. Had I wished, I could have stayed at the Burning Shore, ten minutes south of Swakopmund at Langstrand, a lodge that advertised itself as the place where the actress (and humanitarian, her biography adds) Angelina Jolie had brooded for a few months in 2006 before shuttling to the Cottage Private Hospital, now also on the map as a result of the birth of her child there. The Burning Shore lodge was a newish but fairly ordinary set of walled-in buildings by the beach, and the whole of it had been commandeered and occupied for the prologue to the birth. The discovery of Brad Pitt and Angelina Jolie in Swakopmund had been an event of greater significance to the world than the discovery in the same year of a vast deposit of uranium that became the Langer Heinrich uranium mine, near the town.

The promenade in Swakopmund, like its long wooden jetty, its neatly planted palms, its villagy look, and most of all its many villas with walled gardens, made the town feel like a bourgeois refuge from the world, which in fact it was, and had been for a hundred years, hugging the shore, its back turned to the desert.

But I did not sneer at the efficiency, the order, the mildness, the streets that had no litter. Such qualities were so rare in an African city or town—certainly I had seen very few like it—I felt they should be celebrated. The dining room at the Hansa served Wiener schnitzel and carpaccio of kudu, game dumplings and springbok loin. Yet it made me restless. The whole time I was there I felt I was on vacation, an intimation that made me feel uncomfortable and frivolous and lonely.

What I had seen of Namibia, and Swakopmund, was tame. The tourists seemed fastidious, and the smooth walls of the buildings —the old German ones and the newer villas—looked prim, as if they'd been exfoliated.

After a day of walking around the town, I hired a man, Linus, of the Damara people, to take me into the desert, thinking that the wilderness might lift my spirits, but bumping along the moonscape in the Land Rover among the weird vegetation depressed me. Linus plucked medicinal plants and explained their properties, but these dusty shrubs seemed just another example of desert lifelessness.

Aloe, he said. Welwitschia. Stinkbush. Thorn scrub. Tiny moldlike growths and crumpled lichens. And the rest—for miles—sand and gravel.

We continued up the Windhoek Road back to Usakos and then to Spitzkoppe, to hike to the rock paintings. The stone mountains all stood alone, some like recumbent animals, others like creatures breaking through the desert, surfacing from beneath the earth, still others like the toothy lower jaws of predators.

"My people live here," he said, but he meant the Damara people, not the San who had done the paintings a few thousand years ago, and had dispersed.

More stinkbush, more spiky plants, and a singular rugged tooth rising in the desert, Gross Spitzkoppe. We left the vehicle, walked around the bare mountain of rock, and climbed up a steep side, clinging to a fixed chain. We came to an overhang, Paradise Cave. It was just the sort of shallow cave you see in the cracked and reddened stone canyons around Sedona, Arizona, and similarly serving as a sheltered gallery for petroglyphs and paintings.

"They are in bad shape," Linus said without much interest.

The images had been vandalized, rubbed, and scraped, but even smudged, they were impressive. It is impossible to see a whole coherent shape carefully drawn in ancient stone—by an artist setting down a vision, or a dream, or the memory of a beast—and not think back to the people who had flourished in this landscape, all of them now gone, having left behind these animated figures.

Rhinos, elephants, great cats, animals with curved horns, others with tails, and—in a row—human figures wielding bows and arrows, a troop of clearly painted hunters. The vitality, the movement, in this art—none of it was static—was striking: the figures leaped across the wall in a spirited panorama of bravado and companionship.

In spite of the deterioration and neglect, what I saw was more than a mural depicting a glimpse of human life from the Neolithic; it was a language. It occurred to me that Chinese characters are based on pictures. So are hieroglyphics, and so are the lines of glyphs carved into the Rosetta stone. These cave paintings served as words too, the whole wall of pictographs.

I had not realized that this cave art was closer to written language than to the mere sketching of animals. Something was shown, but more important, something was being said. Taken together, it was a statement about hunting — terrors and stratagems, the rows of images set out like sentences.

"There is a Damara village near here," Linus said. "I can take you. It is traditional."

But darkness was falling, and I hated African roads at night. I asked him where he lived.

"Mondesa," he said, and explained that it was a township just outside Swakopmund.

"Let's go there tomorrow."

"We don't have a tour," he said.

"But you can show me where you live and where other people live."

He laughed, because the concept of township tours had just recently begun in Namibia, so it had yet to become an established sightseeing feature as it was in South Africa. It seemed a pure novelty to Linus. But he said, for a fee, he would take me.

The following morning, we drove to the far end of Swakopmund, where the edge of town met the desert and the industrial area. On bare ground were rows of square, flat-topped cinderblock huts, dusted brown from the blowing grit. Beyond these cement huts were clusters of cobbled-together shacks and shanties. After spick-and-span Swakopmund this large settlement of about thirty thousand people was a dose of reality, a place of obvious poverty.

"This is Mondesa, the black township," Linus said.

"Are there others?"

"Tamariskia. It is colored."

Like most African townships, Mondesa had begun as a shantytown. This was in the strictly segregated 1950s, when Swakopmund needed domestic workers and manual laborers but did not want them living in the white town. "In the desert on the northern edge of [Swakopmund] are the shanties of the Africans," Jon Manchip White wrote in 1971, and went on, "'Man is a wolf to man.' The tag [from Plautus] was much on my mind at Swakopmund." Segregation had officially ended with independence in 1990, yet the racial division had continued, with further subdivisions. Mondesa was carved up along tribal lines, with some streets occupied by Damara people, others by Herero or Oshiwambo people. The rutted dirt streets were lined by low, squarish, two-room huts. Some of the huts had indoor plumbing, but not many, Linus said. Public toilets and bathhouses stood on street corners.

We passed a forlorn building he identified as an orphanage, and some others, looking like holding pens, he said were kindergartens that operated on handouts. One of the more ambitious educational projects in the township, called Mondesa Youth Opportunities, had been started by an American in 2003 and was mainly run by non-Namibians and funded by foreign donations. All of this poverty and disorder and charity was a far cry from the brisk Teutonic discipline and spotless streets and five-course meals in Swakopmund, which I now found more and more misleading.

Linus's house was much like the others, built of cinderblocks but slightly enlarged to accommodate his extended family—his nephews and other relations, all of them (so he said) unemployed.

"Your neighbor is doing some serious work on his house," I said.

I could see the beginnings of a sheltered area, a projection of beams over the dirt yard, and a picket fence.

"He wants to turn his house into a shebeen, to make more money."

Just what you want on your street in the edge-of-desert Mondesa township—a beer joint, with loud music, shouting, and the occasional drunken brawl for which shebeens are well known. No visual relief brightened the place, no grass anywhere, no trees. The playing fields were mere rectangles of dust and gravel, and over the whole sprawling settlement hung a chilly air of desolation.

Tamariskia, an adjacent township named for the tamarisk tree (though none grew here), was a step up — larger houses, also of cinderblock but many of them painted. They were bigger than the ones at Mondesa, and some had garages, and cars parked in driveways.

"Just coloreds here?"

"Just coloreds," Linus said, and pointed. We were walking toward a main road. Before we crossed the road we passed Cottage Private Hospital, where Linus proudly said that Angelina Jolie had given birth. Then he pointed to the other side of this road, at bigger, brighter houses, some of them two-story bungalows with tile roofs, and many with landscaped grounds, bushes and palm trees behind the perimeter walls. "That is Vineta."

Vineta, nearer the ocean, Linus said was "white mostly, and some colored."

These three communities existed within a one-mile radius: the whitest nearest the shore, with the best houses and stands of trees; the darkest and most tribal inland, at the bleakest fringe of the desert. As they said in South Africa, you could take one look at a person here and tell precisely where he or she lived. And the inhabitants of the communities worked in the half-dozen mines, either in management or digging in the open pits, scooping the uranium oxide that was sifted, treated, and carted away, to be sold to countries with nuclear reactors. (There was only one in Africa, at Koeberg, near Cape Town.)

The sight of these subdivisions, and especially the long look at Mondesa township, took the bloom off my rosy view of Swakopmund, the town of German retirees and European snowbirds and tourists from all over.

Linus said that some of the schools in Mondesa were partly staffed with volunteer teachers from Britain and America; that some offered programs to combat teen pregnancy and to raise awareness about HIV/AIDS, which infected a fifth of Namibia's population. If you stood facing the ocean, or strolled under the fan palms along the Arnold Schad Promenade (named for a nineteenth-century merchant) or down Am Zoll by the strand, it was easy to convince yourself that it was the desirable waterhole of the brochures. The reality was bleaker; it was an oasis surrounded by unemployment, poverty, neglect, and disease.

But everyone I encountered, including the ones I questioned about the bleakness, was friendly, and many — locals and foreigners both — were optimistic about the future. Pierre, a man of fifty or so, was a bookseller. His business was slow but not bad. His shop in the center of the town was also a café. He had known much worse times. He was South African, from a farming family, and in the mid-1970s his parents decided that life in South Africa was growing dangerous, so they migrated to Rhodesia, where they had relatives. They bought some land in the south of the country, near Victoria, built a house, and planted various crops — maize, wheat, alfalfa — and as Pierre's mother was a gardener, she laid out an elaborate formal garden, for the pleasure of the flowers, roses mostly. They had fled uncertainty in South Africa only to arrive in Rhodesia at the beginning of the Bush War.

"The war started to heat up," Pierre said, speaking of the independence struggle, the guerrilla soldiers of the liberation movements and the Rhodesian army sniping at each other. "It surprised my parents, the violence of it, but they kept farming. Life was precarious, but they could feed themselves — and mother had her beautiful garden."

After independence, Rhodesia becoming Zimbabwe, Victoria renamed Masvingo, Pierre's parents went on farming. But they began to be pestered by men who wanted portions of their land — men sent by President Robert Mugabe. The men called themselves war veterans, but in reality they were landless people from overcrowded villages. Pierre's father made concessions, signed over corners and margins of their farmland to the squatters, who put up shacks and planted vegetables. This went on for fifteen years, the farm chipped away by more and more men, some pleading, others threatening.

"Then my parents were served an eviction notice by the government," Pierre said. "This was round about 2000. 'Get out or else.'"

His mother called him in South Africa — now, after its own upheaval, being governed by Nelson Mandela — and asked him to come immediately and help them pack. They were losing the farm, the house, the crops in the fields — being thrown out, without compensation; a cabinet minister high up in the Zimbabwe government would be taking everything.

"I went," Pierre said. He took a deep breath and gazed into the middle distance. "The sight that I cannot forget — and the saddest thing I have ever seen in my life — was my mother, on the day she left her house forever, standing with a hose in her hand, watering her garden. Knowing she would never see it again. Standing there on that sunny day, spraying the hose on her flowers."[*]

Another man I met, Michael, who had a shop near Pierre's, had migrated from Germany in 1986. Namibia was better then, he said — no crime, you could leave your door open. But now, with high unemployment, petty theft was common. And he was dismayed by the parsimony of the tourists. Of the tens of thousands of Germans resident in Namibia Michael said, "They never spend money, my countrymen." He was looking forward to Oktoberfest, a big celebration in Swakopmund and Windhoek, with music and dancing and drunkenness.

---

[*] I had written about the Zimbabwe government violently seizing these farms in *Dark Star Safari*. Eight months after Pierre told me this story, the *New York Times* reported, in 2012, that the maize harvest had been reduced by a third, 1.6 million Zimbabweans faced starvation, and the UN's World Food Program would need to distribute emergency food aid. Before 2000, Zimbabwe had a surplus of maize, the staple food of the people.

"I keep my German passport." Nodding toward the street, as though at all the other Germans, Michael added, "They do the same. There are no Namibians in this country. There are Herero, Damara, Oshiwambo, Afrikaners, Basters — that's what they say first, if you ask. Then afterward they say, 'Oh, yes, I'm also Namibian.'"

There was something colonial about Swakopmund, and perhaps it was this that the Germans liked. The old buildings still stood, some of the town looked much as it had a century before, there were no high-rises, and — owing to the hard-up townships — there was no servant problem. There were many good restaurants, the wine lists were lengthy, the prices were reasonable, the hospitality was convincing. Every evening when I returned from my forays, Herr Wacker, the general manager of the Hansa Hotel, greeted me warmly.

"You must stay longer," he said.

I would have, but I had a train to catch.

It wasn't easy leaving the hotel. As all the other guests were filing into the dining room, I made my way by taxi to the now obscure railway station, the driver reminding me of the all-night journey through the desert and repeating that, for a hundred dollars or so, he would whisk me to Windhoek in the morning.

But I had resolved to ride the train, and the more it was denounced ("Only black people take the train"), the greater my desire to see it. Like much in Swakopmund — many houses, the banks, some hotels, the layout of streets — the railway, too, was a hundred years old.

I found a seat that canted back and would allow me to sleep. Among my fellow passengers, some were burdened with bundles, some with small children, family groups already settling in for the night. Across the aisle was a great fat Afrikaner reading a newspaper in his language. He was sitting alone, and his entire bulging midsection was swathed in a heavy bandage, as if to prevent him from exploding.

In the seat ahead, a German, Klaus. He said he was ill. "I passed a bad night," he explained. And he made the vomit gesture, his hand mimicking a flow from his wide-open mouth. "It was the biltong [cured meat] I ate."

Then we left the station, and when the lights in the coach went out, the desert was lit, and glittered for hours in the light of the cold moon.

6

The Bush Track to Tsumkwe

AN EARNEST, HIGH-MINDED, well-funded, foreign-sponsored event — the sort I always either avoided or mocked — was being held in Tsumkwe, a small town in the remote northeast of Namibia. Much less than a town, Tsumkwe was a village crossroads in the Kaokoveld, a region in the center of Nyae Nyae, which was eighteen thousand square miles of infertile, drought-prone, famine-haunted, thinly populated bush — an unpromising area, it seemed, for such an expensive and scholarly effort. Yet I knew such places to be the beating heart of Africa.

The event would be a full day's program of talks and films, billed as "World Day for Celebrating Audio-Visual Heritage in Namibia," organized by the Windhoek office of UNESCO. You cannot hear such a pompous title without imagining a long hot day of yawning and paper shuffling and protocol, discussion groups, noble projects ("We could start a workshop . . . form a committee . . . apply for a grant"), and endless talk — the jargonized gabbing about plans that would never amount to anything more than words on the wind. You think: What's the use?

I was asked if I would be willing to speak at this Tsumkwe event, at a forum devoted to the theme for the day, "Preserving a Cultural Heritage."

The subject, however vague, interested me, and I had nothing else to do except stay on the road. I welcomed the idea of a ride to Tsumkwe, which was 454 miles from Windhoek, the last third of it on a gravel road through uncultivated and featureless bush. And I might have something to add to the discussion.

I said yes, fighting my skepticism, and was glad afterward.

No train, no bus, hardly even a bush taxi went to Tsumkwe. Trucks traveled to the place at irregular intervals. At the end of the dusty road and near the Botswana border, Tsumkwe was closer in miles (about a hundred or so) to the Okavango Delta and the small town of Nokaneng in Botswana than to any place of substance in Namibia. It was home to the Ju/'hoansi, a subgroup of the !Kung, and near many of their settlements, and was regarded as a center of the last of the hunter-gatherers, who had lived thereabouts for almost forty thousand years.

In return for two talks at the event, I'd get a ride from Windhoek. In my travel, I used no transport other than public buses and trains, and I was determined to proceed overland, though it was awkward at times. In any case, no commercial planes flew to Tsumkwe either; an airstrip had been bulldozed in the bush to accommodate the private planes and ministerial helicopters of Namibian politicians.

Though it was only a dot on the map, in a historical sense Tsumkwe was important. It was near the base of operations chosen by the ethnographer Lorna Marshall for her pioneering study of the Ju/'hoansi, the Real People. In a fit of restless inspiration combined with wanderlust, Lorna's husband, Laurence Marshall, a wealthy businessman and cofounder of Raytheon Corporation, took his wife and children to southern Africa in 1950. Newly retired, he said he wanted to do something constructive that would include spending time traveling with his family. He devised an ambitious—

some would say reckless — plan to relocate to the remote Nyae Nyae Conservancy area and get to know the indigenous people, at that time an overlooked and undifferentiated folk called simply, and unhelpfully, Bushmen. Until that time these despised people had barely been studied, and had been pushed to the margins and ignored by the South African government, which administered what was then the mandated territory of South-West Africa. Laurence and Lorna Marshall and their teenage children, Elizabeth and John, penetrated the trackless bush in a Chevy truck, a difficult journey now, almost unimaginable in the 1950s.

Tsumkwe then was not any kind of formal settlement. No more than a waterhole near a large black baobab tree, it was a mere unsurveyed landholding, a patch of bush (called a *n!ore*) that supported the hunting and foraging of a tiny group of Ju/'hoansi people. The Marshalls located themselves about thirty miles to the southeast, near a pan — a seasonal waterhole — called Gautscha. There they stayed for two years, and kept returning for more than a decade. On the face of it, the Marshalls resembled the Swiss Family Robinson on wheels; in practice, it was family rustication provoked by intellectual curiosity that bore rich anthropological fruit.

Lorna Marshall's book, *The !Kung of Nyae Nyae* (1976), was one of the earliest scholarly studies of these people. Lorna's children were similarly inspired. John Marshall, traditionally initiated while still in his teens and fluent in the language, was to spend the rest of his life, off and on, among the Ju/'hoansi, hunting with them, studying them, filming them. Elizabeth Marshall Thomas, a novelist, has written two nonfiction accounts of the Ju/'hoansi ("Ju/wasi" in her spelling): *The Harmless People* (1991), a mild and hopeful account of the people, and *The Old Way* (2006), a more sober look at the drastic changes in their culture and at the myths about their lives that are harbored by romantic voyeurs like me.

Over a period of fifty years, from 1950 to 2000, John Marshall, a man of luminous sensibility, recorded the Ju/'hoansi extensively on film. His five-part documentary, *A Kalahari Family,* in which he interviewed Ju/'hoansi in footage now considered very rare, is regarded as a classic ethnographic visual record. He made many other films about them and their disappearing culture, chronicling the dramatic recent history of these people who, living the old way, undisturbed for 1,500 centuries, have been confronted by the outer world of bureaucrats, traders, politicians, missionaries, miners, tourists, opportunists, educators, and all the paraphernalia that the outsiders brought with them — legal briefs, guns, money, canned food, alcohol, candy, books, Bibles, and new diseases. They also brought extravagant promises, if not of prosperity in this world than glory in the afterlife. The Marshalls witnessed the Ju/'hoansi change from self-sufficient and strong to mostly dependent and much weakened. The timeline of Tsumkwe, this outpost in the bush, was like the timeline of sub-Saharan Africa, the history of Africa in a parable of exploitation and decline.

Something else that persuaded me to participate in this Audio-Visual Heritage Day in Tsumkwe was the news that two of John Marshall's films, recently discovered in the Namibian National Archives, would be shown there — where they were made — for the first time. I wanted to see the place, view the films, and meet the people, and I was eager to travel into the bush.

So far my trip had been fairly straightforward. Though many South Africans had warned of physical danger, and Namibians warned of theft, I had not been seriously inconvenienced. All I had experienced were a few shouted threats, some mild racial abuse, petty thievery (sunglasses, a small amount of money), and the pleading of hungry people — but you might encounter these annoyances anywhere in the world.

People said, "Wait till you get to Angola!"

I asked, "When were you last in Angola?"

They said never, that no one went to Angola because it was so dreadful. No eyewitnesses, no firsthand accounts; I was not deterred.

I never looked for trouble and usually took the path of least resistance, though the simplest trip in Africa can be trouble for someone traveling alone. I hated taking risks, I tried to avoid them, but sometimes they were unavoidable. Going solo, I always had problems to solve. I had no car, so I had to rely on public transport. I did not make plans very far in advance, so I was always in need of a hotel room or a meal at short notice. Because of that, I sometimes had to sleep on a bus, or not sleep at all, and now and then went without meals. But I could hardly complain about such irksome outcomes in countries where so many people were destitute and slept under trees and endured long periods without food. I am not by nature a networker or a looker-up of people, so I am always dependent on chance meetings, on dumb luck, on the kindness of strangers.

Tony, an American diplomat in Namibia, was one of those helpful strangers. He had invited me to the Tsumkwe event, and he too would be a participant. Briefing me beforehand over dinner in a Portuguese restaurant in Windhoek, he proved reassuringly amiable and well read ("You know, Thomas Pynchon wrote about the Hereros in *Gravity's Rainbow* and *V*"). Tony was also unflappable, and he had access to a fairly new four-wheel-drive vehicle. All the best qualities for a ten-hour road trip into the bush.

We set off early in the morning from Windhoek, driving into the sunrise. We talked about Pynchon's books. I mentioned that, sentence by glowing sentence, the man was brilliant, but his high-density pages and wandering, infolding plot lines gave the books a bloodless literary affectation that made them almost unreadable to me. Tony, educated as a literature major, had an academic's patience, a stomach for solving monotonous literary puzzles, and a delight in lessons learned: a difficult literary text to him was a problem in dissection, like a biology student in a lab hovering over a gutted rodent. Tony read for the challenge and possible reward of identifying obscurities and making connections. This was not my temperament at all. I hate studying books and chewing through teasingly contrived texts, the obstacle courses of deliberate difficulty. If a book doesn't engage me, I toss it aside. I read for the visceral pleasure of it.

Driving past browsing cattle in the savanna of the great sunbaked heartland, Tony urged me to treat the Pynchon books more sympathetically. They were fiction but historically accurate, dramatizing a period of German colonialism and atrocities that had been suppressed by German politicians and not written about much elsewhere. But in the past few years this brutal era has received much more notice and, as well, deeper and detailed scholarship.

Germany—the last European country to acquire colonies, and the first to lose them—had attempted to exterminate an entire native population, the Herero, in South-West Africa in 1904. The wipeout had almost succeeded, in what has been called the first genocide of the twentieth century. This was largely the effort of one man, General Lothar von Trotha, charged by Kaiser Wilhelm II to carry out a *Vernichtungsbefehl* ("extermination order"), an actual printed document, dated October 2, 1904, a copy of which is kept in the Botswana National Archives. To von Trotha, the Herero were *Unmenschen*—nonhuman. They were—and a small number still are—a pastoral nomadic people. Herero seeking to cling to their traditional lands, and occasionally raiding the intrusive colonists, infuriated von Trotha.

"All the tribes of Africa share the same mentality, in that they only retreat when confronted by violence," von Trotha wrote to his superiors, sounding like Mr. Kurtz. "My policy was and is, to apply such violence with the utmost degree of terrorism and brutality. I will exterminate the rebellious tribes with rivers of blood."

Pushed by the Germans, the Herero resisted. One of the results was the Waterberg massacre, and in this and other battles (the rapid-fire Maxim guns against arrows and old single-shot rifles) it is estimated that as many as ninety thousand Herero — the great majority of the Herero people — were killed.

Tony and I talked about this as we traveled in glorious sunshine toward the town of Otjiwarongo, passing the very spot, Waterberg, a bluish ridge in the distance, where the massacre took place.

Somehow — in exile, scattered, in concentration camps, as slave laborers — the remnant Herero had survived. Herero women are easily identifiable by their distinctive clothing: a billowy ankle-length dress with full sleeves and an extravagant headpiece of folded cloth, called an *otjikaiva*, with two pointed ends that look like a flattened admiral's hat which is said to mimic the horns of a cow.

"I see Hereros all over the place," I said. The Herero men were unremarkable in their clothes, but the women were unmistakable. "I saw a lot of them in Windhoek, which is full of Germans. They don't seem to bear any grudges."

"The people in Namibia are generally easygoing," Tony said. "They're gentle. You seldom hear anyone shouting. It's the Angolans here who have a reputation for being lively and excitable."

But we saw no one on the roadside or in the landscape, nothing to suggest human habitation except the cattle fences strung along the road. Now and then we saw wild game — a springbok or an ostrich or an occasional raptor hung in the sky — but there were no people, no houses, nothing but the vast hot land, yellow in the drought that had gripped it.

Tony said, "The people in Tsumkwe are really glad you're coming."

"I'm grateful they asked me," I said, and meant it. And I smiled to think that I, who usually mocked such events, would be taking part in an NGO effort at enlightenment in this remote place.

"What's it like there?"

"I don't know," he said. "This is my first time."

We came to the town of Otjiwarongo ("Place of Fat Cattle" in the Herero language), still a center of cattle ranching. One of the German outrages had been to push the cattle-owning tribes off the land and to engage in cattle ranching themselves. When challenged on this by right-thinking people, the Germans, and after them the South Africans, said that what the natives needed in order to achieve self-sufficiency was education.

"My great-grandfather, the late Chief Kambazembi, had never been to school, but he had 25,000 cattle in 1903 before we were conquered," a Herero man, Zedekia Ngavirue, told a UN commission in Dar es Salaam in 1961 (quoted in Ruth First, *South West Africa*, 1963). "I have a college diploma but do not possess even a chicken." This statement was prescient: many Africans today could make this sort of claim.

The ancestral graves of this chiefly Kambazembi family were not far away, on the slopes of the Waterberg Plateau. Some disinterred remains had been returned from Botswana (where the family had been exiled) and ceremonially reburied as recently as 2006.

Otjiwarongo had a German and Afrikaner population of around three thousand, mostly farmers and shopkeepers, when the writer Jon Manchip White passed through in the 1960s and found it an outpost of fussiness — Rotarianism, parking signs, and plaster garden gnomes. The number of whites had not much diminished, though a great number seemed to live in a neighborhood of walled-in bungalows two blocks from the main street. The town remained a center of ranching and farming, so on the main street was a big supermarket, repair shops, feed stores, small hotels, and many churches, including a large Lutheran church with an enormous square-sided steeple, which was also a clock tower.

"You could probably find a cell phone here at one of these shops," Tony said.

I had mentioned my lack of a cell phone on our drive. I sometimes felt that I was the only person in Namibia without one, and it occurred to me that it might be a good idea to phone home.

Some helpful directions from friendly Otjiwarongans brought us to the small roadside shop of Mr. Khan, who had an array of electronic goods in his display case. Mr. Khan explained that for about $20 I could buy a phone, and for another $20 a SIM card and usable minutes, which he would program into the phone. I now understood, rather late in the day, why rickshaw wallahs, Cambodian fishermen, and Masai warriors were sometimes seen talking on a tiny plastic phone.

A young Herero woman, Grace, helped with the transaction.

I said, "Grace, tell me, where can I find some fun in Otjiwarongo?"

"There is no fun here!" she said, laughing, and Mr. Khan, who was from Pakistan, agreed: "No fun, sir."

With this bargain phone in my hand I called home, and for many weeks after that, all I needed to do was dial the number, say "Call me back," and I could talk to the loved one I had left behind. Occasionally, in the most unlikely place — on a bus, in a thatched hut, in a chicken shack, slapping at tsetse flies or kicking through the dust — I would feel a buzzing in my pocket against my thigh: Hawaii on the line.

Grootfontein was a hundred miles up the road, still in the Waterberg region of smooth-featured hills, sun-bleached plains of grass and stubble, and stony swales. The landscape was immense and simple — no forests, no water, few villages. This emptiness and apparent simplicity is the glory of Namibia and a consequence of its small population. The number of people in the country in 1904 was tiny — perhaps a few hundred thousand in this region — so it seems an even greater crime that the Germans, not satisfied to share, were intent on extermination to the last woman and child, to have the whole desert colony to themselves.

Nowadays, most people go to Namibia to see the animals at the waterholes in Etosha Pan (part of Etosha National Park) and nothing more. But this northeasterly part of the country, lovely as it was, and rich in bird life, was not on that route and not visited much.

Grootfontein, the site of a significant German defeat in 1915, was more famous for its object visible from space, the Hoba meteorite, a blocky, sixty-six-ton slab of iron enshrined in a nearby field. The town existed to serve the cattle ranches, the game farms, and the small township population. As with many of the bush towns I saw in Namibia, it seemed a place fighting for survival, a pit stop for anyone headed north to Angola and the Caprivi Strip or traveling northeast on the gravel road to Tsumkwe, neither of them well-traveled routes.

The center of activity in Grootfontein was the supermarket on the main road. It was a place of loungers and panhandlers and little old Afrikaner women in long, faded, 1930s-style frocks, holding umbrellas against the bright sun, strange, yellowish, Dutch-faced ladies, like artifacts from an earlier time. I approached two of them with questions, but they smiled and murmured, "*Mynheer, ek verstaan nie.*" Unlike the Herero and Ovambo, these isolated Afrikaners spoke only their own language.

A troupe of nine young singers, Herero perhaps, were performing at the edge of the parking lot — dancing, harmonizing, while a small boy passed a hat for contributions. They represented an evangelical church in Grootfontein, they were shouting gleeful syncopated hymns, and they seemed at home among the streetside beggars, fruit hawkers, and basket sellers, reminding me that much of the commercial activity in rural Africa resembles a medieval market. How people live in market towns in the bush is how people once lived in Europe — congregating to flirt, to sell their wares and show off their animals, to dazzle onlookers, to make music, to find a wife or husband.

The only place that offered meals was a corner of the supermarket with chairs and tables that sold meat pies and chicken schnitzel and fried potatoes. Tony and I sat down with our food and I chatted with the server, who was also the restaurant manager — Helena, a thin, sallow-faced woman with bony bitten fingers and lank hair and a sad, slightly exasperated manner. She seemed harassed, obscurely burdened, and a glaze of melancholy showed in her pale gray eyes.

"There's no fun in Otjiwarongo," I said, teasing. "Where's the fun in Grootfontein?"

"No fun here," she said with that jaw-twisting Afrikaner *yeauh* for "here." "No life. No life at all."

She said she'd been born in Grootfontein, with a gargle on the *Groot*, and knew what she was talking about.

"What about the weekends?"

"Well, the Golf Club. It's mainly drinking."

"I'll buy you a drink, Helena. All I ask is that you tell me about growing up in Grootfontein."

"I don't need you to buy me a drink," she said, defiant but smiling. "I've got me own money."

"Tell me about the club."

"It's just whites at the club," she said, not so much stating a fact as suggesting an atmosphere. "It's not bad—it's okay."

"We could talk. Unless you're spoken for."

"I'm single," she said, and hesitated, looking distressed, and I feared what was coming next. "My husband died six months ago. I'm all alone now."

Tony winced and shook his head. I had talked too much, and now felt terrible, and tried to be sympathetic. But it was too late. She was a poor, small, bereaved woman in a remote and dusty cattle town in the middle of Namibia—well known for its thievery, I was to learn. So I regretted being facetious, and tried to ease my conscience by giving her a large tip and asking her some ignorant questions about Tsumkwe.

She sighed at the thought of Tsumkwe and said she had never been there. She added, "But I know one thing. It's hot there. I saw on the telly—it was forty-two up there yesterday."

"That's over a hundred Fahrenheit," Tony said when we were back in the car.

It was 107 degrees in the shade.

Thirty miles up the paved road we came to a turnoff, a narrow track of whitish gravel, and then we were clattering on loose stones in dry earth, traveling through low yellow bush for the rest of the afternoon, slowly bumping and sliding, the windows coated with the grime of risen dust. No other cars, no people, no animals, no settlements, not even any paths, nothing but sand and the tangle of dark thornbush.

"The Vet Fence," Tony said, peering ahead and slowing down after about three hours of driving.

No fence was immediately visible to me, though I could see a wall of high dusty trees and a metal barrier across the road. A man mopping his face with a white rag was apparently guarding it. Closer, I could see a wire fence strung on widely spaced poles that stretched to the horizon.

"This fence goes entirely across the country," Tony said. "Amazing, eh?"

Now the khaki-uniformed guard, yawning in the heat, approached our car and began to frown at us through the side window as he sedulously examined the back seat—for what? For contraband?

He yawned again, sweltering in a hot depression in the road. "You have milk? You have meat?"

"No milk, no meat," Tony said.

"Where you are going?" The man chewed on his white rag.

"Tsumkwe."

"It is too hot there. It is too hot here too. What is your country?"

We told him. He was friendly. We chatted a little. He said he wanted to go to Chicago. He raised the iron bar and let us through the fence. On the other side we were in a different Africa.

I saw at once that the Veterinary Fence, also called the Animal Control Fence, put in place in the early 1960s to prevent the spread of disease, was much more than a *cordon sanitaire*. The original problem had been a rinderpest pandemic that was being spread by the wild southern savanna buffalo. This heavy, dangerous, thick-horned beast was a favorite of hunters (for its ferocious aspect as a mounted head on a wall) and poachers (for its meat). The erection of the fence, which traversed all of northern Namibia and on the east the frontier of Botswana, contained the wildlife and the infected cattle, preventing them from going farther south into the heart of the country.

The fence that had solved some problems had also created others. Certain species, specialized feeders such as roan and sable antelopes, unable to get to waterholes during droughts, were trapped and died of thirst. At all checkpoints in the Vet Fence it was routine to confiscate milk and meat from inspected cars entering and leaving. The entrapment and confinement of wildlife had caused a subsequent decline in their numbers, as well as the creation of new ecosystems and patterns of settlement.

But, crucially, the Vet Fence was a distinct cultural frontier, separating people, creating division. Beyond the wire was the more familiar Africa of skinny, hungry-looking children wincing in sunlight, of men drinking beer under trees, of straggling villages and frantic chickens and cattle wandering on the roads, of blowing paper and flimsy plastic bags snagged on trees, of piles of castoff rags and trampled beer cans, the improvised, slapped-together Africa of tumbled fences and cooking fires, of mud and thatch. This was an Africa unknown in the Teutonic order of downtown Swakopmund and Windhoek, and quite different even from the small-town haplessness of Grootfontein, which was only a few hours away. The landscape across the fence was different too — bumpier, haphazardly plowed and planted, irregularly divided, in all ways like a new faltering country. It was also, strangely, more affecting, more hospitable, more congenial.

The fence that isolated animals also isolated people. Nothing behind this thousand-mile barrier remotely resembled anything I had seen in the south of the country. The texture of life was different here on the far side, poorer, meaner, but—the word "authentic" seems patronizing—more human and real. If you didn't cross the Vet Fence, you would have no idea what a struggle it was for the rural poor in Namibia—probably the majority of the population—to stay alive. The Red Line, as it was less often called, might be a better name, for being appropriately dramatic.

Down the bumpy road, a signboard with an arrow indicated a Ju/'hoansi village. We turned onto a narrow track and traveled slowly through foot-deep unforgiving sand for several miles, occasionally becoming mired in it. We briefly lost heart, started back, then resumed the search for the village.

We came to a clearing: on one side a traditional village with thatched huts and twig fences, on the other side a new village of shacks. The traditional huts were for show, like the teepees displayed for tourists of Plains Indians; the shacks were where the San people actually lived.

Three small men trotted toward us, smiling, gesturing. I was always irrationally moved and felt tender toward anyone I saw running fast in Africa.

One of the men spoke haltingly in English—hospitable words. "Please—welcome—yes, yes."

It was for me like encountering three unicorns. They were the first I had seen of the folk—!Kung-speaking San—who called themselves Ju/'hoansi, the Real People. Though they were dressed neatly in short-sleeved shirts and long pants, I beheld their unusual, friendly faces with a kind of rapture, as though gazing upon mythical ancestors. It is said that the features of these people are a combination of all the racial characteristics of the world — Asian eyes, African faces, European skin tones — and if there was a human synthesis of all the world's ethnic groups, the resulting example would probably be a Ju/'hoansi person. They were small-boned, short of stature — no more than five feet tall — and eager to show us their village. We asked for details.

"But it is too late," the man said.

He meant it was after four, too late in the day. This, my first glimpse of the San, gave me the wild thought that they looked like extraterrestrials — the narrow chin, the hooded eyes, the large, domelike, well-formed cranium. I knew I was in the presence of our oldest living ancestors, and they radiated a kind of innocence and kindliness. It was no illusion. Everyone who had studied these people had remarked on their gentleness, that they don't fight, don't raise their voices, don't steal, never scold their children.

When Francis Galton encountered such people south of here — Hottentots, he called them — he characterized them in a different manner, remarking on "the felon face" and explaining: "I mean that they have prominent cheek bones, bullet shaped head, cowering but restless eyes, and heavy sensual lips, and added to this a shackling dress and manner." Later he found some other related people with "remarkably pleasing Chinese-looking faces." At least that part was true: the faces of the men also had an Asian cast.

I said, "We'll come back."

"Buy something, please. There." He indicated a path that led to a small clearing.

In the clearing a twig fence was hung with trinkets, bead necklaces and bracelets, clusters of feathers, leather pouches, wooden pipes, and the pierced and polished fragments of ostrich shells. No one was hawking them; the artifacts were dangling like wind chimes or Christmas ornaments, with prices inked on paper tags. It was the honor system, appropriate to people in whose culture theft was unknown. "Stealing without being discovered is practically impossible in !Kung life, because the !Kung know everybody's footprints and every object. Respect for ownership is strong, but apart from that, 'Stealing would cause nothing but trouble. It might cause fighting'" (Lorna Marshall, *The !Kung of Nyae Nyae*). You chose the trinkets you wanted and left your money in a box.

We had arrived in Tsumkwe at dusk, described by the San as "the hour when everything is beautiful."

7

Ceremony at the Crossroads

I**N ITS SMALLNESS,** frying in the desert heat, torpid, disheveled Tsumkwe illustrated in the simplest manner a number of African economic and demographic dilemmas. In the nearby bush, village life was sustainable but oldfangled, and access to water was a problem. The irregularly settled town, growing larger by the year from people leaving the bush, was a picture of filth and futility and bad management. Tsumkwe had a police station, two churches, and a school. The school educated hundreds of students, but it was hard-up, the teachers were poorly compensated, the students needed to find money for fees, and what lay at the end of their education in this severely unemployed country?

The shanties of indigent newcomers to the place were scattered on one side of the crossroads, and on the other side, beyond the shops, were two stinking shebeens where drunken men squatted on the dirt floor, drooling over their home-brewed beer, while a haggard woman ladled more of it into tin cans from a plastic barrel. Outside under a tree, a man in rags, either drunk or exhausted, lay in a posture of crucifixion. Nearby were seven stalls made of rough planks. Two sold used clothes, and one sold new clothes. One offered vegetables, another milky tea and stale bread rolls for the schoolchildren. In a butcher's shack the stallholder hacked with a machete at the black, flyblown leg of a goat. The last and most salubrious stall, labeled *Real Hair*, sold wigs and foot-long hair extensions. Near the shops was a shade tree under which a dozen women and about ten children sat in a friendly chatting group, some of them pounding ostrich shells into small discs, while others, using homemade tools, drilled holes in the middle, and still others threaded the punctured discs into bracelets and necklaces to sell to tourists.

But I saw no tourists in Tsumkwe; few travelers or stragglers made it to this distant and forlorn place. I now knew why: Tsumkwe lay 180 miles down a dusty gravel road through the bush that shimmered in the heat; and the nearest town, Grootfontein, was nothing much — a supermarket, a bank, a gas station, some back streets, and a sports club that, as Helena suggested, had a largely white membership and hosted weekend keggers and crapulosities.

To the north of Tsumkwe was the border of Angola and the Caprivi Strip, a narrow panhandle that protruded east neatly on the map and contained one road to the riverside border of Zambia. (This oddity was a concession to the German colonizers, who drew the border in 1890 and wanted access to the Zambezi River and what was then German East Africa.) To the west was desert, to the east about eighty miles more desert, and Botswana — some Ju/'hoansi settlements and the small town of Nokaneng, at the edge of the Okavango Delta, a lush water world rich in game where wealthy tourists, paying thousands of dollars a day, were flown in private planes to luxury camps. At one of these camps you could splash through the swamps on the backs of elephants, in what was one of Africa's most expensive safaris.

Tsumkwe, a crossroads, had always been negligible. What we know of the place is due almost entirely to the writing of the

Marshalls. In *The Old Way*, Elizabeth Marshall Thomas described how the waterhole was selected as the spot for a government agency to monitor the movements of cattle, to prevent poaching, to protect the area against incursions by diamond prospectors, and to allow the raiding by Boer farmers of Ju/'hoansi settlements for farm workers — treated as little more than slave labor. The government post was established in 1960, and the area was designated a "Homeland for Bushmen" in 1970. Tsumkwe got a police station and jail in 1975 when it was deemed a crime for local people to hunt or start bush fires.

The crossroads appeared more boldly on the map at the time the South African Defense Force built an army post there. This was in 1978, when the South African government, which administered South-West Africa as a colony of white domination, was vainly attempting to suppress the well-armed Namibian liberation struggle. Some !Kung were co-opted by the South African army, which used them as trackers and spotters and even as regular gun-toting recruits. After the success of the struggle, and Namibia's independence in 1990, this apparent collaboration with the enemies of the nationalists tainted relations between the !Kung and the Namibian politicians who saw their desperate bid for employment as the treachery of counterrevolutionaries.

This being Namibia, the people in and around Tsumkwe were probably not particularly healthy. USE A CONDOM was painted in brightly colored foot-high letters in two languages on the outside wall of the Tsumkwe community center, and for anyone who missed the point or might be illiterate, a condom was also drawn on the wall, five feet long, like a large and flapping windsock.

The only sounds in the Ju/'hoansi villages were the crackle and screech of insects. At the Tsumkwe crossroads the prevailing sound was the shout and thump of rap music. Rap and hip-hop now dominate African pop music. Much of it is imported unchanged from the United States, some of it comes from Brazil or is adapted locally, all of it blasting at full volume from car radios or from inside bars, even in this tiny place.

Because it is predictably fogeyish — and useless in any case — to object to loud music, especially the music of the young, I merely wondered, in a sour and squinting way, about the appeal of this semiliterate music here. And not just here: rap music is played all over sub-Saharan Africa. Nearly every country has its own rap groups. When I inquired, I discovered that Namibia alone had more than twenty hip-hop singers or groups, with names such as Contract Killers, Snazzy, L'il D, and, in the small town I had just passed through, Otjiwarongo, a group called Krazie D. Obviously something in this music speaks to the urban African, who is typically unemployed, overlooked, idle, very poor, lonely, and alienated from village traditions and pieties.

Rap is the howl of the underclass, the music of menace, of hostility, of aggression. Intentionally offensive, much of the language is so obscene that it is unplayable on radio stations. So naturally you wonder what is in the heads of the young here who have adopted these songs as their anthems. Are they merely idle, their minds colonized by the alien lyrics? And along with the music is a whole style of dress. Any Tsumkwe youths who could afford to buy clothes wore brand-new rap-themed T-shirts and shorts. Faded ones were also available at the used-clothes stalls, courtesy of Americans who offloaded their kids' old clothes, giving them to charities and perhaps never guessing that the T-shirt with the portrait of The Notorious B.I.G. or Heavy D or Snoop Dogg, or the one lettered *Thug Life* in homage to the murdered rapper Tupac Shakur, was just what they wanted. And they now had the music to match it. They had the words, too, and could say, with Caliban in *The Tempest*, "You taught me language, and my profit on't / Is I know how to curse."

In countries where baseball was unknown, the most common headgear was a baseball cap. Hip-hop music has inspired skateboarding, break dancing, and graffiti. A skateboard is unusable on an African road, but I sometimes saw break dancing in villages or townships, and it was a rare public wall in Africa that had not been tagged with graffiti. The sound of urban Africa is not the harmonious and hypnotic rhythm of a drum, but the shout of rap and its opposite, the hoarse hymn singing of evangelicals — both sorts heard in remote Tsumkwe.

The community center with the windsock-sized condom painted on the side was officially designated the Captain Kxao Kxami Community Learning and Development Centre. (To clarify, words like Kxao, #Oma, !Kung, and /'hoansi each convey a specific sound — a tsk, a click, a tongue-suck, or a cluck mimicking the clopping of a horse or the cheek-suck a rider uses to command a horse to giddyup — four distinct "velaric suction stops" that no written phonetic form can begin to approximate.) Far from being a Namibian government effort, the center had been built in 2006 with funds from the Namibia Association of Norway (NAMAS), which also supplied it with computers and an Internet connection. This Norwegian group was also deeply involved in village education and health projects. The Redbush Tea Company chipped in with money, and a charity in South Africa donated books. In 2009, the Texas chapter of the Explorers Club collected money to construct the seminar room where I was to deliver my talk.

On the face of it, Tsumkwe — solitary, remote, poor — was the classic example of a hard-up outpost in Africa, adopted by foreigners as a recipient of funds and the idealistic efforts of outsiders to improve education and health. The three churches there also played a role, though I did not discover how successful they were.

Tsumkwe had been neglected, if not ignored altogether, by the Namibian government, though two ministries — water and agriculture — had offices near the crossroads. For this reason, and its poverty and need, Tsumkwe had become a cause and a rallying point for the virtue industry, in which for a few days I was playing an active part. The intrusion of outsiders in the day-to-day lives of Africans was the sort of thing I had always criticized. The Norwegians had been at it for thirty years, funneling money into the place and producing extensive and scholarly self-financed surveys of the hardships and goals of the local people.

And this was a lesson to me, because my first impression of Namibia, from the border to Windhoek and the coast, was of a place that did not need anyone from outside the country to tell the people how to live their lives, that Namibians themselves had set an example in development and decorum. But that was a snap judgment, from before I crossed the Vet Fence.

At the lodge in Tsumkwe, which was actually a little camp, Tony and I met the UNESCO people: Jaco, a South African; his coworker, Andrea; and Werner, a German, head of the Namibian archives in Windhoek. We each had a small cabin—Tony's was next door to mine—and we observed the subdued routine of campers. Sunset was sudden, the nights were hot, and the generator went off at ten, plunging the whole place into darkness and silence. The first night, though, I heard a pattering that in seconds became a torrent of rain. A phantom downpour, it seemed. In the morning there was no sign of dampness anywhere, only pockmarked dust and withered plants.

We gathered at the Captain Kxao Kxami Community Learning and Development Centre in the morning for what was billed as the opening ceremony. The room filled with officials, chiefs and their retinues, advisers, people from the Ministry of Education, the governor of the region, the delegation from Windhoek—of which I was one—and some clergymen. There were about thirty of us altogether, the women in bright dresses, and all the men—except for me—wearing ties and dark suits.

We began by singing the Namibian national anthem ("Namibia, land of the brave / Freedom fight we have won . . .") and the African Union anthem ("Let us all unite and celebrate together / The victories won for our liberation . . ."), and then the oldest of the clergymen led us in a prayer in the !Kung language and in Afrikaans. I caught the word "Moses," and at the end, in English, "We all belong to God."

This was followed by messages and remarks about the importance of Audio-Visual Heritage Day, though I wondered what meaning "audio-visual" had here; no one had mentioned that Tsumkwe was a place without television, without a movie theater, and with only irregular Internet access.

With great formality and chiefly protocol, the attendees were introduced, and the governor gave his keynote address.

"I must also welcome myself!" Governor Kamehozu of Otjozondjupa said teasingly, after his solemn welcome to the visitors. He went on, "This is one of the remotest areas of Namibia. But Tsumkwe has its own beauty, and we must take advantage of the opportunities our heavenly father has given us. We are lucky in many ways. Our elephants are bigger than elephants elsewhere. Our lions are also bigger . . ."

Speaker after speaker took the podium, making remarks, ponderously handing over historic photographs to the Namibian National Archives, declaiming messages of congratulation, reading introductions, until the closing homily of Chief Tsamkxao #Oma. I kept reminding myself in this hall — with windows too high to see through — that all this talk and ceremony was taking place at the end of a gravel road in a distant bush settlement at the edge of the Kalahari Desert.

That was just the morning I had feared, rarefied and overformal. But after lunch (sandwiches and fruit punch under the thorn tree) the event acquired greater meaning. In the first session students from the nearby school filled the room. They were only in their early teens, yet they looked well developed, and the heavy-bosomed schoolgirls seemed on the verge of womanhood. They were all polite, fluent in English, well behaved, and responsive, in their intensity reminding me of the hopeful, hard-working students I had taught almost fifty years ago in Malawi. They sat attentively in neat uniforms, as my own students had done, the girls in white blouses and dark skirts, the boys in white shirts and dark trousers.

I gave my talk. I explained—because they said they didn't have a clue—the meaning of the words "audio" and "visual" and "heritage." Then I launched into my assigned theme, "Preserving a Cultural Heritage." My message to the students was simple enough: talk to the oldest people in the village; ask them about their experiences and skills and folktales; write them down. Gathered together, these stories were the history of the region. This was something I wished I had done long ago in Malawi. Though I had talked to villagers and written down some of their stories, I should have been more methodical, using a tape recorder, interviewing all the elders I could find. The ones who were over sixty, and there were many, would have had memories of the nineteenth century, of the earliest colonials, of their first glimpses of missionaries, travelers, and white settlers; they might have heard family stories of the Arab slave trade. Oral history of this kind was invaluable, and that, in brief, was my pep talk on cultural preservation.

Afterward, the lights were dimmed. John Marshall's short film *Children Throw Toy Assegais* (1974) was shown. It was a glimpse into the recent past, six or seven boys, no more than ten years old, practicing the throwing of a shortened spearlike weapon, some of them succeeding in making the sharp thing penetrate a tree. The boys were gleeful, competing to see who would succeed as the best shot. The assegais were mere toys, but this play had a serious intention; when a boy grew older, his assegai would be a blade hafted to a throwing stick and used to kill animals. So it was not just competitive play—it was preparation for their lives as hunters.

None of the boys in the film wore more than a perfunctory wrap around his hips, and the sight of them half naked made the neatly uniformed schoolchildren giggle, if not in embarrassment, then in awkwardness. Although the Ju/'hoansi wore very little, they were averse to displaying their bodies to outsiders. Some of the women were prominently steatopygous — huge-buttocked — but "we were unable to observe to what extent steatopygia existed among the women in the Nyae Nyae area," Lorna Marshall wrote, "because the women there flatly refused to take off their karosses [antelope-hide capes] from around their backs." The schoolchildren watching the film squirmed because we outsiders were present, but they were excited, too, with this glimpse into their animated history.

"I saw my own brother in those pictures!" old Chief Tsamkxao #Oma exclaimed in the !Kung language when the lights went up. He was tearful with excitement, gesturing to the blank screen, clumsily passionate. "This is something like a dream. That was my brother when he was young!" He bowed to the visitors and touched his heart. "Thank you for this film. This is like a dream for me."

The schoolchildren stared at the chief with what seemed a new curiosity, as though he himself were an artifact. And he was, in a sense, because he had been raised in the old way, in the bush, without school, but living by the assegai and the arrow. And consider: it was less than forty years ago, but from all appearances it could have been a thousand.

The next film was *A Rite of Passage,* which had been made by John Marshall in 1972. This riveted the children because it was not so remote from them. Many of their fathers would have participated in this ritual, the Rite of the First Kill, the occasion on which a boy in a hunting party kills his first large animal. Until that point, the boy would have killed only a bird or a rabbit, but killing a full-grown giraffe, a heavy antelope, a buffalo, or a wildebeest — a game animal killed for meat — was a matter of importance, a stage in the passage from boy to man.

A small group of Ju/'hoansi danced through the tall grass, seeking an animal, and /Ti!kay, the boy to be initiated, crept at the head of the column of hunters. The schoolchildren in the room watched closely, occasionally yelping in excitement.

"A mature wildebeest is seen in the tall grass," John Marshall said, narrating his film, as the hunting party became alert and watchful.

The progress of the hunt and the chase and the kill, revealed by John Marshall in his voice-over, and the later testimony of his mother, Lorna, in her book on these people, described this first big kill as essential in proving manhood. A young man could not court a woman and marry her until he had slaughtered a powerful animal, and only then, when he had displayed his hunting prowess, could he undergo the Rite of the First Kill.

In the movie a full-grown wildebeest—horned, humpbacked, hairy-flanked—was flushed from the tall grass, pursued by the young, slim, spear-carrying /Ti!kay, the adults shadowing him in the chase. Out of sight of the camera the heavy animal was brought down by the boy's spear and, to the rejoicing of the elders, finished off with stabs from his assegai. Just as quickly the animal was butchered, chopped into irregular bleeding chunks, its legs were hacked and jointed, and a dish of blobby wildebeest fat was set aside,

A fire was lit near the slabs of meat, and a lump of fatty flesh sizzled on it, while /Ti!kay the boy hunter underwent scarification, ritual knife cuts to his arms and chest and forehead. The boy's father, Khan//, did the cutting—frowning but clearly proud—and these cuts were slathered and rubbed with the hot fat.

At this point in their viewing of the film, the schoolchildren screeched, because it was obviously painful to the boy, and just as obviously /Ti!kay endured it stoically. If the hunt had been a test of prowess, this scarification was a test of nerve. /Ti!kay was probably in his early teens, yet through this ordeal he was entering manhood.

The ritual of rubbing the charred meat and hot fat into the cuts, Lorna Marshall wrote, served "to insure that he will not be lazy, that his heart will say to him, 'Why am I sitting here at my fire? Why am I not out hunting?'"

The wildebeest was a male, John Marshall said in his narration, and therefore /Ti!kay was scarified on his right side. "When eventually he kills a large female animal he will be cut on his left side."

Initiated this way, he had greater powers. The anointed scars gave him protection — made it easier for him to find an animal, and would make him invisible to animals. Perhaps more important than this, the ceremony gave him the right to marry, which would not necessarily happen soon, but was certain in the fullness of time; and on the big day, because hunting and marriage were linked, his bride would share an animal that he had recently killed. "The primary sources of physical life — sex and food," Lorna Marshall wrote of this event. "Power as a male and worthiness and dignity are associated with hunting . . . The bride's people can capture at once the sexual and the hunting powers of the young man."

When the lights went on, the children were whispering to each other. The film about playing with the assegais seemed to have a greater effect than this film of hunting, butchering, ritual scarification, and pain.

"What did you think of this film?" the UNESCO man asked.

They stopped whispering, lapsed into silence, and simply watched the white man who was repeating his question.

They had spaniel eyes, long lashes, smooth serious faces, intense expressions.

"Was it interesting to you?"

They murmured yes, a rising hum.

"She has cuts!" one of the girls said, and pointed behind her to a girl who was wriggling timidly in her chair.

"And he has cuts!" another said, indicating a frowning boy.

The wriggling girl stood up and showed her facial scarring.

I asked what it meant.

"It is for protection."

I asked how many of them had been cut in this way. About a third of them put their hands up, more girls than boys. It was curious to see this assembled group of schoolchildren, in their neatly pressed

and laundered uniforms, proudly acknowledging their ritual scarification, showing the slash marks on their faces and arms.

The session was just about over, but as my brief had been to talk
about cultural preservation, I asked whether any of them had a story
to tell — perhaps one they'd heard at home, in the village, or related
by an elder. Several stood and told a short story, but the one that
made the most impact was told by a tall, smiling, self-possessed
girl, first in !Kung, her language, and then in English.

"Two men were out hunting," she began in English, after she had
made a great success of the story in !Kung — laughter all around.
"They were deep in the bush, and it became night, and so they decided to sleep just there, under a tree. The first man fell asleep. But
it was a cool night. The other man used a cheetah skin as a blanket,
and he pulled it over himself. In the middle of the night, the first
man woke up — eh! He saw the cheetah skin. He took his knife and
stabbed at it, and slashed his friend's leg."

The students yelled with delight, as they had the first time they'd
heard it in their own language.

"The friend began to cry out. When the man with the knife saw
what he had done to his friend's leg, he held his own face" — and the
girl held her face and gestured madly — "and stabbed his eyes, he
was so upset. So one was lame and the other was blind."

The children howled at this irony, perhaps for the symmetry of it,
perhaps for the sheer gory horror of it.

"Morning came." The girl was smiling. She wasn't done. "The
blind one carried the crippled one on his shoulders back to the village."

When the laughter died down, I asked, "Is there a moral to this
story?"

"I don't know."

There was, I discovered, a Ju/'hoansi story called "The Beautiful
Elephant Girl." A folktale, it concerned the strange and sudden
birth of the elephant girl, her meaningless murder by two brothers,

the butchering of her corpse and her whole body cannibalized, the setting aside of her blood, the mystical opening of an anthill as a refuge, the blood swelling to create a rebirth of the Elephant Girl, a magic gemsbok horn, the reappearance of the murderous brothers, and the revenge on them: "When the two brothers had entered the village, she took out her magical gemsbok horn and blew on it, saying, 'These two brothers and their village shall be broken apart and ruined!' The horn blew down the village, flattened it to the ground. Then the beautiful elephant girl walked home."

This weird disjointed tale, characteristic of traditional Ju/'hoansi stories, was not greatly different from the short gory tale the schoolgirl had told. The only difference was that the girl was extemporizing, and amusing her friends; and "The Beautiful Elephant Girl" was a tale that had been told by an elder and transcribed by a team of bilingual Ju/'hoansi.

It was what I had advocated to the students that morning.

And that was how I learned about the transcription project in Tsumkwe, the Kalahari Peoples Fund, and the enormous number of foreigners who had contributed to keeping this culture alive, while the indigenous people were helped along and looked after.

The Ju/'hoan Transcription Group had been active in Tsumkwe since 2002, but the tales had been collected since 1971, some of them recorded almost forty years ago by the distinguished Harvard anthropologist Megan Biesele, and the stories (printed in both English and Ju/'hoan) were faithful translations of recordings that had been made in villages. Much of this work was supported by the Kalahari Peoples Fund (based in Austin, Texas), which dated to the 1970s and operated throughout the apartheid era, creating homegrown reading materials for the local schools. There was no government involvement in the fund; in fact, the Namibian educational authorities had always resisted mother-tongue instruction in this area.

The Village Schools Project had been created within the Kalahari Peoples Fund in order to lobby the Namibian Ministry of Education to have the Ju/'hoan language used in schools and in printed materials. All of this information was available on the Kalahari Peoples Network, and the whole initiative was funded with foreign donations.

Over the years, the project had become more and more ambitious. The idea was to create a database of traditional stories, to codify the text by creating a user-friendly orthography for this phonetically complex language. Another goal was the updating of a Ju/'hoan dictionary. A Youth Transcription Group was started in order to pass on skills. This meant the training of transcribers to be computer savvy, the raising of money to buy equipment, and a collective effort to encourage anthropologists, volunteer teachers, writers, and aides to help run the center, guide the project, and see the work into print and onto the Internet.

Foreign aid! From afar came webmasters, tech assistants, linguists from Germany, donations of laptops and solar panels by foreign companies. After 2007 the Norwegian-funded Captain Kxao Kxami Community Centre became available, and now it had electricity and an Internet connection.

These aid givers from abroad engaged the whole community, starting with village-based students who would encourage elders to speak about the past and share stories. Some of the elders were healers, who would pass on their experiences of "psychic healing." But the stories of local leaders who had participated in the struggle for Namibian independence were also recorded. The transcription group was a memory project, the oral history I had described in my talk—but I was a latecomer to this effort.

In the foreign-funded center with the foreign-funded equipment —computers, digital tape recorders, video cameras—the goal was "technological empowerment"—to protect the culture, produce educational materials for schools, and build an archive. The stated mission was for the Ju/'hoansi people to tell their own stories.

When I was asked to speak on "Preserving a Cultural Heritage," this is what I had in mind. It saddened me to think that so much in Africa had been lost—the skills of building and farming, the arts of carving and ornamenting, of music and dance, of storytelling. I had not realized that the preservation had already been under way for so many years, and that the whole Ju/'hoansi community and a large foreign community of supporters were also involved.

If these foreigners hadn't done it, no one would have done it. And preserving this history was an important matter—as important as providing water or food. It was all a lesson to me: none of it would have happened if it had been left to the Namibian government, which seemed to regard Tsumkwe and the lands beyond the Vet Fence as beneath notice. Without the inspired meddling of outsiders, Tsumkwe would have subsided into its own dust in silence. Because of this foreign involvement it had pride in its language, an oral history, a growing archive of stories, and a place to meet and make plans.

In Tsumkwe I met an American, a man from Seattle, who had been teaching in Namibia for fifteen years, the past two in the school at the crossroads.

"Lots of challenges here," he said, because I had asked. "Remoteness, drunkenness, teen pregnancy." But he was not dismayed; he was hoping to stay a few more years.

I saw that I had been hasty in judging some efforts by outsiders. This was necessary and timely. Yet you cannot see such hope and high spirits in the young and not think: What will happen to them?

The next day I voiced my anxiety to one of the South Africans, who simply shrugged.

"They'll go to the cities. To Grootfontein. To Windhoek."

"What will they do there?" I asked.

"They'll be servants. Domestic service."

It sounded crueler in that accent: *dimisteek*.

At the end of my last day, the children in a large group made their way back to the school compound, which was at the far side of the crossroads. They saw me watching from under a shade tree and called out, "Sir!"

I walked with them for a while and was heartened by their vitality — their humor, their teasing, their intelligence. Each of them carried a copybook with notes they'd taken at the event. When we parted, they called out, "Come back to Tsumkwe, sir!" and then they continued on their way, in the heat, attached to long shadows.

8

Among the Real People

IT WAS ON THE FOLLOWING day, in the hot flat bush some miles north of Tsumkwe, that—as I began this narrative by saying—I crossed the bulging termite mound of smooth, ant-chewed sand, and with just the slightest elevation of this swelling under my foot soles the landscape opened in a majestic fan, like the fluttered pages of a whole unread book.

I then resumed kicking behind a file of small-bodied, mostly naked men and women who were quick-stepping under a sky fretted with golden fire through the dry scrub of what was once coarsely called in Afrikaans Boesmanland (Bushman Land), and generally known as the Kaokoveld. This had been redesignated Nyae Nyae, a homeland for the !Kung and subgroups like the Ju/'hoansi—hard to utter, click-thickened names for the ancient race that still inhabited the region.

An old dream of mine had been to meet and talk with some of these people in their own village, though "village" is the wrong word for a *n!ore,* the expanse of land they claimed to keep themselves alive—a portion of the landscape with vague boundaries they called home. It was an area of bush where there was water, wild game, and sufficient edible bulbs, tubers, roots, seeds, and man-ketti nuts for their diet. In that place they would have a campsite, called a *tshu/ko*, and build shelters — hardly more than windbreaks or twiggy lean-tos — just sleeping places, not for living in or shuf-fling around inside. They lived under the sky, they lived around the fire. That was the accepted notion of the Ju/'hoansi by travelers like me, many of us romantic voyeurs.

Long ago, in the freest period of my life, I had worked as a teacher in Africa for six years straight. I had revisited the conti-nent every few years after that, sometimes staying for months. I had been up and down half a dozen great rivers, including the Nile and the Zambezi, hiked the foothills of the Mountains of the Moon, and crossed Lake Victoria and Lake Malawi. I had traveled over-land from Cairo to Cape Town. I had fraternized with, and worked among, Angoni people, Baganda, Nubians, Karomojong, Watutsi, WaGogo, Masai, Zulus, Kikuyu, the Sena people of the Lower River, the Batwa Pygmies of the Ituri Forest, and scores of other peoples. Yet in all that time I had never met a Ju/'hoansi — elusive, dwelling in small related groups — on his or her own turf.

But I had glimpsed them with fascination, the way you see a bird of passage flashing onto a nearby branch and twitching its brilliant tail. Their physiognomy — the look of these people, their whole physical being — was unmistakable. Now and then, on a busy Cape Town street or in a sleepy *dorp* in the countryside, I would see that light-hued, faintly Asiatic face, the narrow eyes, the delicate hands, the small stature, a distinct upright way of standing and a swift, almost skipping way of walking — and, even if the person happened to be wrapped in a heavy coat and scarf against the wind blowing from Table Bay or the Great Karoo, I knew whom I was looking at.

I always suspected that these people, oblique in answers to my direct questions, were far from home. And I felt there was some-thing radiant about them. It was no illusion. It was the radiance of peacefulness from the core of their being, what Elizabeth Marshall Thomas called "their magnificent nonviolence." They are known as, in a rendering of their own name for themselves, the Harmless People.

These were the people who had endured, and they had a claim to being the living remnant of the first humans on earth, with an ancient pedigree that was an unbroken link to the present. Bands of other Africans, mainly Bantu, those who were rovers and conquerors, had traveled — some settling, others moving on — through the forests in the heart of Africa, at first clockwise through the Congo and then fanning out and descending, percolating east and south as far as the Great Fish River. That river became a traditional boundary of the Cape Colony, where in the late eighteenth century a confrontation between the Xhosa on one bank and the Dutch and English settlers on the opposite bank led to a series of bloody wars. But both the Bantu and the whites were another story; they were migrants or the children of migrants.

The Ju/'hoansi were not migrants. Some had scattered because of persecution and land grabbing, but most of them had remained pretty much where they had always been, in this southern part of Africa, since the Upper Pleistocene, loyal to each other and clinging to their skills and traditions, famously peaceful and accommodating — no thieving, no fighting, and divorce so simple a matter that adultery was almost unknown among them.

Celebrated as trackers of game, masters of the hunt — just a small hunting party could bring down and butcher a fleet-footed, full-grown giraffe, as John Marshall had shown them doing in one of his earliest films. Brilliant as botanists, they recognized an enormous taxonomy of bush and savanna plants — used for food, for medicine, as fetishes, as ornaments. They knew the entomological chemistry of poison and the art of weapon making, the skills of using arrows and spears and snares. Despite all this, they hardly fought or raised their voices, had never gone to war with each other, nor had they become inflamed by bellicosity even against the greatest provocation — slave raids, intruding white settlers, and predatory Bantu hunters.

It was amazing, in the face of all the encroachments — they lived in a land where diamonds littered the ground like pebbles, where trophy animals might be slaughtered, where cattle might graze — amazing that the Ju/'hoansi still existed. Yet they did, though in dwindling numbers, and they had become the obsessive subjects, even the darlings, of ethnographers, for what they were able to tell us about how we as humans had lived in prehistory, and also as "noble savages" — "one of the most heavily scientifically commoditized human groups in the annals of science," wrote Robert J. Gordon in *The Bushman Myth: The Making of a Namibian Underclass.*

They seemed a timeless people, as eternal as the features of the landscape — the rocks, the gullies, the termite mounds. They didn't grow old, they didn't change, they endured in their ancestral land. That was the impression I had gotten from the first books I read.

It was, of course, all wrong, but what did I know?

Decades ago, the only books about the Ju/'hoansi I could find were the works of Laurens van der Post, but I soon learned to be wary of him. He had published *Venture to the Interior* in 1952, an account of his surveying trip to Nyasaland, and when I began to live there a little more than ten years later, I saw that he had made a crepuscular and existential narrative out of a fairly conventional few months of bushwhacking with a team of hearties in the Mlanje region of tea estates. I realized from that book and his others that he was something of a mythomaniac.

I once visited van der Post in England in 1975, for a magazine interview, and found him humorless and vain, monologuing to me, mostly about the highly colored life he had led, in the dry, imperious tone of a headmaster. His life had indeed been extraordinary in many respects (prisoner of the Japanese, friend of Carl Jung's, patron of the Bushmen), but in his telling it was a succession of sullen boasts. He had an odd pout, his wet lower lip protruding as if in disbelief, staring blue eyes, and a severe, somewhat reluctant manner.

In a large wing chair he looked like an old auntie interrupted in her knitting, and had an auntie's lined and tetchy face. He refused to see me alone, but remained canted sideways in his chair, surrounded by sycophants and handmaidens who treated him as a sage. (Later he would become a mentor to a similarly bedazzled Prince Charles.) Starring in his own films, he saw himself as a pioneer interpreter of the Bushmen, and though he had no language proficiency and no deep knowledge of the people, only a romantic enthusiasm for their tenacity and their culture, he was instrumental in helping to frame South African government policy that granted them a homeland.

I came to see that he was a posturing fantasist and fake mystic in the field, and as a writer he was an impressionist using colors, rather than a social scientist using facts. It was easy to understand and almost forgivable, because the people in the mid-1950s when he first visited them were still (we have the Marshalls' work as proof) culturally coherent, self-sufficient, remote, and wonderful physical specimens. But van der Post tended to get carried away in describing them; his self-regard and his Jungian glosses impeded his narratives. His work, full of breathless mystery or plain inaccuracy, is either not mentioned or dismissed by later scholars, who seem to regard him, with reason, as a little more than a village explainer (*The Lost World of the Kalahari*) or fabulist (*The Face Beside the Fire*) — an unreliable witness.

The most complete book I found, the bible of Bushman culture, was the classic *Specimens of Bushman Folklore* by Wilhelm Bleek and Lucy Lloyd, the earliest study of the people and their language. (Van der Post had created one of his Bushman books, *The Heart of the Hunter,* by rehashing the folktales in *Specimens.*) Bleek — stout, hairy, ursine, even to a lumbering bearish untidiness — was a linguistic genius, a Prussian philologist who migrated to South Africa in 1855 with the aim of compiling a Zulu grammar. But while a young student at the University of Berlin, in 1850, he was, as Neil Bennun wrote in *The Broken String: The Last Words of an Extinct People* (2004), "the world's greatest expert on the languages of southern Africa." He suspected, and tried to prove, that the Bushmen's languages might be related (because of the northward push of prehistoric peoples) to ancient Egyptian. He was scholarly but sickly — tubercular, easily fatigued, prone to chills, and habitually coughing up blood. He married Jemima Lloyd, daughter of a Welsh clergyman, but it was his sister-in-law Lucy Lloyd who became his collaborator on the project of writing down and piecing together the elements of the Bushman language /Xam, and recording the stories and beliefs of these unknown and unregarded people.

How this happened is a good story, and a short one. Bleek did not have the stomach or the constitution for arduous travel. He could not meet the Bushmen on their own terms in their distant hinterland. But the Bushmen were routinely arrested for minor transgressions — drunkenness, loitering, theft, cattle rustling, trespassing, poaching ("Hunger had made criminals out of the /Xam men," wrote Bennun). This was in the 1860s and 1870s. The captured men were brought in chains to Cape Town, put on trial, sentenced to hard labor, and jailed. Hearing of this, Bleek volunteered to house one of them at his little estate, The Hill, in Mowbray, a rustic village just outside the Cape Town city limits. This wish was granted, and other prisoners joined the Bleeks. As residents at The Hill, the convicts became their language teachers, and over time these Bushmen divulged their *kukummi* — their oral history, their traditions, their cosmology, their stories. The Bleek archive of Bushman lore, dictated by the prisoners, grew to twelve thousand pages.

Many of the stories were harsh, some bitter and violent. "If you were learning the language of the indigenous hunting and gathering people of South Africa in the second half of the nineteenth century," Bennun wrote, "the first words and sentences you learned were to do with hunger, dispossession and crime."

Wilhelm Bleek died in 1875 at the age of forty-eight. Lucy Lloyd and Bleek's daughter Dorothea carried on his work, deepening their understanding, relying on prisoner informants. After many trials, some of this material—groundbreaking ethnology of the earliest people—was published in *Specimens of Bushman Folklore* in 1911. Through the twenties and thirties curious travelers made forays into the Kalahari, yet these expeditions were largely touristic, not adding much to what Bleek and Lloyd had learned but only confirming the stereotype that the Bushmen were naked semisavage Stone Age hunters who slept under trees, grubbed for roots, chased down antelopes, and ate insects.

Much later, choosing to live among them and know them better, the Marshall family were the pioneers: Lorna in *The !Kung of Nyae Nyae,* the subtle and detailed study of the people, then her children, who documented the change and decay in the people's circumstances—John in his many films, Elizabeth in her two evocative books. Ultimately, many other books appeared, and the titles alone are offputting: *Land Filled with Flies, The Land God Made in Anger, The Bushman Myth, Women Like Meat*—helpful, well-informed books, actually, but they kept the people two-dimensional, odorless, unphysical, out of focus, in sepia tones, as books of anthropology often do.

Reading about a far-off place can be a satisfaction in itself, and you might be thankful you're reading about the bad trip without the dust in your nose and the sun burning your head, not having to endure the unrewarding nuisance and delay of the road. But reading can also be a powerful stimulus to travel. That was the case for me from the beginning. Reading and restlessness — dissatisfaction at home, a sourness at being indoors, and a notion that the real world was elsewhere — made me a traveler. If the Internet were everything it is cracked up to be, we would all stay home and be brilliantly witty and insightful. Yet with so much contradictory information available, there is more reason to travel than ever before: to look closer, to dig deeper, to sort the authentic from the fake; to verify, to smell, to touch, to taste, to hear, and sometimes — importantly — to suffer the effects of this curiosity.

That was what compelled me to travel through a desiccated landscape from Tsumkwe to the Ju/'hoansi village on this very hot day.

Some Ju/'hoansi men were drying and curing slashed hunks of meat — thicker than mere strips; great black sinewy belts of it — that looked more like old leather than flesh, turning it into the jerky known all over southern Africa as biltong. They had food and water on their minds.

The settlement of shacks and shelters was up a narrow road of sand so soft and deep our vehicle plowed and butted it clumsily into heaps like a tipped-forward and wobbling wheelbarrow. We became stuck several times, the useless wheels scouring deeper ruts until the axles rested against the road. The sand was hot, too, as I found out when I knelt in it to push against the back bumper. I thought of walking the rest of the way to the settlement, but the driver, who was himself a town-dwelling Ju/'hoansi, and calm, urged me to be patient. After a while, the vehicle was plowing the sand again, and we swayed and slewed into the village.

A dozen small people wearing skins and beads rushed to greet us, all smiles.

But at the far side of the village, a group of five children, none older than ten or twelve, barefoot, dressed in conventional clothes, were sorting an array of plastic buckets and tin basins. In Tsumkwe, most children of that age, many of them Ju/'hoansi, would have been in school this morning, in blue-and-white uniforms, wearing shoes, scribbling in copybooks.

"They are going for water," one of the men said through an interpreter, whose name was John.

As he spoke, the children shouldered their containers and set off through the low thornbush. I noticed that the man who had spoken was dressed in a traditional leather breechclout, called a *chuana,* and handsewn leather sandals, and that he carried a wooden staff. The water-seeking Ju/'hoansi children wore castoff Western clothes that are found all over sub-Saharan Africa. The boys had on torn shirts and shorts, the two small girls pink and blue dresses. Far from seeming like hunter-gatherers, they looked like urchins in any rural African village. And like most African urchins they were skinny and overworked.

"Where's the water — is there a creek nearby?" I asked.

"No water! The children are going two kilometers for water!" I could see grievance on the man's face as he spoke in his language. "The government promised us a water pipe three years ago, but it hasn't come."

The drought had lasted for years. Weather was often blamed for Africa's troubles, but "what is the use of ascribing any catastrophe to nature?" Rebecca West asked herself in *Black Lamb and Grey Falcon,* and answered, "Nearly always man's inherent malignity comes in and uses the opportunities it offers to create a graver catastrophe."

Chickens were pecking in the sand near us, and a little distance away a crudely made shed looked more substantial than the shelters of tree branches and thatch I had seen in the black-and-white photo plates in anthropology books. This was not a seasonal camp but seemed more like a permanent settlement, and to say it was a poor one was an understatement.

I asked about the belts of meat blackening in the sun, about thirty pounds of it draped on a wooden rack.

"It is elephant meat."

"You killed an elephant? Tell me how."

This made the Ju/'hoansi man laugh. "No, no," he said. "We don't kill elephants."

"Where did the meat come from?"

"From a trophy hunter."

"A Ju/'hoansi man?" I knew it could not have been. No village hunter anywhere here was interested in killing an elephant or a lion or a buffalo as a trophy. "Who was it?"

"Hunter!"

"From where?"

"White man!"

I wanted to know the word he'd used. It was *!hû* — white person. Trying it out, I said I was a *!hû*, and they agreed, yes, but I was also a *ju-s-a-!gaa* — a red man, and they confirmed what Lorna Marshall had discovered and explained, that black Africans are called *ju-s-a-djo* — black people.

"And what are you — red or black or white?"

"We are Ju/'hoansi!" And he gave the name the emphasis of its true aboriginal meaning: *We are Real People!*

"Was this a big elephant?"

"Very big," the man said, flinging his arms out, "with big tusks."

"Why don't the trophy hunters kill small, weak elephants?" I asked, another leading question — but he knew I was testing him.

"The big one with tusks is the only elephant they want."

As the Ju/'hoansi man led me around the compound, the interpreter and some women followed us. The women, young and old, also wearing animal skins and shell and ostrich egg beads as ornaments, were bare-breasted, and one carried a child in a sling.

"Look, Mr. Paul," John, the interpreter, said — and by the way, this dapper Ju/'hoansi man was wearing a T-shirt, sunglasses, and blue jeans, with sturdy shoes on his feet. As he walked he jingled his car keys, which were chained to a plastic tag. "He wants to show you this hook."

The Ju/'hoansi man in the leather clout snatched a pole resting against a stump. A long stiff wire was attached to one end of the pole and a wicked-looking hook to the other end. Shaking it, thrusting it, he explained how it was used to capture any small animal that had retreated into a hole in the ground. The hook was pushed into the hole — sometimes to its entire length, which was seven or eight feet — until the animal was spiked and yanked out bleeding.

"What animal are you after?"

"The springhare."

"Are there many here?"

"No. Just a few." The man looked downcast, and I had the impression there were no springhares at all to catch, because the pole looked lethal but unused — no blood on the hook — perhaps just a curiosity to show to a credulous visitor like me.

Jingling his keys again, John said, "Mr. Paul, you want to go for a bush walk?"

"Not now," I said. "Maybe later."

I had seen an old man standing in the shade of a tree, holding a sturdy, well-strung bow. He wore an apron of animal skin and had been watching us making the rounds of the drying meat and the weapons. He was slight but sinewy, as they all were. I was attracted by his stance — not leaning against the tree but standing lightly on his feet under its boughs, dappled by the filtered sunlight, just staring at us, unmoving, as though we were no more than unheeding animals, browsing in his compound.

"I want to talk to him," I said.

I am making this sound sober and deliberate, and there might be an unintentional note of ponderous solemnity in these descriptions. It was a very hot morning, over a hundred degrees once again. I was writing notes and asking questions at the same time, and all the while tramping through the sand. This seems to have all the bitter ingredients of a hard day. But it was not hard at all. I was happy.

I was happier than I could remember being when so far from home. Happiness had removed all obstacles. I hardly noticed the heat, I was excited, I wasn't hungry. The fulfillment of an old dream can be that way if the reality matches the dream. Some people who have dreamed of the pyramids and finally manage to travel to Giza are disappointed at the sight of them. "I hadn't realized they were so small," a man once said to me in Egypt, because the pyramids had towered in his imagination. But most people are blown away by their first sight of the Grand Canyon; their first experience of the Balinese Monkey Dance, the *Ketjak*; their first glimpse of a breaching humpback whale. That was how I felt. Being among these people exceeded my dream. And maybe happiness is the wrong word; perhaps what I felt was bliss bordering on rapture.

"Please ask that man if I can speak to him."

When the man was asked, he didn't change his posture or his expression, nor did he blink, and I was afraid the answer would be no.

"He will speak to you."

A stranger, whether black or white, among these people was called *ju dole* — a bad or harmful person. "The strange is potentially harmful in !Kung thinking," wrote Lorna Marshall. Strange places, strange people, and strange situations make the Ju/'hoansi apprehensive. Yet as a peaceable people they have ways of dealing with the alien and the odd. First they put down their weapons before greeting a stranger, because they believe that approaching someone while armed might provoke trouble. They are polite even toward a person who is obnoxiously *ju dole*; they maintain restraint, modesty, and deference.

So the old man, observing the ritual courtesies of his people, could not reasonably refuse to talk to me, although he had kept himself away from the eager group that had welcomed me, and looked wary and oblique as I approached him.

He was a *ju n!a,* an old person, and this expression, like *mzee* in Swahili and *bambo* in Chichewa, is a term of respect, meaning "elder" or "father." The elderly in Africa, men more than women, are generally accorded a special status — age demands deference. But the age of a person who has lived a hard life is always difficult to reckon; an elder in such a society might be no more than forty or fifty. I had the impression that this man was much older than that, and that he might be willing to share *kukummi* — talk, stories, history.

His name was Dambó. He did not know how old he was. John translated for me.

"Seventy or eighty," Dambó said, and admitted he was guessing. This excited me further. If he was seventy, he would have been nine in 1950, the year the Marshalls first came and found the culture intact, unviolated. He might have memories of the old ways.

"Did the Christian missionaries come here?"

"Yes," Dambó said, "long ago. I was myself a Christian for a while." He shrugged as he spoke. "But I gave it up."

"What about the mantis. Do you believe in the power of the mantis?"

I asked because the green praying mantis is one of the dominant creatures in the stories collected by Bleek and Lloyd; the mantis is a supernatural being, called /Kaggen, who was a creator and, through the dazzle of his dreams, a bringer of fire and tools. The mantis was also creator of the /Xam people, the group to which Bleek's convict informants belonged, and this creator was not always an insect but sometimes an old man. Nothing in the /Xam or Ju/'hoansi (to whom the /Xam are related) mythology is simple. In this it resembles many of the world's mythologies, full of transformation, where animals become people or cohabit with them. In Hindu mythology, a deity might give birth to an elephant, as in the case of Ganesh, the four-armed, one-tusked, elephant-headed god whose mother is the voluptuous Parvati (but even that is not the whole story). And the Ju/'hoansi believe, as do many other peoples on earth, that humans were once animals, and still retain the characteristics of wild creatures. And the other way around: certain animals can be tricky and selfish like humans, because their ancestors were human.

"The beasts of prey were once people," a Bushman told Lucy Lloyd, and she entered this in a notebook, which remained in the archives until Neil Bennun transcribed and published it. The rest of the fragment Bennun found is tantalizing. "[The people] became beasts of prey because of the Lynx and the Anteater — they were the ones responsible. They cursed each other because of the little Springbok's doings. They cursed each other.

"All things were once people."

The Anteater made laws that ended immortality for most creatures, but not /Kaggen (the mantis), who survived as a hero, a trickster, and a shape-shifter, because /Kaggen was immortal.

"Yes, I know this mantis," Dambó said. He called it by its Ju/'hoansi name, G//auan — the "//" sound was the giddyup click.

"Please tell me about the mantis," I asked, through John.

"It is a devil," Dambó said. "It brings illness."

"But is it always bad?"

"It is strong. It knows everything."

"It's just a small insect," I said, in the way I might bait a Hindu by saying that Ganesh was just a jolly elephant with one tusk who often rode or danced on a mouse.

"The mantis can kill anything," Dambó said.

"You could kill it if you wanted to, with that stick," I said, because in addition to his bow, Dambó had a short staff jammed into his woven belt, and the thing had a thickened top like the knobkerries that Zulus and Boers used for whacking people on the head.

"If you kill the mantis, you will be in trouble."

"What sort of trouble?"

"You will get sick. You will die."

This was interesting, because here we were in the bush, where wildebeest, warthogs, jackals, and hyenas were common, and lions and cheetahs, though rarer, might turn up too, not to mention the snakes that thrived in this hot desert: the mamba, the python, the puff adder. A hyena had prowled around the Ju/'hoansi shelters the previous night, probably attracted by the hanging elephant meat. But the fragile-looking praying mantis was feared more than any of these.

"Do the young people here know about the mantis?"

"The young people here don't know anything of this," Dambó said.

Some of the youths were watching us talk, and five women sat apart from them, the youngest a shy, elfin-faced girl of sixteen or so, the others much older, one of them a crone and partially blind. Another young woman joined them, and this one carried a dazed infant in a sling.

Dambó, too, had poor vision — pale, clotted, unfocused eyes that were glazed and weepy. His skin was smooth and lined like glove leather. His narrow twisted mustache gave him a look of almost dandified elegance.

"Have you traveled far from here?" I asked.

"I went to Windhoek once," he said, and when I prodded him he added, "Some years ago."

He was as vague about the time he'd been there as he was about his age. The Ju/'hoansi observe the seasons but not the years — and only the recent dry or rainy seasons. Years have no meaning, history has no meaning; the past is simply gone and largely unremembered.

"What did you think when you saw Windhoek?"

"I liked it. It was very good. It was so big."

"What did you like most about the city?"

"The best part" — and for the first time in this little talk he smiled and showed his small darkened teeth—"you don't have to worry about getting food. There is plenty of food." He continued smiling at the memory of meals in distant Windhoek. "There is everything to eat."

I asked for details—how and why he had made the long trip—but he was unforthcoming. I had the impression that it might have been political. He was *ju n!a,* an elder, and since elders were held in high esteem, his visit might have been part of a government initiative. In spite of the fact that the Ju/'hoansi were marginalized, advocates for their development worked in affirmative action programs, put in place by Namibia's first prime minister, Sam Nujoma, who had taken an interest in uplifting the Ju/'hoansi after independence. Delegations from rural villages made numerous visits to the capital; Dambó might have been a member of one of these groups, reporting a grievance, offering testimony, or giving an opinion. Such a group would be comfortably housed and well fed. But all that was in the past. Windhoek for him was a place where no one went hungry, unlike here, where finding food was always difficult.

Then he volunteered another memory, that among his travels, as a small boy he had been to Rundu. This town, due north, on the Namibia-Angola border, was several hundred miles away, and there was no direct road, only a bush track through the semidesert and the wilderness of Kaudom, now a remote game park.

"We went on foot and by truck," he said, and I worked out that "small boy" meant he might have been eight or nine. It could have been 1950 or earlier, when, as all the anthropologists testified, the foraging and hunting culture had been intact, the people ignored, unchanged, still following the old ways.

"Dambó, what do you remember of Rundu?"

"I saw a white man."

I seemed to hear the word *!hû.* I verified this and asked him why he used this particular word and not the one for red man, which I thought was interchangeable.

He said, "He was white like you. We call you white because your skin is white."

"You were a small boy then. Had you seen a white man before that?"

"Never."

"What did you think when you saw the man?"

"I was with my father. My father took me to Rundu. He explained everything to me."

"What did he say?"

"My father said, 'The white people are the people you have to work for.'"

Forced labor, amounting to blackbirding, was common as late as the 1960s, with many instances of white Afrikaner farmers raiding Ju/'hoansi settlements and forcing the men into their trucks to work their farms, keeping them in harsh servitude, if not semi-slavery, as harshly treated farm workers. By putting pressure on the Pretoria government, Laurence Marshall helped put a stop to this brutal practice.

"When your father said that you had to work for them, how did you feel?"

"We were afraid of the white people."

"Were you afraid because they would force you onto their farms?"

He thought hard before he answered, and finally said, "They were not good people for us."

"Did you think the white people might hurt you?"

"We thought, 'They will kill us.'" His face was grayish in the shadows, and he gazed into the middle distance with his glazed and clotted eyes. He said, "Herero people were also killing San people."

Also true. The animosity had a long history, certainly since pre-colonial times and probably much further back. Early-nineteenth-century explorers had described the pitched battles between the two peoples. As the Herero had been pastoral and the San hunter-gatherers, the two modes of life inevitably came into conflict. The

Herero driving their cattle before them had encroached on traditional Bushman lands, and the intrusion had resulted in submission, exploitation, and bloodshed.

"Are the Herero your enemies now?"

"No. We have no enemies now."

"Everything's peaceful?"

Standing stock-still seemed to be his way of taking exception to my generalization. He said, "We have problems."

"Tell me some of your problems."

"The main one in this village is water," Dambó said. But "village" seemed a misnomer for the small cluster of huts and sheds in the immensity of low thorn scrub. "We have to walk so far to find water."

"The children go for the water." I had been struck by the small kids setting off with their buckets and basins on the hot weekday morning.

"That is the children's work."

"What about other problems?" I asked. "How do people get along?"

"We get along," he said.

Practically all observers of the Ju/'hoansi spoke of their acceptance of adultery, because divorce was a simple matter. An adulterous partner was separated from the marriage and, suddenly single, allowed to continue without the taint of transgression.

So I asked Dambó about this, and he gave me a surprising answer.

"If your wife has sex with another man, you beat her," he said. "You might beat the man, too. Or kill him."

"Do such things happen here?"

"A few years ago a man killed his wife in this village."

It seemed uncouth to ask for details, so I let it pass. Many of the violent crimes among the Ju/'hoansi were attributed to drunkenness, which was a scourge of Ju/'hoansi life today. According to one recent researcher, as much as a third of a family's income might be spent on alcohol.

Recalling the film *Rite of Passage,* which I had seen in Tsumkwe, I asked Dambó about his first kill. The memory of this successful hunt animated him, and though it was said that the Ju/'hoansi did not dwell in the past, and were unmoved by historical events, it was a different matter — if Dambó was an example — in the case of personal history, where ritual was involved.

"My first kill was an oryx," he said. The usual name for this large antelope (*Oryx gazella*) is the gemsbok. A mature male can weigh over four hundred pounds, and its long sharp horns, like a pair of samurai swords, make the oryx more than a match for an attacking lion. Dambó raised his arm and said, "He was bigger than this."

"And how big were you?"

"I was small."

"How did you kill him?"

He hoisted his bow and made the gesture of nocking an arrow and letting it fly. He said, "Then I used my assegais."

"What happened after you killed the oryx?"

"They cut my arm — see?" He showed me the ritual scars of the slashes on his forearm that his father had made and pressed with hot fat and oryx flesh.

We talked some more, and out of idle curiosity I wanted to ask about the Ju/'hoansi word for orgasm, which was *tain.* I had read (in Richard B. Lee's *The Dobe Ju/'hoansi*) that *tain* was also the word used to describe the intense sweetness of wild honey. I resisted inquiring because I thought he might be offended, and rightly so, by something so indelicate. Otherwise, I was so happy talking to this old man I had not noticed the time. He seemed content to answer my questions, and perhaps because he was so venerable, no one was emboldened to interrupt.

But during a long pause in the conversation, John tapped his watch and mouthed the words "bush walk."

Dambó stayed behind, frowning in the dappled shade, as we set off into the low thorn scrub in a long file of men and women wearing skins who seemed to dance through the bush. They pointed out the plants they used for medicine, the berries they ate, and the branches that were the hardest and straightest for arrow shafts.

The young elfin-faced woman found a vine and dug up a finger-shaped tuber from the dark, strangely moist hole she'd made and cradled it in her hand. As she flicked dust from the root, it paled beneath her fingertips, and, smiling, she offered the first bite to me. Then everyone shared it, as they shared everything.

Farther on, two men knelt in the leaf litter facing each other. They took turns spinning a two-foot-long stick between their palms, which raised a puff of smoke from the friction of its bottom end in a darkening piece of soft wood, and in the dust of the drilled block some sparks were lit. One man lifted the glowing, gently smoking wood and blew on it with lips framed in a kissing expression, and we had fire.

The women sat in the shade and watched, one of them nursing her baby, as an older man made, out of twisted vine and a bent-over branch, a snare for a guinea hen or any other unwary bird.

They named the trees, they identified a lizard and chased it, they called out to each other, they laughed. The sun beat down. The heat was tremendous and seemed life-giving, and everything was golden.

And though it was all a charade, my mood of happiness persisted.

Back at the clearing and the rack of drying elephant meat, the shelters and sheds looked more depressing and shantylike after the light and air of the bush walk. All the men and women had vanished, and soon others appeared, dressed in faded used clothes. But what I took to be a whole new crew were the same people, who had changed from their animal skins into Western clothes that had been handed out by foreign charities, T-shirts lettered *Tommy Hilfiger* and *Springfield Hockey,* and old pleated skirts and threadbare pink pajama tops with bunny rabbits printed on them.

They all hung back, looking a bit apprehensive, because they had a favor to ask.

John, the dapper interpreter and driver, said, "They are asking if you can take some of them to Tsumkwe. That one" — and he pointed to a thin teenage girl in a blue blouse and plaid skirt — "she is sick and wants to go to the clinic."

"Tell them they can come with us," I said. Five of them climbed into the Land Rover, the ailing girl helped by the others into the back seat, where she lay as if sorrowful, and she did not move even when farther down the road the vehicle became stuck in deep sand and we struggled to push it.

What I had seen, all of my happiness, my bliss bordering on rapture, was the result of witnessing a reenactment.

"Today, nobody lives in the old way," Elizabeth Marshall Thomas wrote in 2006. "All Bushmen, unless they put on skins for a photographer, wear the clothing of the dominant cultures . . . and none live by hunting and gathering, although with these activities they sometimes supplement their meager diet, which today is often cornmeal provided by the Namibian government as a welfare ration."

A German charitable organization, the Living Culture Foundation, sponsored some of these Ju/'hoansi villages as "Living Museums" (*Lebende Museen*). As the foundation elaborated on its website and in its brochures, "A Living Museum is an interesting and authentic way of presenting traditional culture," and "guests can learn a lot about . . . the original way of living of the San."

"The Living Culture Foundation's three aims are to protect traditional culture, to encourage intercultural dialogue, and to fight poverty." Toward the realization of the last aim, the foundation encouraged "the establishment of sustainable projects for the tourism industry, for example our 'Living Museums.'"

In the mid-1930s, when the Ju/'hoansi were still known as Bushmen, a white South African named Donald Bain mounted a campaign to protect their way of life, put some of them on display at the Empire Exhibition in Johannesburg, and promoted them (for their "Stone Age" reputation) as "living fossils." What he managed to do, to realize his vision of the people, was not very different from the creation of the Living Museums.

What I saw — what visitors in general see — is a travesty in the precise meaning of the word: a parody, a dressing up in unnatural clothes. The Ju/'hoansi were costumed, misrepresenting themselves to cater to the imaginations of fantasists, of which I was one. It was like taking the reenactment at Plimoth Plantation, and its employees dressed as Pilgrims, for the reality of life south of Boston today. Ultimately, I saw the reality of Tsumkwe, and read more of the Ju/'hoansi's travails, which were extreme. "Far from being 'beautiful people living in a primeval paradise,'" one anthropologist has written, "they are in reality the most victimized and brutalized people in the bloody history that is southern Africa."

If I was a latecomer to the world of the Ju/'hoansi, I was not alone. Anthropologists agree that the hunter-gatherer lifestyle ended in the 1970s, largely as a result of the South African army's installing itself in Tsumkwe and recruiting Ju/'hoansi into its ranks to fight the Namibian nationalists. The South Africans spread money around; they doled out free food; they discouraged hunting in some areas and made it unlawful in others. Deprived of their traditional livelihood, the Ju/'hoansi moved closer to the growing town, and with their army money they bought food at the store and alcohol from the shebeens. And for the first time in tens of thousands of years they began to suffer from Western diseases — high blood pressure, diabetes, heart ailments, and alcoholism.

The Kalahari Peoples Fund was started in 1973, the moving force behind it being the anthropologists and linguists who had observed the decline of the traditional lifestyle. In 1981 John Marshall and

Claire Ritchie started the Nyae Nyae Development Fund and began drilling boreholes to supply water to family compounds. One hope for the people's survival lay in learning agricultural and stock-raising skills to become small farmers, as well as earning wages and doing occasional foraging. To that end, the Nyae Nyae Farmers' Cooperative was established.

At about the time the Ju/'hoansi had nearly abandoned hunting and gathering, a South African filmmaker shot *The Gods Must Be Crazy* in and around Tsumkwe, using Ju/'hoansi actors and celebrating the "living fossil" aspect of the people. This was in 1984, and though the gimmick of the film — the McGuffin — was a Coca-Cola can that was chucked from a plane into the unviolated Eden of Bushman Land, it was a time when in fact Western soft drinks and beer were freely available, when alcoholism and poverty were eating away at the culture.

The Ju/'hoansi lost their land in the cause of nature conservation, tourist safaris, and expanding game reserves where elephants (like the fillets and biltong of the one I had seen) were killed by wealthy foreigners. Robert Gordon, in *The Bushman Myth* — his subtitle, *The Making of a Namibian Underclass*, says it all — gives a detailed chronology of the loss of Ju/'hoansi lands and describes how tourism robs the people of their dignity, exploits and suppresses them, and leaves them manipulated and unprepared for new ways of life.

But there is near unanimity in the belief that the Ju/'hoansi no longer want the traditional lifestyle for themselves. "Is it right that we should still be wearing loincloths?" one elder asks, referring to a planned government game reserve for tourists in which the Ju/'hoansi would be part of the colorful foreground (described in Lee, *The Dobe Ju/'hoansi*): "[Eating well] is a good thing, but it doesn't mean our women should have to expose their stomachs and buttocks again by wearing skin clothing."

In the aftermath of the anachronistic *The Gods Must Be Crazy* — which made anthropologists apoplectic with rage — John Marshall compared the Ju/'hoansi, in the way they were stereotyped, to the conventional image of the Hollywood redskin. Almost thirty years ago he wrote, "Among the simplest and dangerous [misconceptions] is the widespread conviction that, somewhere in the Kalahari, Bushman people still live skillfully and peacefully by hunting and gathering. The danger lies in the belief that these mythical people both can and want to live their ancient life in isolation" (John Marshall and Claire Ritchie, *Where Are the Ju/'wasi of Nyae Nyae?*).

The process of this misunderstanding he calls "Death by Myth," the title of one of his last films. It is the myth that they are still hunter-gatherers, that they can go back to it and flourish that way. "The myth is inherent in our thinking about Bushmen."

The traditional mode of living is long gone. A Ju/'hoansi born after 1950 would know little or nothing about hunting and gathering. "The cycle of knowledge was broken." Apart from a handful of Ju/'hoansi who allowed themselves to be co-opted into the choreographed charade I had seen, the vast majority want to join the mainstream, go to school, work, live in a stable and safe place, and never again have to depend on the insecure life in the bush. They have drifted to town, where manual labor, even pick-and-shovel work, is easier than hunting. Some welfare was available at Tsumkwe, and the new clinic was installed to deal with the new diseases.

In this grim fate, the Ju/'hoansi had gone from a fleet-footed bush-dwelling people who chased down game, to sedentary town dwellers plagued by drunkenness and hunger. In the past they had been able to move their settlement, to search for animals or water. But by living in a static way, in a cash economy, in a house on a small plot of land, this was not possible, so they became more dependent on government assistance.

The myth of the Bushman has shaped the plans of the NGOs that try to help them. For the many charities and NGOs (the Living Museums program was the most visible one), which were sentimental like me, hankering for the days Before the Fall, Elizabeth

Marshall Thomas had a shrewd rejoinder: "Such organizations have no choice but to carry out their missions," she wrote in *The Old Way.* "No wonder that they wish to save traditional Nyae Nyae, a place where an indigenous population occupied an ecosystem for 35,000 years without ruining it. Who would not want the survival of a life style that could accomplish that?" And she added, "The myth was that the Ju/'hoansi wanted it."

So they don't hunt as they once did. They eat junk food and too much refined sugar, and they drink themselves into stupefaction, yet even in dysfunctional Tsumkwe the Ju/'hoansi retain their social culture of interdependency. With this mode of survival and generosity, they help each other through hard times.

There was no future for them in being dependent on tourists' visits, or the leftovers from trophy hunting, or government handouts. It seemed to me that, at bottom, Tsumkwe was one vast welfare scheme funded by NGOs. But in the face of an indifferent government, what was the alternative? I had seen that in the recording of oral histories and folktales, and with the health programs, some success had been achieved by the agents of virtue from foreign countries.

And perhaps the Ju/'hoansi would manage to become small sustainable farmers, keeping cattle, feeding themselves, and overcoming the new diseases and the old hardships of hunger and lack of water.

I was disillusioned, of course, as anyone would be, knowing what I knew now. I had been wrong. Being wrong and disillusioned seems an inevitable consequence of any serious African journey. But I felt lucky in one respect. I had met the old man Dambó. He was undoubtedly a man from the past, and knowledgeable — wise, experienced, a patriarch. That part of my visit, I was convinced, was neither a travesty nor a charade. Dambó was a true relic who had somehow survived from an earlier age. He could have said, with Job and Ishmael, *And I only am escaped alone to tell thee.*

The image of the Ju/'hoansi we cling to—I did anyway—is that of a wild-dwelling, self-sufficient people. We seem to need them to be that way, not merely different from us, and purer, but more different than they really are—tenacious, resourceful, generous, peaceful, as if inhabiting Eden. They are reminders of who we once were, our ancient better selves. At one time, long ago, all of us were foragers on earth. What a relief it is in a world yearning for authenticity to know that though we have blighted our habitat, there is an unspoiled place on the planet, and a people who have defied modernity by clinging to their old ways. The past recaptured. Isn't it pretty to think so?

9

Riding an Elephant: The Ultimate Safari

THE ENORMOUS EMPTY SKY over the Kaokoveld Desert teased my mind with the prospect of freedom, and the flat land of grit and crumble was inspiring too — you could go anywhere under all this untroubled air and dazzling sunlight. Even on the worst day in the African bush the sky and the space offer relief.

At the end of a simple bumpy drive on a bad road east from Tsumkwe, just over the Namibia-Botswana border, the small stony town of Dobe baked like a biscuit in the sun — more hard-up Ju/'hoansi looking for a livelihood, anthropologists searching for subjects, and baboons with tragic faces picking through road-side garbage. Not far from Dobe, still easterly, in a channel of the Okavango Delta, there was a luxury camp for people who paid large sums of money to ride elephants across mushy ground, and through tall grass and swamps, to look at birds and big animals. No one else in Africa rode elephants. At Abu Camp all they rode were elephants.

I have a hatred of the taming of animals, especially large ones that are so contented in the wild. I abominate circus acts that involve big befooled beasts — cowed tigers or helplessly roaring lions pawing the air and teetering on small stools. I deplore zoos and anything to do with animal confinement or restraint. "A robin redbreast in a cage / Puts all heaven in a rage" — I agree, and canaries and parrots, pythons and panthers, too. Even drooling, needy, yappy dogs seem a bit sad to me. Early in the last century, Lord Rothschild broke four zebras and harnessed them to pull his carriage through London; Michael Jackson kept a demented orangutan in a barred cell at Neverland; a Chinese fruit vendor in my former neighborhood in Singapore trained his macaque to pick coconuts. Some people consider bull riding, or the sight of synchronized swimming of killer whales in a pool, a thrill.

There is a hint of sadism in all of this. But the notion of African elephants submitting to the conveying of tourists through the bush was something I felt I had to see, because it seemed overwhelmingly absurd, and besides, the man who ran the operation was a friend of mine. Knowing how I felt about domesticating wild animals, he had encouraged me to pay a visit to his safari operation, called Abu Camp.

After miles of gravel, upright spinning funnels of dust devils, the light brown scrub of the bush, and an immensity of woodland and camel thorns — after all that thirst, the Okavango Delta is unexpectedly drenched, as the desert deliquesces into a watery mirage, a deep green marvel that bubbles up and sprawls over the left shoulder of Botswana as a succession of swamps. Most river deltas — perhaps all of them in the world — occur at the edge of a landmass, widening and dumping soil and water, enlarging the shore, pouring the river current into a body of water, the sea or a lake. The Okavango is unusual in being landlocked; the stream of the river, fed by numerous watercourses draining from a catchment area in the *planalto* of Angola, the wooded highlands of the far north, becomes a delta hundreds of miles wide. This river, lush and sodden and silted, empties its flow into the middle of the Kalahari Desert. The precise and pretty term for this natural wonder of watery interstices and spreading rivulets is an alluvial fan.

The results of the sprawling torrent of water are channels, flood zones, lagoons, islands of palms, and water so clean from percolating through the papyrus beds that it is drinkable. Also seasonal swamps, wide trenches called fossil rivers that once carried water, ephemeral rivers, and permanent rivers — it is a water world. This fertile habitat for animals, birds, and flowers, one of the glories of Africa, is without traditional villages; the Tswana people live almost entirely on the perimeter, entering the delta only to fish or hunt.

In Africa, animals large and small are found at waterholes. The Okavango Delta, teeming with wildlife and still pristine, might be considered one of the great waterholes of the continent.

Abu Camp ("Meet your inner elephant") advertised itself as a "unique opportunity to bond with elephants firsthand," and went on, "Situated in a vast private reserve of 400,000 acres, guests interact with the resident elephant herd, whether riding or walking with them through the bush. The ultimate elephant education safari!"

The camp had originally been conceived in the late 1980s as a refuge for "rescue elephants" — elephants that had survived a cull, or had been orphaned in the wild as a result of the mother being killed, or had suffered the torments and teasing of a circus, or had been confined in a zoo or wildlife park. The elephant refuge was the idea of Randall Moore, an American who had begun his working life shoveling great crumbly muffins of elephant dung at an animal training school in Oregon. By an odd set of circumstances he had come to possess three elephants.

It happened this way. A pair of animal trainers, a man and woman who were his mentors at the school, were killed separately, but in quick succession, a consequence of the bull elephants being in musth, a condition of high-testosterone aggression. The woman was gored and transfixed by the tusks of an enraged elephant — this occurred during a circus act, before a large crowd of horrified Québécois in a small Canadian town. Later, in Oregon, the man was stomped to death by his favorite elephant.

Since he was on the payroll and knew the ropes, Randall Moore inherited his trainers' elephants, which — stigmatized and vilified as "killer elephants" — he resolved to save by relocating them to Africa, as he describes in his book, *Back to Africa* (1989). Failing to find a home for them in Kenya (red tape, obstinate officialdom, bush confusion), he was welcomed in Botswana, where as a wildlife entrepreneur he started a training program for rescue elephants and pioneered his unusual safaris. The idea for elephant-back safaris was initially that of the photographer, socialite, and Africa hand Peter Beard, who suggested to Moore in the 1980s that riding elephants through the bush was unprecedented and would be an incomparable safari.

Abu ("Father" in Arabic), for whom the camp was named, was one of the first rescued elephants, brought from a wildlife park in Texas. As the star of the camp and a natural performer, Abu had appeared in several feature films. Other elephants — enough to create a substantial herd — were added over the years, from distant parts of Africa and as far afield as Canada and Sri Lanka. They had names and pedigrees, they had distinct profiles and personalities; some were quite old, others were babies, either born at the camp within the motley herd or recently orphaned. They were attended to and trained by a large team of mahouts — they used this Hindi term for an elephant whisperer — mainly African, each one bonded to a particular elephant.

The appeal of Abu Camp was its remoteness in the delta, the uniqueness of an elephant-back safari, and the luxury of its accommodations. One of the boasts of the camp was that the purring refrigeration of its extensive wine cellar was inaudible outside the kitchen compound. The camp was also eco-friendly, depending on solar panels for electricity and reducing all its kitchen waste into compost to fertilize its extensive vegetable gardens. The staff quarters amounted to a rather prim village with its own dining hall and recreation room—nearly all the workers had permanent homes in Maun, the Okavango's main town and only substantial airport, at the southeastern edge of the delta. Most guests were flown from Maun to bush airstrips in small planes over startled herds of zebra and wildebeest.

The camp had only six tents, but "tents" gives a mistaken impression. They were more like canvas bungalows on high platforms, with showers and tubs and double beds with mosquito nets like wedding veils. From your tent at the edge of the lagoon you could prop yourself up on one elbow in a big soft bed and watch the resident herd of hippos gasping and spewing in the water below.

Michael Lorentz, who ran Abu, was my friend. He called himself a safari guide—and he was an inspired one—but he was also the moving force behind a reconceived and upgraded Abu, and was a great lover of the wild, with a particular affection for elephants. I had met him ten years before in Johannesburg, at the end of my *Dark Star Safari* trip, and we had kept in touch. His fortunes had risen in that decade: he had become an entrepreneur with his own high-end safari company. He was now married, his wife was an academic, and they had two small boys. He was clearly prospering in a competitive business—he still conducted safaris of his own all over the wilds of South Africa and Botswana, as well as in Zambia, Kenya, and Ethiopia.

A stout, imposing figure in bush hat and khakis, Michael was a perfectionist with a strong work ethic who had grown up in a large family—his father a surgeon, his mother a landscape gardener. Abandoning a career in law to be a trainee guide in Kruger Park, in South Africa, he rose through the ranks, started his own company, and had worked among the elephants at Abu for twenty years. And he was not much older than forty.

"I intend Abu to be the premier safari lodge in Africa," Michael said. "I want it to be like an English house party—a great house party—to eat together, sit around the fire together, five nights ideally, sharing experiences. Luxury without excess."

Michael said he was drawn to the African elephant for what he called its deep level of emotional intelligence and its ability to elicit a wide range of responses in the people who encounter it—awe, excitement, happiness, fear, wonder, laughter, respect, humility.

"Abu is a complete immersion in a single species," he said, "which also happens to be one of the most charismatic of all land mammals, the African elephant." Complete immersion meant sharing five days of your life with a single herd—physically interacting with the elephants, riding them, walking with them, game viewing from atop their backs, even sleeping near them on a raised platform while the elephants browsed and snorted below. These creatures inspired fear in some people, Michael said, but it was his view that they were to be respected, not feared.

"I've been slapped by an elephant—by its trunk," he told me. "It sent me flying! Why? I was probably being inappropriate."

Michael was an enthusiast—intelligent, well read, congenial, physically strong, and happiest outdoors in the bush. He seemed to have a genuine gift for working with large mammals, and that extended to his ability to get on with people. I was delighted to see him again after so long.

"There's something I want you to see. Just do exactly what I tell you to do," he said minutes after my arrival, then checked his watch. "Want a beer? Go over to the platform at the front of the property. Have a beer and wait for me."

This was the highest level of safari Africa, a day's drive but a world away from the hard-up Ju/'hoansi, the squalor and drought and drunkards at Tsumkwe, the aid schemes and charities, the squabbling politicians and the shantytowns. Abu Camp was the Africa of the travel magazine article that promotes expensive holidays, the multicolored brochure brought to life in the form of an elegant lodge, with comfortable chairs, gourmet food, and "Would you care for a cold towel?" as you're proffered a chilled and folded face cloth held with silver tongs. Abu Camp represented that rare thing in rural Africa, comfort and cleanliness. For most tourists it was the only Africa they knew; for most Africans it was something utterly unknown.

The platform at the edge of the lodge had been built around the tower of a high smooth termite mound, fat and cylindrical and so sculptural it could have been an artwork. The lodge itself was situated in a grove of trees — African ebony, sycamore fig, and jackalberry. I was greeted by the staff and offered sushi — *sushi!* — from a tray, and I sat down to drink a cold bottle of St. Louis beer.

Past the cushions and the lounge chairs, beyond the rails of the wide platform, the lagoon on this reach of the Okavango was dark and depthless-seeming, in shadow as the sun dipped behind it. But the slanting sun gilded the reeds of the marsh and glittered on the boughs of the acacia trees on what looked like floating islands in the distance. Streaks of pink and purple had begun to appear low in the sky. Usually nightfall in rural Africa is the end of everything — nothing to do, time to sleep, to await the dawn. But I was confident in the comfort of this sumptuous camp, able to enjoy the growing dusk and the expectation of nightfall. Food! Wine! Lamps were lit, torches blazed, and then came an unusual noise from the marsh.

It was the sound of heavy footfalls plopping in water, squishing in mud, and kicking against thicknesses of dense grass. I looked up and saw a herd of elephants parting the reeds in front of them, trunks upraised. They were approaching the camp in the golden light, framed by dark trees and the pinky purple sky, kicking through the swamp water and the brush, some of them trumpeting. Each rounded, advancing creature was ridden by an upright man, sitting just behind its flapping ears, and though the men held a goad, a stick with a hook that Indians call an *ankusha*, none of them used it. Instead, to direct the elephants they called out commands in English — though not many commands were needed for elephants headed to the security of their enclosure and the expectation of cakes of food.

At sunset, the quietest time of day, the loud and sudden arrival of the elephants in a welter of splashing was an impressive display. The herd filed in front of the platform like disciplined troops past a reviewing stand.

I was witnessing this royal progress for the first time, but the other guests, who had seen it all the previous evening, were beaming with pleasure and expressing their renewed astonishment.

"They told me this would be the experience of a lifetime — and it is," a woman near me said. She was a photographer, a New Yorker, her first time in Africa. "Africa is just amazing."

I resisted telling her that this was an experience that only a handful of people knew. I said, truthfully, "I had no idea that anyone in Africa actually trained and rode elephants."

"I rode one yesterday," she said. "We're going out again tomorrow. I can hardly wait."

Her name was Alexandra, and she was taking pictures for a magazine article. Because she was a first-timer to Africa she was all nerves, hyperalert and intensely watchful.

"I can't sleep I'm so excited," she said. "And the noises from the swamp keep me awake."

"Funny. I have that problem in New York."

Of the arrival of the herd at dusk, she said, "The sounds are as interesting as the visual experience." And that day, on the elephant, she had noticed a guide with a rifle just ahead of her. "It was a strange juxtaposition. I'm the elephant and I see the guy with the gun." And she added, "You have no idea how much these mahouts adore the elephants."

After drinks in front of a campfire, we gathered on the veranda for dinner, about ten of us around a long refectory table; four courses, with wine, Michael at the head of the table answering questions and calming the more anxious guests.

"Elephants are emotionally highly complex," he said. "Never lose your respect and never assume too much, but don't be afraid."

"You must have had some amazing experiences," someone said.

"Want to know one of the best ones?" Michael said. "It was lying on the ground for hours watching the antics of dung beetles as they battled over a pile of elephant dung, with the brood pairs frantically rolling away the nuptial ball."

The strangeness of being in an open-sided room, around a linen-covered dining table, in the middle of an African swamp kept the conversation somewhat subdued. It was a situation daunting even to the much-traveled millionaires at the table, humbled by the surrounding darkness. The meal was delicious, but past the torches and lanterns at the edge of the platform we could hear the snorts and grumbles of hippos thrashing in the reeds, the squawking of birds, and the crackle of insects frying on the bug zapper.

After dinner, Michael took me aside and introduced me to Star, a young Tswana woman, all smiles, who was the chef, and to his managerial staff, his colleagues, the people who ran the operation in his absence. One, a man of about thirty, had been at dinner, listening intently but saying nothing. Because of his reticence I said hello.

"This is Nathan Jamieson," Michael said. "He was traveling around Africa and visited us. He discovered he liked what we were doing. He found us, not the other way around."

His friendly bluster made Nathan smile, but he still seemed rather shy. I introduced myself and we talked awhile. He said he'd been at Abu just a few months, and that his girlfriend, Jen, also worked here.

"Nathan's one of our trainers," Michael said, because Nathan had not yet said so.

His shyness showed in his faintly smiling downcast face, the sideways tilt of his head, his deferential posture, the way he planted his feet. This shy man trained five-ton elephants! But really, it wasn't so odd. Shyness is not timidity; he was a confident, collected man. The rifle-toting safari guides, so bold and in their element in the bush, stalking lions or leopards, were often unforthcoming indoors, among the booming, well-heeled clients, whose natural element was the dinner table.

I said, "So, Nathan, how do you like it here at Abu?"

"It's great, yes. It's brilliant."

I heard the slightest inflection, the nasal Australian haw and the short smiling vowel in the affirmative *yiss*.

"Where are you from in Australia?"

"Sydney, originally, but I was at a zoo at a place—you wouldn't know it."

"Try me."

"Dubbo?" he said in that rising tone of Australians offering information.

"I've been there—half a day's drive from Sydney."

"I worked at the Western Plains Zoo."

"God, I hate zoos."

"This one isn't like that. It's open range. The animals have a lot of freedom."

"I went to Dubbo because there's a character in a novel with that name, Alf Dubbo, in *Riders in the Chariot*. I love that novel and I really like Alf Dubbo, the aboriginal painter."

An airless awkward silence descended on us, the embarrassment of intelligent people when a book is mentioned that no one has read, as though you've suddenly lapsed into a foreign language. I never know in such circumstances whether to describe the book with an exhortation to read it or simply shut up.

I did neither. I said, "I never hear a good word about Patrick White from Australians, and he was one of your best writers."

"I know who you mean," Nathan said. "We read him at school."

When the subject turned to elephants, Nathan brightened. He was like Michael, an enthusiast. He had worked with elephants in Thailand and Canada too, and seemed determined to know everything about elephant behavior. I realized that I was talking about them as large shadowy creatures seen at a distance, but for Nathan they were distinct and definable. He had strong opinions about their behavior, how teachable they were, how they responded. He reminded me of a horse owner who speaks of the subtlety of horses' responses—how they're smarter than their rider; or of the dog owner who says, "Nugget is always a little nervous around really selfish people."

One by one, the guests were escorted to their tents by a guide holding a powerful flashlight, looking out for a snake or a scorpion or possibly a hippo—hippos leave the water every evening to climb ashore and feed on vegetation.

The night air crackled with the slapping of bats and the *fit-fit-fit* of insects and the hoots of herons and the thrashing of hippos browsing in the reeds under my sleeping platform.

Dawn is sudden in the water world of the Okavango, without any hills or heights to delay the sunrise, and the shimmering mirrors of the lagoons and channels intensified the light, which is all gold.

After breakfast, Michael showed me around the camp—the staff quarters, the composting field, the solar panels—and at the elephant compound he introduced me to the mahouts. Big Joe, George, Itaki, Collet, Frank, and Nathan—the one non-African—were leading the elephants from their stockade to an open area where each one, with an iron cuff shackling its foot, was chained to a large eyebolt. The clanking of the long heavy chains, the bang of the bolts, and the shouted orders of the mahouts as the elephants shuffled were at odds with the idyllic place—a courtyard with a canopy of high foliage, the sunlight filtered through the dust kicked up by the elephants. The mahouts were nimble in their task of chaining the huge animals — and it took two of them to drag the heavy chains. I had last seen the elephants the previous evening, splashing through the swamp in the failing light of day. How different they seemed in the glare of morning, bolted to the ground to receive their riders; they looked impatient and vexed.

I mentioned this to Nathan, who was securing his elephant, helped by Big Joe.

"She's a good girl," Nathan said, and he rested his head against the thick gray post of her leg. "Aren't you, Sukiri?"

"How old is she?"

"Eighteen," he said in the Australian way, *ay-deen*. "She was orphaned from a cull at Kruger with Thandi and Seeni. They were brought to Gaberone. That's where we got them. Steady, girl!"

Now the seating platform — a howdah-like contraption — was lifted onto their backs and strapped around the elephant's middle, and when this was done each elephant was verbally hectored until it knelt, its whole body flat to the ground. This was accomplished by a slow folding of the legs beneath it and a sagging collapse of the big gray belly.

Michael approached and said, "Isn't it incredible?"

"I've never seen anything like it."

"You're riding Cathy today. That's her over there."

"What's her story?"

"Captured in Uganda when her family was culled. She was sent to a zoo in Toronto. That's where we got her from. She's about fifty years old, the matriarch of the herd."

Another kneeling elephant snorted dust as a group of men fussed around her, fastening a wooden seating platform to her back.

"This operation is amazing," I said. "All these workers, all these animals, and just a few guests."

"That's why we're expensive," Michael said. "But we have wonderful owners and great clients." He was smoking a cigarette and admiring the activity. "A team created it. You can build whatever you want. But if you don't have the human element, you've got nothing."

"How many elephants altogether?"

"The ones we ride—about a dozen. But there are lots more, big and small, that are part of the herd. They'll go out and follow. It's a dysfunctional, put-together family of elephants."

"In what way dysfunctional?"

"They're from all over. We created the herd, so there's all sorts of dynamics." He was still looking across the compound. "Our plan is to release some of them back into the wild."

A little while later, speaking to the guests before the ride, he said, "The elephants embody so much of Africa . . ."

This peroration about the glory of African elephants reminded me of the passion of Morel, the idealistic hero of Romain Gary's *The Roots of Heaven.* In this early (1956) environmental-themed novel (later a John Huston film), Morel mounts a campaign in Africa to save elephants from the big guns of hunters, and fails.

While the elephants knelt on the ground, we took turns getting onto the seats. There was no delicate way of climbing the elephant's back and squirming into place, so this was another job for the mahouts and the trainers—easing the timid and top-heavy guests into position. Wealthy dignified clients, paying $4,000 a day, scrambled clumsily onto the elephants, their wide, khaki-clad buttocks raised for all to see.

We set out in a long and straggling line, heading across the swamp water, looking for animals. Each mahout, seated on the elephant's neck, talked much of the time to the elephant, urging it onward, cautioning it, mildly scolding it when—as frequently happened—the elephant took a hunger-determined detour from the route and, tearing at bunches of palm leaves, decided to eat a whole tree. We were aimed in a general direction, a long file of elephants, great and small, some of them with humans on their backs. We saw impalas, zebras, warthogs, and a profusion of birds, but the strongest impression I had of this outing was of a herd of elephants idly grazing.

"Move up, move up. Come on, Cathy, move up," Big Joe called out. And I could hear the other mahouts exhorting their elephants.

But the elephants were hungry, and there was no way to dissuade a famished animal from its food — and in this glittering swamp, food was abundant as far as the eye could see. The elephants wrenched at leafy boughs and crammed palm fronds into their pink mouths. They twirled tall stands of grass with their trunks and uprooted whole sheaves of it to eat.

"Move it up!"

All along the file, the mahouts were calling out in English. Pet owners and trainers talk to their animals constantly. I am struck by these earnest appeals. Do animals understand English, and if so, how much? I suppose "Beg" and "Roll over" and "Heel" might elicit a response. What about "You're a good boy" and "No, Nugget, whine all you like, you're not getting any more munchies"?

The cry "Move it up" did very little to provoke Cathy to move from her meal, and I could not see the point of trying to convince this snorting and masticating beast that it was a better idea to keep moving than to finish eating the tree she was stabbing with her tusks and tearing apart with her trunk.

But the experience of riding an elephant past the wildlife on the grassy banks and the herons in the channels under the high blue sky was something unimaginable to me, and though objectively I could see that the elephant was enormous, and I had always felt elephants were dangerous, I felt safe from any predators. What animal would dare attack this big-tusked creature? Its only true enemy was a human, armed with an enormous gun.

We proceeded to an island between two channels where there was a mud wallow, where we dismounted. The elephants, relieved of their riders and seats, rolled in the soft muck and sprayed water over themselves while we few guests sat in camp chairs, sipping mineral water, snapping pictures, or making notes in a journal or for a magazine piece. *Close encounters of the herd kind!* and *Clamber onto an African elephant for the ultimate safari!*

I had been on safaris before. It is always a ticklish and often an infantilizing business. First come the detailed instructions — what to wear, how to move, how to talk, what to expect; all power and initiative are taken from you in the interest of safety. You are reduced to being a child on a school trip, reminded that you are very small and strange and vulnerable, that there are dangers all around. And this is demonstrably true. Look, a croc on the riverbank, the glimpse of a lion, a leopard up a tree, a buffalo pawing the dust, fresh bales of elephant dung littering the road — evidence of a nearby herd.

So you put yourself in the hands of experienced guides who lead you from sight to sight, from animal to animal. As a child again, you are closely supervised by an adult, and you rediscover a child's sense of wonder. But the Abu Camp safari was something new. I was in the care of a guide and on the back of an elephant, now being shown a zebra, now an eagle, and now taken home to have my lunch, then a nap in my sumptuous tent.

Riding on a trained elephant, gazing on wild elephants — it was like nothing I had ever done or seen, and as far as I knew it had no parallel in Africa. Added to the fact that Abu Camp was an island of luxury in the bush was the novelty of elephants for transport and the staff working so hard to please the guests. I could understand the travel writer gushing for a magazine, writing pieces about *Where pachyderms play* and recalling the meals: *Antelope steaks sizzled on the grill as we were plied with wild mushroom risotto, cauliflower gratin, tiramisù, Veuve Clicquot . . . And as we sat drinking and talking an enormous hyena appeared out of nowhere . . .*

A dreamy-bosomed woman in stylish khaki and a bush hat was tapping her pretty pouting lips with a blunt pen and preparing to write, *We soon discovered that riding an elephant is not terribly com-*

fortable — after sitting sideways on the saddle for an hour or two I felt restless and sticky. And then she added, *The cheekiest of the herd, and our favorite, was Paseka, aged two.*

At the wallow, Nathan and Big Joe were drinking coffee and watching their elephants. I wandered over to them. Nathan had told me that he had an identical twin brother, Heath, who lived in Australia. Twins fascinate me for many reasons, especially the obvious literary examples in Mark Twain and Dickens, in *The Comedy of Errors* and Tweedledum and Tweedledee.

"The Yoruba in Nigeria have an unusually high incidence of twins," I said. "Twins figure in their belief system. Yoruba carve special twin images to represent them — they believe that twins share the same soul."

"I understand that. Heath and I get along great," Nathan said. Then, "We were just talking about our trip," he said. "Big Joe and Collet and I are going to the States on a marketing trip pretty soon."

Big Joe laughed. "My first time in America!"

"Where are you going?"

"New York City?" Nathan said in a querying voice. "Toronto? A few other places. It's mainly for Abu, but we'll be visiting some elephant facilities too. What do you think?"

"You'll have the time of your life," I said. "If you can get these elephants to behave, you can do anything."

I had seen elephants in Africa before. They are unmissable features of the landscape, visible from a mile away, and they are dauntless, never hurrying or circumspect or hunted-looking as most other African game seems. Elephants own the bush, where they are right at home, ambling in family groups, going wherever they wish. If they decide to eat a tree, they will do so, and are well known for tearing a baobab to pieces with their tusks to get at the juicy pulp. If you are in their way, they will trample you and keep going. They never give the impression that they need anyone or anything. Because of their size and their appetite they spend much of the day eating. The oddity of Abu was that these elephants, born in the wild, had been captured and dominated, taught to submit to humans climbing on them.

Riding an Indian elephant (*Elephas maximus indicus*) in Rajasthan is not unusual. In India they are traditionally used as beasts of burden, as workers in the fields, and in combat; this has been the case for thousands of years. Alexander the Great used elephants in his campaign of conquest as he battled into India, and so did the armies opposing him, as did Hannibal later, crossing the Alps. But these were Asian or Syrian war elephants — smaller, tractable varieties.

A big-eared African elephant (*Loxodonta africana*) is another matter altogether. For one thing, it is the largest land animal in the world, highly intelligent, independent, and family-minded. I easily understood the purpose of Abu Camp as a refuge for lost and orphaned elephants. But it was harder for me to grasp the hubristic intention of creating a program to bully elephants into obedience, to dominate them so thoroughly that they would allow themselves to be harnessed to a riding platform. Some of these heavy wooden platforms held two anxious people, and with the mahout loudly urging the creature along, that meant three vociferating adult humans balancing on the elephant's bristly spine while it moved through the swamp among the other animals.

I was thinking that Africa, which was losing its wildness by the day to urban encroachment and land grabbers, was also sacrificing the wildness of these powerful elephants as well, in the interest of tourism, and exploiting them as drudges, to be led back and forth like pack animals.

When I mentioned this to Michael, he repeated that his ultimate intention was to reintroduce most of these elephants into the wild so they could join a herd and live as free creatures again. This seemed to me a worthy aim.

On another day at Abu, we climbed onto the elephants and were taken for a picnic in a clearing by a backwater at the side of one of the wider river channels. This picnic by the lagoon stands out in my memory as the highest level of comfort one could find in the African bush while still retaining all the elements of the safari experience. The clearing was a lovely setting, in a grove of tall mopane and fig trees, well shaded but looking onto the water coursing through the thick reed beds of the Okavango. In all essentials we were outdoors in the heart of Africa, among small darting birds and tall fish-hunting herons. We were seated in camp chairs and served cold drinks by the Abu staff, and on an expanse of white linen, a buffet table had been laid — yellow curries, bowls of purple vegetables, a tureen of soup, platters of sliced fruit, and beer and wine in chests of ice.

Nathan — his usual serene self, chatting with the other mahouts — told me that he had recently taken the mahouts and elephants out camping for the night. What fun they had swimming and playing soccer. "We were sleeping with the elephants in a circle around us." He made it sound like Boy Scout camp. But one of the cautions in Randall Moore's *Back to Africa* — the whole Abu Camp rationale — was that it was crucial that the trainer continually remind the elephant who was boss. "Dominance . . . must prevail," Moore writes. The trainer "must make it known from the start who has the best means of domination at his disposal."

Nathan spoke of the elephants, and especially Sukiri, with a matey affection, but his tone also contained a note of reverential awe, granting them a sort of sacredness. I noticed that no one at Abu ever joked about the elephants.

I said, "I'm trying to imagine what Big Joe and Collet will make of New York City."

Michael said, "They might fancy it. They've never been out of the Okavango, much less Botswana. They might decide to stay there for years." And saying *yeurs*, he raised his glass to the three men sitting together.

"Safe travels," I said, toasting them.

"And if the Americans don't understand an Aussie accent, Big Joe can translate." *Tronslate.*

Sighing, Alexandra said, "Isn't this magical? Look at us. It's a living Manet, *Déjeuner sur l'herbe.*"

It was a transcendent experience and an unexpected thrill. Such experiences are so exceptional in Africa that few people know them — and those people are nearly all outsiders who have flown at great expense from Europe or America to pay thousands a day for this. Five days at Abu must have cost in the tens of thousands — I didn't know, since Michael was too tactful to tell me. These thrills will become rarer as the game diminishes and the wild places are overrun with camps and lodges, the rivers dammed, the savannas fenced, the land carved up and exploited, and the bush animals eaten to extinction. Peter Beard's landmark book *The End of the Game: The Last Word from Paradise* was early (1965) but prophetic. The doom of the animals was inevitable: "Death is the patiently awaited, unfeared fact of delicately poised African life."

I admired the order of Abu Camp and the integrity of Michael's wish to release the elephants, and hoped that he would prosper. I liked the harmony and found it funny that although the mahout might yell and cajole, the elephant stood its ground, yanking at trees, stuffing its mouth with leafy boughs, doing exactly what it wanted to do, taking its time, resuming its walk only when it had eaten its fill. So much for the trainer's superiority or dominance.

On my last evening, Michael asked where I was going next. I said back to Namibia, and north to Etosha.

"Etosha's another story."

For him, Etosha Pan was mass tourism in a large regulated game park: busloads of gawkers, herds of budget-minded tourists, sprawling hotel compounds.

"I'm seeing a man who's doling out American aid," I said.

Michael said that he would stay in touch, and he did. I got news of

Nathan, Collet, and Big Joe in New York. The three friends, bonded by their months of working together, stayed at the elegant Pierre Hotel and were interviewed by awed journalists about their life in the bush and their elephant experiences with the herd at Abu. They visited zoos in Toronto, Indianapolis, Pittsburgh, and Baltimore, looking at elephants and studying the breeding programs. They were photographed and quoted as though they themselves were marvels from Africa. They were away for six weeks.

On his return to Abu, Nathan Jamieson began working again with his elephant, Sukiri. A few days after he'd arrived back, he left her untethered, and when he walked a little distance to fetch her chains and manacles, turning his back on her, she followed him in the nodding and plodding way of an elephant on a mission, and knocked him flat, crushing him to death with her huge head. Nathan was thirty-two years old.

There was a further shock. When his identical twin brother Heath showed up at the camp to take Nathan's body away, the whole African staff stared in fascinated horror and then abject fear, scared rigid by the sight of what appeared to be an incarnation of Nathan, claiming his ghost.

Later, Michael told me, "He died doing what he loved." I remembered how happy Nathan had been at Abu Camp, how fond he was of the elephants, how much he knew of them. Perhaps it was true that he'd had a happy death.

On hearing of Nathan's death, the Botswana government ordered that Sukiri be destroyed. Michael Lorentz vigorously opposed this, and thus began an imbroglio that ended with Michael quitting Abu for good, the camp resuming business under new management. Sukiri and the two elephants that had been orphaned with her were trucked to Johannesburg and flown in elephantine crates to the United States, where they are now housed together in a cage at the Pittsburgh Zoo.

10

━ ━ ━ ━

The Hungry Herds at Etosha

I CROSSED THE BORDER into Namibia again, got a lift, and descended to the crumbly yellow middle of the country, staying first at a bush camp and then at a hotel. It was one of those inevitable transitions of travel—not travel at all, but stringent captivity and enforced delay. Months later, I couldn't help but think of what Michael had said of Nathan Jamieson: "He died doing what he loved." I wondered—and who wouldn't?—in what circumstances that hopeful consolation might be uttered of my death, and whether it would be true.

The bush camp, north of Grootfontein, had only one other guest, except after dark when five large, well-formed eland crept through the thorn trees to drink at the waterhole near the lodge. The woman manager, who had seemed so taciturn, softened at the sight of them, as misanthropes often do in the presence of animals, saying, "Lovely, aren't they?" The next day she brightened again, pointing out a golden oriole and a parrot-sized hornbill flitting through those same trees.

An American in charge of an aid program had agreed to meet me in Otjiwarongo, take me to Etosha Pan, and drop me on the road to Angola. From there I would be on my own. I saw the thin and sad widow Helena ("No fun here. No life at all") again at the Grootfontein supermarket, and in Otjiwarongo stopped in to see Mr. Khan and buy more minutes for my phone. And, welcomed by these friendly people, I was reminded that in much of Africa there are so few main roads that people's lives continually converge, and there occurs a repeating experience of crossed paths and familiar faces.

Otjiwarongo had seemed a welcoming enough place when I'd breezed through with Tony, the American diplomat and my traveling companion. But after a day and a half there it proved to be somnolent to the point of melancholy, or was this the predictable effect of a rainy weekend in a country town in Namibia? In the bar of my hotel a multiracial crowd howled at a South African rugby match on the wide-screen TV. Some were ranchers, as beefy as their cattle; others worked in the fluorite mine or were farmers. It was their day to drink. My bedroom stank of mildew. The desert rain fell intermittently from the sort of low grimy sky I associated with heavy industry, yet there was no industry in Otjiwarongo.

I asked the hotel clerk the way to the main street. She told me, and added, "Yes, go for a walk. But it's Saturday. Be careful. There will be drunks."

Into the drizzle I went, down the dirt sidewalk, past the one-story houses surrounded by high walls — and the perimeter walls made the houses seem more depressing than if they had been shacks. I scuffed through the litter to the only businesses that were open, the gas station and the Shoprite supermarket, where staggering boys and men shouted at passing cars, and at me.

"You!" one of the boys called out, and because he was in a group idling at the side of the Shoprite parking lot, I decided to ask him what he wanted. Seeing me approach, he skulked among the others, just as a singled-out animal in a herd might do, for camouflage and protection.

"Did you want to ask me a question?" I asked. But he was shy now.

"Where do you come from?" one of the others asked. He was glassy-eyed and a bit unsteady, yet did not seem threatening.

I told them where I was from.

"I want to go to America," that boy said.

"What will you do there?"

"I can do anything."

This prompt reply made the others laugh.

"And me, I want to go," another said. "For work and for enjoying."

"You can work in Otjiwarongo, or Windhoek," I said.

"There is no work here. There is nothing here. We have no money."

"Give us money," one of the younger ones said.

"Maybe tomorrow," I said, because they were growing in confidence, and insolence, and were now beginning to surround me.

"He is a clever man," the first boy said. "He is telling us lies. He is lying because he is fearing us."

Now I realized it had been a mistake to engage them in any sort of talk. I said, "Thank you! See you tomorrow," and walked briskly away, down the empty road under the gray sky. I was thinking of the futility of such an encounter, because although we were in Namibia, they were boys I might have met anywhere in the world—aimless, idle, with little education and no work.

I walked for an hour and then returned by a different route to wait out the weekend. It was one of those empty interludes in travel, an airless unrewarding delay, when nothing occurs except a rising sense of loneliness and uncertainty, a darkening of prospects, the condition of being an outsider with all of a stranger's suspicions.

To take the curse off the rest of the day I sat and read to pass the time — Melville's *Benito Cereno* (ships, ocean, deception, mutiny). At such times I am so drawn into the detailed life of the novel that I am startled when I look up from the fiction and see gravel and cactuses and palm trees that remind me I am elsewhere.

I was glad when Oliver showed up in his four-wheel-drive vehicle. It meant a few days of companionship and the pleasure of being on the road again, as well as a chance to find out about his aid mission. His role in Africa involved giving large amounts of money away and supervising its use.

Oliver was the resident country director in Namibia of the American Millennial Challenge Corporation, an agency that financed foreign aid and development. The total fund was considerable, currently running at about $1 billion, and the projects were spread all over Africa — indeed, all over the globe, the dispensing of American taxpayers' money in an effort to improve other people's lives. One of the projects in Namibia was helping the tourism infrastructure. In an era of financial hardship for Americans, I wanted to know more.

"Oliver goes everywhere in Namibia," I had been told. "He loads up his vehicle with food and water and extra gas and drives into the wilderness. If there's no road, he drives up dry riverbeds. He spends weeks in the bush."

He was young, mid-thirties, and quietly hearty. I liked his energy and admired his disposition. He biked and ran, even on the hottest Namibian days. He was married, with an infant son, and lived in Windhoek when he was not traveling. He had been associated with the Millennial Challenge for four years.

Also in the car was Trevor, a lanky, good-humored Texan whose wife was a medical officer in Windhoek, specializing in the administration of HIV/AIDS programs. Trevor was contemplating his next move, but was not sure what that might be. He was nearer my age, well traveled, ironical, and, as I was to find out, knowledgeable about African wildlife. His mellow mood showed in his loose and jaunty way of walking. He was a thoughtful person but not a worrier. He said he was just coming along for the ride, interested that I was eventually heading to Angola.

"Have you been up there?" I asked him.

He said no. Neither he nor Oliver had been over the border, nor did they know anyone who had. Oliver had been in touch with an Angolan on the other side who said he might be able to help me, but when pressed for a definite answer, the Angolan lapsed into silence and became unobtainable.

We drove north through small, narrow, road-straddling cattle towns, Hartseer and Vrindskap and Outjo, past the gravy-colored ridge of Fransfonteinberge, and after sixty miles or so we were rolling through the bush. The terrain was the unchanging semidesert and low thornbush that characterized much of Namibia, and it looked sterile until an ostrich strutted into view or a herd of buffalo shadowed forth to flare their nostrils. Passing not far from here 150 years ago, Francis Galton wrote in his diary, "The country is remarkably uniform, intersected with paths, and quite destitute of natural features to guide us. It is also slightly undulating, enough so to limit the view to a mile or two ahead."

That was true today. The few Victorian travelers who had dared to march across these parts would find much of rural Namibia unchanged, because it is so thinly populated and undeveloped. Many of Galton's descriptions in *Narrative of an Explorer in Tropical South Africa,* the account of his 1851 journey in what was then an unmapped country, would still apply to this enduring, crystalline, and seemingly steamrolled landscape.

Nowhere was that truer than at Etosha, which we entered a few hours later. Apart from the gate and checkpoint, it was as Galton had sketched it:

May 30th — We passed the grave of the god Omakuru . . .
Came to Etosha, a great salt-pan. It is very remarkable

in many ways. The borders are defined and wooded; its surface is flat and effloresced, and the mirage excessive over it; it was about nine miles in breadth, but the mirage prevented my guessing at its length; it certainly exceeded fifteen miles [actually more like eighty]. Chik said it was quite impassable after the rainy season, and it must form a rather pretty lake at that time. We arrived late in the evening at another *werft* [or *werf*: Afrikaans for the enclosure around a living area], on the south border of the grand flat, Otchikako-wa-motenya, which appears to extend as a grassy treeless estuary between wooded banks the whole way hence to near the sea.

Galton had gone north with two companions, John Allen and Charles Andersson, and a caravan of bearers following a file of heavily laden oxen. Galton was only twenty-eight, but he was high-spirited, in pursuit of David Livingstone's Lake Ngami. At that time, European travelers in Africa, like Galton, were searching for the source of the Nile and denouncing the slave trade. For almost two years, Galton wandered up and down what is now Namibia, the first Englishman to report on it. He did not find Lake Ngami, but he penetrated deep into the country, very near what is now the Angola border ("four or five days' easy journey ahead"), where slaves were routinely rounded up and shipped to Brazil from the Angolan port of Benguela. Galton noted the customs of the Damara, the Ovambo, and the Bushmen; he inquired about slave trading in Angola; he shot birds and big game; he crossed and recrossed the desert; and in the Victorian manner he asserted himself.

"A man whom I had taken from Chapupa's *werft* became impudent," he wrote. "So I took active measures upon his back and shoulders, to an extent that astonished the Ovampo and reformed the man."

There were a few roads in what was Etosha National Park now, but the rest was bush and water and a salt pan. Galton, who first brought Etosha to the notice of the English-speaking world, would have found much of the area familiar. Twenty-five years after Galton's visit, a young American trader-wanderer named Gerald McKiernan camped at the edge of Etosha and wrote in his diary, "It was the Africa I had read about in books of travel. All the menageries in the world turned loose would not compare to the sight I saw that day."

In prehistory, Etosha had been a vast inland sea and still gave that impression, as if at low tide the sea drained away, leaving the sand and crusted sea floor exposed as flats to glitter under an empty sky. Much of it was now a pan, part of it with year-round water and other sections seasonal lakes. In the open areas it was a vastness of blinding white, and it shimmered as far as the horizon and was so thoroughly bleak it seemed that we had landed on a planet made entirely of crushed coral.

Farther east the land was more varied, with occasional clumps of trees and some parched but wooded glades, where svelte springboks sprinted and white rhinos lowered their armored heads and fitted their wide shovel mouths to the ground to tear at brown grass.

"Giraffe at ten o'clock," Trevor said. He raised his binoculars to his eyes and frowned under them in concentration. "And another. With a baby. Beautiful. She's saying, 'I think I'll try the leaves on this branch up here.'"

Two-toned herds of zebra with stiff, upright, brushlike manes trotted together shoulder to shoulder, then lifting their knees broke into a clopping gallop.

We came to a waterhole where three honey-colored lions lay sleeping, their fatigued bodies slackened on the gravel in the late afternoon sun.

Oliver said, "Siesta time."

Trevor said, "Wait."

We watched for a while: two slender sinewy lionesses and a

broad-shouldered male lying between them with a fluffed-up mane like teased hair.

Trevor said, "Big boy is stirring. He knows what he wants."

Yawning, the big lion got to his feet, tossed his mane, and padded over to the lioness on his left. Then he squatted in a regal pose behind her, raised his noble head, and thrust himself against her. This took but seconds. As he returned to his sleeping spot, the lioness he had covered rolled over and raised her dangling hind legs and shimmied on her back.

Trevor said, "Making sure that sperm gets where it's supposed to."

"That was something," I said.

Trevor said, "Wait. Give big boy ten more minutes."

In less than that time, the lion woke from his doze, yawned again, padded over to the lioness on his right, and squatted over her, knees apart.

As the lion lay sideways and slept again, Trevor said, "He's not done. Wait a little bit. You'll see."

Just as Trevor had said, the lion roused himself and mated again with the first lioness. After this third time, Trevor predicted there would be more couplings, at roughly ten-minute intervals. And it happened. Karen Blixen wrote in *Out of Africa,* "You know you are truly alive when you're living among lions."

"Every man's fantasy," Trevor said. Then, "Oryx."

This sex and sleeping ritual by the three lions was taking place about forty feet from a herd of fifteen oryx, which were lapping at the edge of the waterhole along with a flock of Egyptian geese, two jackals, a file of ostriches, and two giraffes, heads down, canted forward on their wide-apart legs. And it was not a large waterhole; it was hardly bigger than a suburban family's swimming pool. Oliver said it was rare to see all these animals, different species, several of them predators or natural enemies, sharing the water peacefully, if warily, without threatening each other.

At sundown we returned to our lodge at Okaukuejo in time to witness herds of tourists, hundreds of them, alighting from buses and streaming from their rooms. Within minutes they were jostling in the dining room, pushing in a rowdy line to flourish empty plates that they held one-handed at their sides in the fidget of discus throwers, ready to launch themselves at the buffet. They looked fierce, their red faces and bulging eyes gleaming in the heat. There is something terrible about a naked display of hunger, and its nearest passion is perhaps lust.

"Germans," Trevor said, in the same tone as he'd said "Oryx."

They were clamoring for the platters of roast kudu and sliced chicken, basins of pasta, piles of mashed potatoes, and green salad. Four women edged forward, attempting to jump the queue, and the crowd's panting and uneasiness were audible, intimations of appetite, many of them sighing impatiently or muttering with bad grace, and there were words, too. You could not watch all this pushing without thinking of the order at the waterhole, the placidly drinking animals. Of the one million tourists who visit Namibia, most are German, the rest from other European nations, and nearly all swing through Etosha in bulky tour buses.

There is a rule in Africa: do not get between an elephant and the water. Trevor said, "Don't get between a tourist and the buffet."

At the floodlit, fenced-off waterhole at the back of the Okaukuejo lodge, mammals gathered at either side of the barrier, the tourists to watch and whisper, the rhinos and eland to lap at the water.

"Tell me," Trevor said in a rhetorical tone, "what's the difference between this and a zoo?"

We debated this point until we were shushed and reprimanded by a stern German for talking too loud.

We set out early the next morning to drive around the perimeter of the pan. Motoring for hours to spot animals is less interesting to me than happening upon them while en route to a destination. I used to like the sight of hippos that crept past the schoolroom where I was conducting an evening class near Lake Katwe in Uganda, or the hyena that routinely pawed at my compost heap in Malawi at night when I sat reading. I preferred animals as background rather than foreground, like the glimpse of the hefty baboon on the road to Swakopmund, which appeared from the parted grass like a pedestrian, waiting to cross the road.

We came to a place called Halali on my map, but it was merely a dead end and a mud wallow. Nearby was a small cemetery. One of the strictest rules in Etosha was that no one should leave the safety of one's vehicle. I mentioned this.

Trevor said, "But I don't see anyone checking, do you?"

Being out of the car in this great flat sun-struck place was a liberation. The cemetery, surrounded by an old iron fence to discourage animals from violating the graves, contained the remains of seven Boers, their names and dates inscribed in old-style letters on the granite stones. All dated from the 1870s. These were people who had obviously died in this inhospitable salt pan on their way to Angola, during what was called the Dorsland ("Thirstland") Trek, when hundreds of white South African farmers migrated north seeking greener pastures and more elbow room. One gravestone read *Joh. Alberts 1841–1874* — no doubt a relation of Gert Alberts, one of the instigators, and the leader, of the trek. It was the trekkers' fate that they had to cross the Kalahari and hundreds of miles of Etosha Desert and Ovamboland before reaching the great Kunene River and the green uplands of Angola. Just as bad as the fierce animals were the Portuguese, who stipulated that in return for the right to settle, these Dutch Protestants had to convert to Catholicism. Still, many of the renegade Afrikaners ended up farming in Angola.

While we strolled around this small cemetery in the middle of empty glittering Etosha, Trevor suddenly said, "Elephants at two o'clock."

They were tiny in the distance, perhaps a mile away, swaying out of the shadows of a wide grove of trees as though leaving a low building. They moved slowly and at times gingerly, like barefoot children on gravel, because, Trevor said, the broken stones were sharp enough to press into the soft pads on the elephants' tender soles.

We watched, and within half an hour more than forty elephants had gathered at the wallow. Most of them were mothers with babies, some male elephants bullied by the bigger females, and all of them active — rolling in the mud, trumpeting, spraying themselves with squirting trunks of water, the little ones stumbling in the deeper puddles. And there we stood, beholding the marvel of this sudden herd. Seeing so many sociable elephants together while we stood gaping was our reward for visiting Etosha, and I could not help but think of the tamed and obedient, and perhaps resentful, elephants at Abu.

Deeper into Etosha the land was flatter and without any trees, and as the day grew hotter the whole of the pan was blinding white and lifeless.

We came to Namutoni. Francis Galton had been here too, when it was known as a reliable waterhole, "a reedy boggy fountain . . . We were received very hospitably and had a tree assigned to us to camp under." He also complained, "We traveled through everlasting thorns and stones for nine hours, and offpacked at wells — wretched affairs that we had to sit up half the night to clean and dig out."

Some miles to the southeast of Namutoni was Otjikoto Lake, which Galton called "that remarkable tarn, Otchikoto . . . a deep bucket-shaped hole" filled with water. The local Ovambo told him the dark magical stories associated with the lake, "that no living thing that ever got into it could come out again." Hearing this, Galton and his two mates stripped off their clothes, descended the bank to the water, and went swimming. Thus they "dispelled that illusion from the savage mind under the astonished gaze not only of the whole caravan but quantities of Bushmen who lived about the place."

The fort at Namutoni was a set of square whitewashed battlements and watchtowers in the desert that could serve as the backdrop for a foreign-legion movie. Indeed, a foreign legion had once manned it — the German soldiers of the Schutztruppe, which repelled various attacks on the garrison by the Ovambo people in 1904. Ovambo Chief Nehale, who ordered and led the attacks, is remembered by Namibians as one of their earliest anti-colonial heroes. The seven Germans of the Schutztruppe who repulsed the attacks are remembered by the Germans for their colonial heroism. After the attacks, which destroyed most of the structure, the fort was rebuilt and enlarged in 1906 to its present form, and like everything else the Germans built in the colony, it was handed over to the South Africans less than ten years later.

At Namutoni, over cheese sandwiches, Oliver and I swapped stories of the Peace Corps. He had been a teacher in a rural village in Madagascar.

"One day the mailman came with a letter addressed to me," he said. "Funny — I didn't get much mail. This was from someone in a town about twenty kilometers away. It was a very short note saying, 'I would like to see you.' It was from a girl I had said hello to at the market there. How did I know that? Because she included a picture of herself. She was sitting under a bridge — naked."

I said, "I can't top that."

Trevor said, "We want to know more."

"I thought you might," Oliver said, looking inscrutable.

As we had only one more day together, I asked Oliver over dinner about the Millennial Challenge Corporation. Passing the lodges at Etosha — they were large and sprawling and some could accommodate hundreds of tourists — he had mentioned that they were being upgraded. "The staff quarters are going to be moved over there," he had said as he drove around the rundown workers' housing. "This is all going to be cleaned up." Oliver knew the plans and the people involved, and he'd said that one of his tourism projects in the country was being funded with Millennial Challenge money.

The Millennial Challenge Corporation had been started in 2004 during the Bush administration, a consequence of the frustration of people who saw USAID and other agencies pouring money into countries with no tangible results and little oversight. The money either disappeared into the pockets of local politicians or financed projects that were never finished. Anyone who has spent even a short time in a Third World country has seen this waste of money and the futility of a great deal of foreign aid. Africa is the happy hunting ground of donors, also of people seeking funds. The classic African failed state is composed of a busy capital city where politicians on large salaries hold court and drive big cars; dense and hopeless slums surrounding the capital; and the great empty hinterland, ignored by the government and more or less managed by foreign charities, which in many cases are big businesses run by highly paid executives.

In 2007, Oliver, with his Peace Corps zeal, had started working for the Millennial Challenge Corporation in the area of "project appraisal." The following year he became deputy director in Namibia, and in 2011 was appointed the resident country director.

"How much are you giving to Namibia?" I asked.

"A little over three hundred million — but let me explain," he said, because hearing the large number I had started to snort. "The grant is administered in stages over five years, in what we call a compact. And before a country qualifies for a compact it has to pass the eligibility requirements. It takes two years for a country to go through the process. This isn't handing over money, the way it was done in the past. It's a rigorous process."

"What sort of requirements, apart from 'We need money'?" I had my notebook out and was writing down his replies.

"There's three categories we measure them by. Ruling justly. Economic freedom. And investing in people. If these don't exist, no money. Each of the categories is broken down into seventeen indicators—like land rights, civil liberties, control of corruption, freedom of information—and they have to be low- or middle-income countries. Botswana doesn't qualify, because they already have money. After the coup in Madagascar in 2009 their compact was terminated."

"So a country simply applies, and hopes to qualify?"

"We can help a country to qualify by giving a threshold grant —fifteen or twenty million. They'd use this to sort out their policies. That creates a pathway to getting a compact that ranges from two hundred to five hundred million. Like I say, Namibia qualified for three hundred million."

"What's the limit?"

"Tanzania got seven hundred million for roads and energy and some other projects. That's spread over five years. They're now three years into it, and it's working out."

"Almost three quarters of a billion for Tanzania! They don't even like us!"

"Remember when George Bush visited Tanzania in 2008?" Oliver said. "It was a very successful visit. He made promises to them."

"I also remember the 1960s when the Tanzanians claimed they were Maoists. They got the Chinese to build them the Tan-Zam Railway, which is now falling apart," I said. "Anyway, who gets the money? I mean, are American companies hired to do the work— say, on roads?"

"A U.S. company successfully competed for the energy project in Tanzania. I think I can say that we're achieving U.S. development and foreign policy objectives."

I mentioned that I had read in a Namibian newspaper that a Chinese company in the country, financed by American aid money, had underpaid and cheated its Namibian employees.

"You saw that, eh?" Oliver said. It had been a front-page headline. "Chinese government firms once qualified for this money, but that's not the case anymore." But he added that less than 10 percent of Namibia's grant went to American companies. Most of the money went to Namibian or South African firms.

"So we're giving money to foreign companies to do the work. And we used to give it to the Chinese?"

"It's an open bidding process," he said. "And we do audits. There's no evidence that contractors are misappropriating the funds." Slightly exasperated by my questions, he said, "You wouldn't believe how much time we spend in monitoring these grants and double-checking."

"Still, it's a ton of money."

"But there's constant evaluation of performance. We don't take people's word for it, or list numbers as USAID once did — meaningless numbers. We invest money in monitoring, in making sure the money is used the right way, looking at the target, and the performance against that target."

And, he said, sometimes a Millennial Challenge compact is in place and something changes that queers a development deal. Malawi was a recent example. Its government signed on to a $300 million compact for investment in the energy sector, but not long after the signing there was a demonstration in Malawi's capital against the government's human rights abuses. Nineteen demonstrators were shot dead by the army and many were injured.

"So we put an operational hold on the compact," Oliver said. "And then the Malawians hosted Sudan's al-Bashir, who is wanted by the International Criminal Court."

"And what happened?"

"The MCC questioned Malawi's commitment to the principles."

"So no money?"

"No money."

"That's how it should be." But I was not sure what "investment in the energy sector" meant — perhaps speeding the flow of foreign oil, or subsidizing it, or creating alternative sources. One of the problems with the whole discussion was the vagueness of the terms. Even the millions seemed like abstractions.

I remembered the tourist herds at the Etosha lodges and Oliver's showing us the places to be upgraded. Were U.S. funds invested in Namibia's tourism industry?

"Yes." And Oliver elaborated by saying that the tourism project allotment was $67 million, which was for the improvement and management of Etosha National Park and to help in marketing Namibian tourism. The intention was to promote Namibia as a splendid, game-rich, tourist-worthy destination. Some of the money was allotted to develop an interactive website for the Namibia Tourism Board. It was also used to help Namibia in the areas of conservation, ecotourism, and poverty reduction in households within conservancy areas.

All of this was well intentioned in terms of development — even if vague in description — and laudable in the efforts made to ensure the funds weren't stolen or wasted. If the money was misused, the grant would be cut off. But money for *tourism?* Many tourist destinations in the United States, which get nothing from the U.S. government for infrastructure or websites or training, would have been glad to get the $67 million grant Namibia had been awarded. Places I knew well got no money from the government to prop up tourism — Hawaii got nothing, Cape Cod got nothing, but they struggled along. Maine's tourist industry was still in serious trouble in the aftermath of the 2008 economic slump, with high unemployment, high gas prices, and a lack of awareness outside New England of the delights of Downeast Maine, one of the noblest and best-preserved seacoasts on earth.

Were the hard-pressed residents of Maine, many of whom worked in the state's hotels and restaurants, contributing to the improvement of the Namibian tourist industry, helping to lure the herds to Etosha and the Skeleton Coast?

"Let's say I happen to be a Maine lobsterman," I said. "I get up at four-thirty every morning, go out in my boat, and haul hundreds of traps. Some days, fuel is so expensive and there are so few lobsters that I lose money. But I keep hauling, and steering my boat in circles. I pay my stern man. I pay my taxes. I'm wet and cold most of the time." Oliver was smiling, knowing what was coming. "What would you say to my friend Alvin Rackcliff of Wheeler Bay, in Midcoast Maine, about the use of his tax money to attract tourists to Namibia?"

"I'd say we're trying to help create countries that are stable," Oliver said as I scribbled.

"I don't think Alvin would care too much about that. He'd say" —as Alvin said to me once— "human life means nothing in Africa."

"It's less than one percent of the total U.S. budget," Oliver said.

"It's still a lot of money. Alvin is heavily taxed and works very hard and he's pretty old. But he needs to keep working."

"Aid builds good relationships," Oliver said.

"Alvin would want to know what Namibia is doing for itself."

"Each country contributes, up to a half of the total," Oliver said, then, seeing that I was impressed, he added that low-income countries were not required to contribute any money. "Look, it helps make countries viable. It builds infrastructure. Ghana is a good example of how loans and investment help. We had a successful compact there."

At this point Trevor piped up. He had been listening intently throughout my needling interrogation. He said, "How about these politicians in Windhoek who are living like kings? Why are we giving free drugs to the country if they're spending money on themselves for luxuries?"

"Namibia has had regular elections since 1990," Oliver said. "As well as tourist-based development, we're doing education and agriculture. Hey, it's five years, and we keep checking that no one steals."

"I get it," I said, because of all the foreign aid programs I'd come across, this one seemed to be operated in the most efficient way. I remembered the highly critical book *Dead Aid*, and asked, "What does Dambisa Moyo think about it?"

"She's skeptical. She's taken some shots at us," Oliver said. "But the whole idea is that we shouldn't be here forever. There shouldn't be a long-term-donor drip feed."

I was persuaded that the Millennium Challenge Corporation was doing its work well. (And to put the $67 million figure in perspective, soon after my talk with Oliver I heard on the radio that the European Union and the IMF had voted to give a 110-billion-euro bailout loan to Greece, to help write off its debt.) I liked the idea that the MCC would cut off funds to countries that did not live up to their word, and that tyrannies did not qualify. The best news was the close monitoring of the projects and the cash flow. Some nations benefited, and were perhaps grateful and more stable as a result. What did all this mean to the U.S. taxpayer? Not much, I felt.

What did it mean to sorely taxed and hard-working Alvin Rackcliff in Maine? He was well over eighty now and still fishing, still hauling traps. I could see him in his yellow slicker, gloves, and rubber boots in his lobster boat, *Morning Mist*, laughter ringing in my ears.

"If you believe that, Paulie," he would say, "you're crazy as a shit-house rat!" Or perhaps, "The only free cheese is in a mousetrap."

The next day, Oliver dropped me off in the town of Omuthiya, which was so small it did not appear on my map. We met his friend Moses there. Moses was an Ovambo, from Oshikati, near the border. He said he'd take me fifty miles up the road to Ondangwa, where there was a hotel.

I thanked Oliver for enlightening me about his projects, and for putting up with my needling questions, and thanked Trevor for his good humor.

Trevor said, "We're going to miss you, man."

"You'll be fine from here on," Oliver said.

I threw my bag into the back of Moses's truck and climbed into the front seat.

On the road, Moses said, "You're going to the border tomorrow?"

"Yes,"

"You've been to Angola before?"

"No."

"You speak Portuguese?"

"No."

"You have friends there?"

"None."

Moses was a handsome man, but his scowl gave him a fierce mask. He held the steering wheel in both hands, hanging on, ruminating.

"What do you think?" I asked.

He turned his scowling, pained face toward me and said, "It's a nightmare!"

Moses didn't know the half of it, nor did I. Though I was not aware of it until a month later, that day in Namibia, or perhaps earlier, in one of the hotels where I had used my credit card (I had used it only fourteen times in Namibia, always for hotel bills) my personal information was stolen. My name and numbers were printed on a duplicate card, identical to mine ("It's easy," the fraud squad told me), and beginning on my last day in Namibia, and for the next month, this duplicate card was used in more than a hundred fraudulent transactions.

Some of the purchases were substantial ($4,000 worth of furniture from OK Furniture in Windhoek, almost as much at Edgar's Furniture); some were tiny (a $3 meal at an Olympia Quick Shop, $20 for beer at Shoprite). Much more furniture, lots of sunglasses from the Sunglass Hut, numerous computers, a used car, tinted windows, new alloy wheels, $800 worth of new shoes, and many supermarket bills. The total came to just over $48,000 — U.S. dollars.

11

The Frontier of Bad Karma

I TRAVELED UP THE ROAD, the road grew more tortured, and even before I got to Ondangwa, forty miles south of the Angola frontier, I knew I was in a different country, but a nameless one, an ill-defined borderland, a zone of decrepitude and hunger.

Having crossed the Vet Fence again, I was over the Red Line, in the land of skinny cows and poor housing and trash heaps and shredded plastic bags blown against wire fences and fluttering from thornbushes. It was also a land of drunken men, idle boys, and overworked women. Nearly everyone on the other side of the Vet Fence was hard-up, and the best houses were square, miserable, flat-topped huts made of cinderblocks. Most of the blocks were fabricated by recently arrived Chinese immigrants for whom this was a profitable business of simple routines, and they worked in open-sided sheds just off the road using crude mixing machinery and rubber molds. The Chinese employed Namibians, who were coated with cement dust, making them look like an alien race, like exploited, gray-skinned Martians. That was appropriate, because this area seemed like another nation altogether, and at times another planet, the dark star of my anxious dreams.

Though I had heard about them endlessly, I had seen just a few Chinese settlers in Namibia. But here in the north they were numerous (and anonymous), their shops and enterprises shoved up against the border of Angola, the source of much of their business — and they were evasive, usually ducking out of sight when I attempted to ask any questions. Their presence here made me wonder about China's prosperity, because most of the Chinese I was to meet were escapees from the Chinese miracle who in Africa believed themselves to be in a promised land of no regulation, under-the-counter cash transactions, and improvisation. Here, where no one breathed down their necks, they found cheap labor and easy pickings. This free, happy, capitalistic situation is a blessed rarity the Chinese traditionally refer to by intoning a ritual formula (as many must have done in Africa): "Heaven is high and the emperor is far away."

I was soon in a world of roadblocks and mobs, of terrible roads or no roads at all, a world of lies and scamming and crooked policemen. It was also a world of abuse, a world of "Meester, why are you here?" Which was a good question — why *was* I here? Over the following legs of my trip I attempted to answer the question. At first glance, it seemed sheer perversity for me to be here, and foolishness to go farther north.

No tourists ventured into this border area — why would they? The hotels were terrible, the food was filthy, the people were suspicious and occasionally hostile. The roadside was littered with broken glass and crushed soda cans. A foul smell hung over it all — the stink of the latrines of poverty, smoking garbage heaps, diesel fumes, and, at roadside stands, yellow dough balls frying in hot fat. The weather was exhausting — very hot, no shade, no rain.

Still in Namibia, in the ramshackle town of Ondangwa, I looked for travelers but saw none from Angola nor any heading there, except for the desperate people whose extended family or tribe had been bisected by the border, for this was Ovamboland and Ovambo lived on both sides. It was a world of abruptness and rudeness. I was startled when an official would scream "You!" at me and raise a fist, as though on the verge of hitting me in the face.

Until a month after I left, when I learned — too late — that I had been defrauded as a result of identity theft, Namibia had struck me as fairly orderly and reasonably polite. But the farther I traveled on this north-trending road, order and politeness deteriorated, and I began to wonder what I might find at the border and across it. It seemed a hot African world of bad karma, near anarchy, and opportunism. I saw poverty and desperation everywhere, a scavenging culture, and ultimately it made me question the whole purpose of my sentimental journey.

All serious travelers arrive at this doubting, why-bother juncture, stalling on the road, sometime or other. The next question concerned whether there was any point in going on. I had never felt more like an old man, a highly visible alien in a place where no one looked remotely like me, a sitting duck. Perhaps this would provide a good lesson in understanding the vulnerability of a minority, but was it worth the trouble?

In the small hotel, having seen how the little town looked in its dirt and disrepair, I became curious to know how bad things might be farther on, perhaps at the border town of Oshikango and beyond. So far, I could not imagine anything more disorderly or unpromising than the town of Ondangwa.

I write "small hotel" and "little town" and "dirt and disrepair" and it's possible to read into those words a certain seedy charm, as if I am describing a tropical locale in a novel of intrigue — the dark saloon, the warren of back streets, the overhanging foliage, the colorful inhabitants of Ovamboland.

It was not like that at all. The sultry backwater of fiction is never a total slum; it always has a cozy refuge — a hotel with a veranda, a riverboat tied up at a jetty, a quaint old house, a compliant woman or wisecracking local. And here in the comfortable shadows, the hero sips a drink, and eyes the woman, and contemplates the derelict town. This fantasy is complete because as a romance (and much of Graham Greene's fiction, for example, is misleadingly romantic in this flawed way) it includes a safe place to hide and maybe someone to fall in love with, or depend on. The stink of the place, the hopelessness, the vile indifference, do not rise from the page.

There was no refuge here, no vantage point. Ondangwa was a blight of shacks, old cars, and empty shops, of skinny dogs chewing at heaps of trash, of crowds of people, some staring, some casually quarreling. The people had the air of temporariness you see in the desperate poor; they did not appear to belong here, but rather that they were just passing through. Ondangwa was not in any visible sense a community, and its randomness and disorder and bad smell seemed threatening. There was no place to hide, nothing for me to grasp at, and this made me feel somewhat insecure. In fiction, only Paul Bowles writes of such places, and convincingly, because they are truly ugly and uninhabitable, except by his mournful, self-destructive characters who are usually at the end of their tether, and they nearly always die in the awful place.

Ondangwa was built on sand and scrub. There were no trees; it was a town without shade; its people dressed in castoff clothes; nothing worked. The very sunshine made it seem much worse, more bleak and hopeless in its hideous glare, naked to the sky. It was not a destination; it was a place to expire in, or leave quickly. And it was on the way to nowhere.

Ondangwa was near enough to the border for the chaos of Angola to have seeped through and added to its derangement. After his howl of "It's a nightmare!" Moses had dropped me on the town's main road near the only hotel, and raising his large admonitory hand like a cautioning uncle, he gave me repeated warnings: Don't trust anyone. Don't talk to anyone. Don't answer questions from any of the boys or men you see. Keep your hand on your money or your pocket will be picked. Hold on to your bag or it will be stolen. Be careful.

And then he spoke that ominous and fear-inspiring pronouncement that penetrates to the vitals: "There are bad people here."

Moses, a trusted friend of Oliver's, was a shrewd, helpful man; he regarded me as a naïve stranger and a potential victim. He took me for a credulous traveler, and possibly a fool. In these assessments he was perhaps not far wrong. But then he lived in the region and was constantly in the company of aliens and refugees, the usual transients found in border areas. He had been born in, and lived just to the west of, the town of Oshakati.

All national boundaries attract temporary people, as well as rejects and immigrants and fixers. At this, the limit of the country, far from the capital, normal rules did not apply. People did whatever they could get away with. The very presence of a border fence meant that no one really belonged there. Such a fringe area lacked any identity except its own fraying face, and attracted mostly fugitives and hustlers. I was one of the desperadoes, a fugitive. I had no business there. I was just passing through and hoping for the best.

Before he drove away Moses said, "Keep your head down. Don't make eye contact with these people."

This advice was strangely prescient. Eye contact produces aggression. Animal behaviorists agree: Stare at a chimp and he is likely to attack you. Locking eyes with a dog can create hostility. Prolonged eye contact "taps into pack-animal fears." Malevolence is manifested in the gaze. Not just a dirty look but merely meeting a stranger's eyes may be taken as confrontational. "Stink eye," as they say in Hawaii; *malocchio* in Italy. Looking down or averting your eyes signifies submission. You escape from an animal in the wilderness by avoiding eye contact, because a stare is perceived as a challenge, if not an outright threat.

In fact, I felt I was turning into an animal, or perhaps using my animal instincts more than ever. This seemed to shut off a part of my brain, the spongy, gelatinous, reflective part I used for the sake of serenity.

When I checked into the hotel, the back-and-forth with my credit card was clumsier than usual: "The machine's not working" and "I'll be right back with it." In retrospect, it was highly probable that my identity was stolen that day, my last in Namibia, at the Protea Hotel, also known as the Hotel Pandu Ondangwa, a hot cheerless building surrounded by gravel and withered plants, and staffed by a single sly ingratiating man with a toothy smile.

While the day was still light I followed my long shadow to the main road, which was also the main road to Angola. I was stalked by ragged men.

"*Mynheer, mynheer . . .*"

Rural Namibians tended to revert to Afrikaans in the presence of whites.

"I need a ride to the border tomorrow."

Several said, "I can take you, *mynheer.*"

I looked at their cars and, finding one that was in reasonably good shape, began haggling over the cost for the sixty-mile ride.

"Petrol, *mynheer* — so expensive!" This was Joshua, who was fairly presentable and said he could take me to the border. He looked to be in his mid- to late twenties, and there was something reassuring in his manner.

He wasn't exaggerating about the expense — the cost of fuel all over Africa was exorbitant. In Ondangwa that day it was almost $5 a gallon, or about twice what it cost in the United States. I asked him to meet me at seven so we could be at the border at eight, when it opened. Then I took him aside and talked with him about his family — his three children, his home village, his ambitions — and I told him about my wife and children. I wanted us to be human to each other. We shook hands on it, and I repeated the details about the drive, the time, the cost.

Joshua did not appear the following morning. I had risen early and checked out of the hotel. I had my small bag and my briefcase and stood waiting by the entrance for almost an hour.

Then a stranger appeared. "I am Stephen. Joshua is my cousin. His car won't start."

"How will I get to the border?"

"I will take you, *mynheer.*"

This had all the earmarks of a setup. I had no idea who this young man was. He was more ragged than Joshua. His car was such a jalopy, one door had to be held closed with a bent wire coat hanger. The seats were torn, their stuffing exposed. Stephen seemed uneasy, not to say nervous. He did not live in this area but some distance away, at Ogongo, in western Ovamboland. Still — what choice did I have? — I got in and threw my bag into the back seat.

By degrees, it became apparent that Stephen was a good soul — gentle, honest, a proud father, and ambitious to further his education. Like many other young men and women I met in Namibia, he badly wanted to leave the country and find work in the United States. What would he do? I asked. "Anything," he said. I believed him, and I could imagine his coworkers praising him in an American city where Stephen might be a taxi driver or a furniture mover or a functionary in a speedy-oil-change business. "The guy's a ball of fire!" And they would not be able to imagine where Stephen had come from — the poverty and disorder of Ondangwa — and how grateful someone like Stephen would be to have work and a life in that American city.

I was reminded that along borders, populated by transients and opportunists and predators, there were also — and perhaps for the same reason — protectors, shielding the innocent from harm. He was one of those angels. I had encountered many in my life, and I was to meet more of them on this trip.

Like Moses, Stephen was full of warnings, but he assured me that if I followed his advice I would get over the border without a problem.

"What's it like on the other side?"

He shook his head and smiled. No idea. He had never been there.

"Chinese business," he said as we passed warehouses and small factories.

Off to the left, a two-story yellow-painted building with a crimson sign: DRAGON CITY HOTEL AND RESTAURANT. I said, "I think that's a Chinese business. But who goes there?"

"Maybe people from Angola," Stephen said. Then, as we passed more businesses, he enumerated: "Indian man — plastics. Palestinian man — tin sheets for house roofs. Chinese man — textiles — he makes them there. Car and lorry business — South African man. German over there."

All of it because of the proximity to Angola, most of the goods sold to people who traveled across the border. I asked Stephen if this assumption was correct.

"They have nothing in Angola," he said. He thought again. "But they have money."

The shop fronts and businesses became denser, closer together, as we approached the border town of Oshikango, but of course, being a frontier, it was only half a town, walled off from its other side by a high chainlink fence running at a right angle across the main street. Parked on that street, waiting to go through Namibian customs, was a long line of trucks, several cars, even some loaded pushcarts and wheelbarrows. They looked as though they had been sitting there for a year, and the scene was of great, almost riotous disorder.

People milled around the stalled vehicles, shouting, selling food out of baskets — small bread rolls, fried cakes, cold drinks, wilted vegetables, and trays of chewing gum and candy. Beyond the crush of these vendors I could see another large crowd pressing toward an open shed with a high roof. Some of those people, mostly teenage boys, the Artful Dodgers that haunt frontiers, hurried toward us. In such circumstances, you sense being singled out and stalked like a lamed prey animal.

"Be careful," Stephen said. "There are thieves here—and on the other side, many thieves. Don't get out of the car until I give you a signal. I will find someone to help you."

He slipped out of the car and was accosted by a group of boys. He made a circuit of the blocked-off street, returned to the car, and opened the door.

"Lock the door. Don't talk to these boys. Don't look at them."

Then he was gone, hurrying through the mass of people pushing into the shed. Outside the car (my door fastened by the coat hanger), the boys were pressed against the windows, some calling out, others pleading, "*Mynheer! Mynheer!*"

Stephen returned with a girl of about nineteen or twenty, hardly more than five feet tall. She had a serious face set in a scowl, her jaw thrust out, and wore a blue blouse and a pink skirt, and on her head a floppy-brimmed knitted hat of white wool, like a picturesque peasant in a folktale or nursery rhyme.

"This is Vickie," Stephen said. "She will help you."

Seeing her, hearing this, the crowd of boys began to laugh, provoking Vickie to say something sharp to them, which shut them up.

"How much do I owe you?"

"Don't show any money," Stephen said. He palmed the payment —in gratitude for shepherding me, I had given him twice what he asked. He handed Vickie my canvas duffel.

She hoisted my bag onto her head and hung on to it with both hands. I clung to my briefcase. As we walked down the hot street and fought through the crowd to the customs shed, the boys snatched at my shirtsleeves. "*Mynheer!*"

Apart from the pestering boys — and more joined them as we went along — the formalities on the Namibian side were straightforward: presentation of signed forms and passport and the usual bag search, with the singular diversion of a Namibian customs inspector lifting my copy of *Benito Cereno,* squinting at it, then paging through it, his dancing eyes indicating that his head was a hive of subtlety, as if he were looking for an offensive passage.

"You can go." He directed me to the back of the shed, where a narrow walkway with high sides led into a maze.

The same boys followed, about ten of them. I knew their faces by now: the one in the soccer jersey, the one with the woolly Rasta hat, the one with the Emporio Armani T-shirt, the one with the wicked face and broken teeth, the one who kept bumping up against me — his plastic sandals were cracked and his feet were bumped and bruised; several boys had their hats turned backward in the gang-banger style. Customs and immigration did not apply to them, apparently; they pushed and jostled along the narrow passageway, which, I saw afterward, represented no man's land.

At the end of the passageway, Angola was another shed, with a wooden window flap propped open, more people in line, all of it enclosed by chainlink fences and razor wire.

Vickie, surrounded by the mocking boys, pointed to the window and indicated that I should hand in my passport. As I did so, I heard a howl.

"You!" It was a man inside the shed, in a blue uniform. "Get away!"

He meant that I should get in line, which I was happy to do, though I was startled by his snarling tone. I was to hear this same intentionally intimidating voice for the next few weeks, always by policemen or soldiers or petty officials. The Angolan voice of authority is severe, often bitter, usually reproachful, sometimes cruel. When I commented on it or complained, people said, "They've had almost thirty years of war." The war has been over for more than a decade, I would say. "But they were fighting South African soldiers" was the rejoinder. Actually, the South African soldiers had collaborated with one large Angolan faction. It was my belief that the hostility in all this bluster and obstruction usually meant that a bribe was being suggested.

The nastiness was always from an official, seldom from an Angolan civilian, yet the civilians had suffered too. I could not remember having been spoken to with such deliberate rudeness — not in Africa, not anywhere. But of course I was not in an international airport. I was a mere pedestrian in old clothes who had walked across the border from Namibia with old women carrying sacks of vegetables and baskets of chickens, old men shuffling behind them, and loud boys yelling to each other. Also, on that morning I was the only visible alien seeking to enter.

When my turn at the window came, the Angolan immigration official with the mean face and the abusive voice snatched at my passport and found my visa. But instead of stamping it, he put it aside.

"Where is your letter of invitation?"

No foreigner can enter Angola without a formal (and notarized) letter of invitation. I urge anyone in the United States who believes that we treat visitors bureaucratically and with suspicion to consider the obstacle course that Angola (and many other countries) presents to its foreign visitors: a seven-page application, a prepaid hotel reservation, a prepaid round-trip airline ticket, a set of character references, and an invitation letter from a resident of Angola stating exactly what the visitor will be doing in the country. Then you pay $200 for the visa. And you wait for several months. And you might be turned down, as I was, twice, before getting this visa.

"Why bother?" people asked me. But a country that is so hard to enter makes me curious to discover what is on the other side of the fence.

It so happened that I had the letter of invitation in my briefcase, which (in Portuguese) specified that I was in Angola to visit schools and colleges and give some lectures. I was a writer, it explained. All this tedious detail had the singular merit of being true.

I handed over the letter. The fierce-faced man in the shed did not read it. He placed it on his table with my passport.

I waited, breathing hard in the heat. I spoke to Vickie. The loitering boys laughed. After about twenty minutes, I went back to the shed and raised my hand to indicate, *Here I am, sir.* And seeing me, the immigration official, looking offended, swung himself through the door and screamed at me and flicked his hand: "*Você deve esperar!* You wait! You wait over there!"

This display of needless abuse had its effect on the little mob. Seeing how the man had treated me, the loitering boys in their backward caps and rapper T-shirts, emboldened by the tone, began to crowd me, their clothes stinking, muttering to me in Portuguese and Afrikaans, and to one another in their own language.

Twice more the official screamed, "You wait!" And when, about an hour later, he handed me my passport, keeping my letter, deaf to my request for a copy, I realized that I'd had a valuable lesson in border crossing, in Angolan officialdom, in the ways of traveling today.

The official had scowled at me and said, "*Você é professor?*"

"Yes," I had said. "*Sou professor.*"

And he had waved me on. It was a very hot day and the delay was inconvenient, but I could not take it personally. I was an older man of an alien race entering the country by the back door, treated with the casual abuse reserved for the contemptible souls who walked across the remote border. To anyone who breezed through the international airport on the red carpet and praised the country's manners and modernity, I could say: You do not have the slightest idea.

To someone like myself, intending to write a book, this whole morning of serial futility, spent going from Namibia to Angola —

perhaps fifty yards of travel — could not have been a richer or more enlightening experience.

Next I walked into even greater chaos, the Angolan border town of Santa Clara, Vickie quick-stepping behind me with my bag, the boys on either side of us, all of them moving fast, because I was trotting, hoping to discourage them.

"Bus," I said. The boys tugged at me. They knew where I could find a bus. Vickie led the way. We found two buses, but neither were leaving for Lubango, my intended destination, until nightfall. And the buses themselves were in such disrepair I doubted they would leave at all.

Vickie, meanwhile, stood by me. She communicated with me in gestures, and she waved the boys away. She was young, but strong-willed and helpful, and whatever curses or warnings she was muttering to the boys kept them at arm's length.

All I could see of Santa Clara was a potholed main street lined by low shops selling motor oil and Chinese plastic goods — buckets and patio chairs. Here and there stood wooden sheds plastered with signs advertising lottery tickets. The heavily laden women from the Namibian side were mostly traders, and they set out their vegetables by the road or hawked them out of baskets. The town, in its chaos, made Oshikango, just across the border — I could see it through the high border fence — seem peaceful and orderly.

A small boy carrying a bucket filled with bottles of water passed by. I bought one bottle, using Namibian dollars, and the money in my hand attracted a new crowd of jostling men and boys, the moneychangers. As I moved down the street, I found out that the town of Ondjiva was only about twenty miles away. If I got there in a bush taxi or a chicken bus, I could perhaps make a plan.

Then I saw a Land Cruiser ahead, an old one, angular, like a tin breadbox on wheels, and a man beside it. I said, "Ondjiva?"

The man was about thirty and wore a soccer jersey that was already soaked in sweat from the day's heat. His harassed face was made more tragic by his missing front teeth, and a ballpoint pen was stuck into the fat frizz of his dense hair, like a hairpin. He indicated yes. He then enumerated the places he was headed: "Ondjiva. Xangongo. Cahama. Lubango."

Lubango was my destination. I asked when he was leaving. "*Quando vamos?*" In an hour—he indicated on his watch and tapped the time. "*Quanto dinheiro?*"

He mentioned a number, then withdrew the pen from his hair and wrote the price in blue ink on his yellow palm, indicating thousands. This was the amount in Angolan kwanzas. I showed him my Namibian money. He wrote another number. It was a reasonable amount. I paid him. I quietly paid Vickie—and, gratefully as with Stephen, more than she had asked for—and was sorry to see her leave. She went back over the border, her floppy hat crushed and misshapen from her having carried my bag. The whole time she'd been with me, she had never smiled.

Pointing to himself, the driver said, "Camillo."

"Paulo," I said.

If all went well, I would arrive in Lubango that night. But few things in travel are simple, and everything in Angola, even the most straightforward transaction, was so hard as to be inconceivable. I suspected Camillo wanted more passengers. He did. Over the next three hours, in the heat of this border town, he stood by the car howling the names of towns, and one by one, boys, men, a woman with baskets, got into the back of the vehicle. Since I was the first paying passenger, I had taken the front seat, but a young woman slipped through the driver's side. So there would be three of us in the front seat for the three-hundred-mile drive to Lubango.

The woman's name was Paulina, and she was in her early twenties, sweet-faced but silent, wearing a tight black T-shirt and black jeans. She said she was going up the road to her village: "*Minha aldeia está próximo Lubango.*"

I sat, keeping my head down, killing time by making notes that began, *Too tedious to recount the delays . . .*

The seven or eight boys who had been hanging around my side of the car — pesterers, moneychangers, mere gawkers, "*Senhor . . . meestah*" — had wandered away. For me to get out of the car and traipse around would mean being followed, and what was the point? There was no shade. There was nothing to buy. Santa Clara was much worse, more miserable, than Oshikango, fifty yards away. I resigned myself to not eating that day, and I dozed.

In one of those mocking peculiarities of a world I had not gotten used to, my phone buzzed in my pocket. I was still in the telephonic orbit of Namibia. My wife on the line. She missed me. And how was I?

"Lovely day here on the Angolan border. I'm in Santa Clara."

"What a pretty name."

Early in the afternoon, Camillo got into the car and began fussing with his cassette tapes. He found one he wanted and slammed in into the player. Later on, when I had a glimpse of the cassette's label, I saw that it was the Dutch DJ Afrojack, the vocal by Eva Simons, and for the next four hours it played in a loop, Camillo sometimes turning the volume up. Later, when he was drunk and red-eyed and irrational, he played it at a deafening volume and sang along with it, but in a staticky mutter, like a dog gargling at a TV set. *Let's go take a ride in your car . . . I want you to take over control . . . Plug it in and turn me on.*

I came to hate this song, and like many hated songs I could not get the melody or the idiotic words out of my head. We did not leave Santa Clara at once. For reasons Camillo kept to himself, he began the trip by driving along the rutted dirt lanes just off the main road. These contained the slums and squatter camps of the town, with their three-legged dogs and women washing clothes in slop basins of gray water. Perhaps he was looking for someone else to cram into the back of the vehicle. Perhaps he was looking to buy something —

he seemed to make several discreet inquiries. The lanes were so bad the old Land Cruiser swayed back and forth, and the hollow-eyed women and sullen boys watched the vehicle bumping past their shacks. Children played in the dust, and one child tried to maneuver a broken wheelbarrow that held two bruised watermelons. In the heat, the fuzzy stink of human excrement.

I knew that Angola was wealthy, but I did not know then that the country earned billions of dollars a year from its oil, diamond, and gold exports. Later, when I discovered the figures, I recalled that little tour of Santa Clara, in one of the worst slums I had ever seen in my life. I remembered the whole day as an episode of misery; not mine — I was a witness, passing through — but those by the roadside and in the villages, the mute and brutalized Angolans, ignored by the kleptomaniacs in power.

"I'm afraid of what these people will do," an Angolan man was to tell me in Luanda when I mentioned what I'd seen in the south. "Imagine if they realized how they'd been cheated — what they would do if they decided to take their revenge on the government."

To anyone collecting money for the poor in Angola, I would say that before you reach into your pocket, consider Angola's revenues: have a look at the price of a barrel of oil and the fact that the country produces almost two million barrels a day; look at the diamond on your finger, and its gold setting, and reflect that these pretty things also probably originated in Angola.

My first day over the border, and I saw that a lack of money was not the problem in this country — but it seldom is in the hellholes of the world. The paradox was more likely that an excess of money was the problem — or one of them; that, and a government run by thieves.

But I was just learning, and I thought, as one does in such circumstances: Maybe things will improve farther up the road.

This main north-south road, the only one into Namibia and the only one to Angola's capital, was badly broken. The potholes were so wide and deep and numerous that Camillo, normally a speed demon, often had to slow the car to a crawl and make detours around them, and often left the road entirely, driving along the shoulder or through a roadside village.

Up ahead, twenty miles farther on, we came to the town of Ondjiva, where we stopped inexplicably, Camillo revving the engine while someone in the back seat hopped out to run an errand for him. I got out too, to stretch my legs, because I had been confined in the car for hours in Santa Clara and it seemed safe to take a break here. Ondjiva looked new, its buildings well kept. The town had an airport. I saw a hotel sign. This place had none of the menacing ruin of Santa Clara.

I asked Paulina about the place. She said in Portuguese, slowly, for my benefit: "This town was destroyed in the war. All ruined. Bombs, Fires. Guns. *Destruição. Extermínio.* Now it is all new."

Ondjiva, or N'Giva, had been known in Portuguese colonial times as Vila Pereira d'Eça, and after the ghostly and premature independence of 1974 it had been given its old Ovambo name. António Pereira d'Eça (1852–1917) had been a Portuguese colonel, and it was consistent with colonial policy, imposing a culture of famous foreign personalities, that many towns and cities in Angola were named in honor of Portuguese soldiers and statesmen. Pereira d'Eça had been sent on various military expeditions to Mozambique and Cape Verde, and after the outbreak of World War I was appointed commander of the Portuguese expeditionary forces to counter German advances from South-West Africa. But in 1915 the Germans were the least of his troubles, because the Ovambo people in the area, taking advantage of the besieged colonials, rose up under the leadership of their warrior king and went to war with Pereira d'Eça's battalions. The Kwanyama, a subtribe of the Ovambo, were put down in a succession of massacres, and for his butchery and sustained suppression, Pereira d'Eça was rewarded and rose to the rank of general.

One consequence of this brutality was that Pereira d'Eça's name was attached to the village, which was the site of the slaughter; another consequence was the beheading of the warrior king, Mandume Ya Ndemufayo, and his severed head was exhibited for many years in the town. It was the sort of colonial decapitation favored by Mr. Kurtz, as Marlow saw in *Heart of Darkness:* "a half a dozen slim posts remained in a row, roughly trimmed, and with their upper ends ornamented with round carved balls." Not carved balls at all, of course, but the bare, sun-bleached skulls of Kurtz's enemies, put up to discourage anyone who might be tempted to transgress. In Shakespeare's time, the severed heads of wrongdoers were hung on London Bridge. In our own time, as revealed by evidence in the International Criminal Court trial of the warlord Charles Taylor, the bloody heads of villagers, cut off by child soldiers, were exhibited in Liberia and Sierra Leone. Mandume's head was displayed for so many years it too was whitened to bone by the elements and stared with a lipless grin.

The town was renamed, but that was not the end of its troubles. Throughout the 1980s it was the staging post for the South African army's parachute regiment — the Jackals, as they called themselves — in its war against Namibian guerrillas who launched their attacks from Angola. And Ondjiva saw fighting between Angolan factions and Cuban soldiers, too. It was no wonder that by the 1990s the town had been flattened and that so much of it now looked new. It was well supplied because all its building materials and vehicles, and most of its food, came from Namibia, down the road.

Just out of town, going north, the road deteriorated. For many long stretches it was impassable, and Camillo detoured through villages, allowing me a survey of traditional villages in this province of Kunene, featuring a fenced compound and courtyard known as a *kuimbo.* I had not seen anything like these in Namibia, but here in southern Angola not much had changed in spite of four hundred years of slavery, colonialism, military incursion, guerrilla activity, oil revenues, and the extensive charitable work by churches and NGOs. The HIV/AIDS figures were high — nearly 20 percent of the people in this province were infected. But otherwise it was the old Africa of mud huts, twig fences, bony cows, strutting roosters, and no lights — of the barefoot and the hard-up.

Off the road, weaving among the trees, we seemed to make good time. On the road, we were stopped by policemen or soldiers manning roadblocks. These were not the jolly, I-want-to-go-to-Chicago sort of sentries I'd seen in Namibia, but mean-faced, in some cases drunken, and well-armed men to whom Camillo — normally so jaunty and offensive — groveled.

"*Tu-passaporte,*" one of them always said to me, with a clawing of his greedy upraised fingers.

When we pulled off the road, the occupants of the car got out to relieve themselves. No one went far, not more than ten feet or so, all elbow to elbow, like a pissing contest, men with their feet apart and their pants open, women squatting with their skirts hiked up, the spattering sounds against the roadside gravel like water splashing from an old faucet and rivulets running from under them. Amid all this drizzling I saw Camillo conferring with the cops, handing over his papers, covertly passing money to one of the soldiers or policemen. Then I was given my passport back, and off we went.

This happened eight times, and Camillo, whom I had seen as an irritating person and a bad driver, shrank to a pathetic cringing size, and more toothless and poorer with each shakedown. Bribery is a way of life in Angola — the petty intimidation on the dirt road in the south being a reflection of the million-dollar bribes demanded by government ministers of the oil companies and the gold and diamond concessions. For a bribe you get nothing but a perfunctory assurance of safe passage, more like an entry fee or a toll than a payment for services. The sight of bribery on the back road of any country is a clear indication that the whole place is corrupt and the regime a thieving tyranny, as Angola has been for the thirty-five years of its independence — and likely much longer, since Portuguese colonial rule was also an extortion racket.

"Roadblock dictators," the brave journalist Karl Maier calls these men at checkpoints in his account of Angola's recent history of conflict, *Angola: Promises and Lies* (2007). "The [Angolan] checkpoint consists of two small red 'stop' signs facing opposite directions, two pieces of string." And the man there "sports that arrogant half-smile that is typical of Africa's roadblock dictators who have the power to decide whether unfortunate passers-by escape with their money, clothes and even their lives. From his swagger, he would be at home in Liberia, Nigeria, Mozambique or a dozen other countries where the line between police work and banditry is very fine indeed."

The roadblocks and bribes were blatant crookery, but they served a useful purpose too, because I was able to get out of the car, stretch my legs, and check our progress on the map. We had not gone far — I always asked the policemen where a certain town was, and I was surprised at how slowly we were going, how far we were from Lubango. I doubted we would get there anytime soon — certainly not tonight. *I want you to take over control, take over control . . .*

All this while we were passing the residue of the war — blown-up and burned tanks, tipped-over army trucks, rusted-out jeeps. The Cubans had been here, so had the South Africans, and the Namibians with their liberation army, SWAPO, the South West Africa People's Organization. Battles had been fought along this road and in various small towns. The South Africans had held some of the towns for long periods, and so had the Cubans — the Fidel Castro 50th Brigade. And with what result? Death on a huge scale, of course; thousands in Kunene province had died. Destruction too. And this twisted metal, the sort of expensive junk you see in the aftermath of all wars — the litter of it always seems like a deliberate memorial, left there to indicate the uselessness of the whole business. But no, it's just a junkyard with no larger significance, and in time it will all rust to nothing. The young men in this vehicle, Gilberto and João, told me that they had no memory of the war except the loud noises of artillery in the distance.

Then, as we made another stop — "*Cerveja!*" Camillo shouted — I was sure we wouldn't get to Lubango that day. At a small shop, a blockhouse faced with yellow stucco, under a spreading acacia tree, Camillo parked the car and bought a Cuca beer. I bought a soft drink, and would have bought more but there was nothing else, no other drinks, nothing to eat.

It was about five in the afternoon, the sun beginning to slant through the trees, dribbling gilded tints on the leaves and cones of light filled with gold dust. As we stood in the shade of the shop, Camillo began to curse. He walked angrily toward the Land Cruiser, and now I noticed that the Afrojack music had stopped, the idling engine had cut out, and apart from his cursing and the hum of insects we stood in unaccustomed silence.

This Land Cruiser had a diesel engine, was not easily pushable, and was perhaps impossible to restart without another battery. I saw Camillo at the wheel and the others kneeling behind and heaving. They put their shoulders against the rear of the vehicle and shoved it around the bare ground. The engine did not even flutter.

"*Ajuda!*" Camillo called out to me, asking for help, wanting me to kneel and push.

I shook my head and smiled. Sorry, pal.

They kept at it, failing at each attempt. There were no other cars nearby to boost the battery. I was not dismayed. I was sick of this trip and hated the music and now saw that Camillo was half drunk.

The day had gone quiet, the air was mild, the sun dimmed as it had dropped beneath the trees. I knew from the map that we were perhaps at a village called Uia, about thirty miles north of the settlement of Xangongo, which had been no more than a blur when we'd passed it. Too far to walk. Using what remained of the light, I walked to the road, hoping to flag down a car to take me south to Xangongo or north to Cahama—anywhere out from under this tree. But night was falling. I saw the man in the shop light a kerosene lamp, and I knew we were stuck in the bush.

12

—— —— —— ——

Three Pieces of Chicken

I N   T H E   L A S T   S L A N T E D softening of late afternoon light, against the squealy repeated note of one small insect's *cheep*, under the bird-haunted acacia tree towering over the bare trampled compound, and near Camillo's derelict-looking car — dirt footprints on its doors: Camillo had been kicking it barefoot in fury for its refusal to start — an old woman approached through the sun-lit risen dust.

She held a chipped enamel bucket in one hand and a long pair of metal tongs in the other. Her hair was wrapped like a bowl in a yellow cloth, this turban making her an unusual presence, giving her height and dignity and a look of quiet anticipation. She wore a limp blue dress that fell to her ankles ending in a tattered hem, and an apron that had once been white. She was barefoot, but her feet — her only indelicate feature — were as big and battered as shoes. No one paid any attention to her or to what she was carrying. In fact, Camillo stood aside, gripping a Cuca beer bottle as though he were about to throw it. His eyes were empty, and he looked less than futile. His body seemed uninhabited.

We had come north, crossing from Kunene province into Huíla province, but what did it matter? We were stuck for the night at least, and maybe longer. Light was leaking sideways from the sky from membranes of cloud, leaving purpled tissue just above the horizon.

The old woman made directly for me. "Old" was probably inaccurate: she was undoubtedly much younger than me, sixty or less, but had the aged face of a kindly crone. I was standing apart from the others, who were drinking, and perhaps drunk. I looked for a log to rest on, but saw nowhere to sit, and the car seemed cursed.

Holding the bucket up so I could examine its contents, the woman smiled at me and worked the jaws of her rusty tongs.

"*Boa tarde,*" she said, but it seemed more like evening to me.

At the bottom of the bucket were three pieces of chicken — legs attached to thighs. They were skinless, shiny-sinewed, and dark as kippers, as if they'd been smoked. Each one was covered by busy black flies, and flies darted around the hollow of the bucket. It was more a bucket of flies than a bucket of chicken.

Squeezing her rusty tongs again, the woman asked, "*Qual?*"

Which one?

Though I was hungry, I waved her away, retching at the thought of eating any of those chicken legs. Yet I had not eaten all day, and it had been a long and tiring journey, of harassment, of the border crossing, of the sight of misery and naked children playing in dust, flies crawling on their eyes and in the sores on their bodies. The off-road detours had been especially exhausting from the bucking and bumping of the vehicle. And the checkpoints, the shakedowns, the roadblock dictators.

The woman was smiling because I was smiling. The absurdity of "Which one?" had just struck me — three identical pieces of chicken in the dirty bucket, each of them specked by skittering flies; an existential question to the stranger in a strange land.

"*Não,*" I said. "*Obrigado.*"

Something in my smile encouraged her and kept her there, rocking a little, flexing her bruised toes, running her tongue against her lips to show patience. She was gaunt, and she herself looked hungry. But I said no again and, shoulders slackening in resignation, she turned away, making for the others, who were standing in a group still drinking bottles of Cuca beer.

A muscle twisted sharply in my stomach and yanked at my throat: the whip of hunger.

"*Olá!*" I said, and she turned to me, looking hopeful.

"That one," I said, pointing at the one with the fewest flies on it.

"*Frango,*" she said in a gummy voice, as though naming a delicacy, and she wet her lips with her tongue and swallowed, as people often do when handling food. Then the word spoken all over Angola for cool or okay, "*Fixe*" — feesh.

She folded my dollar and tucked it into her apron.

I borrowed Camillo's cigarette lighter and made a small fire of dead grass at the corner of the compound, and I passed the piece of chicken through the fire, believing like a Boy Scout that I was killing the fly-borne germs. Then I found the log I'd been looking for, and sat, and slowly ate the chicken. It was like chewing leather. The straps and thongs of sinew wouldn't break down, and its toughness made it almost indigestible, my chewing turning the meat into a rubber ball. Queasy over a meal he called a "mess of *bouillabaisse,*" Henry James said that it was "a formidable dish, demanding French digestion." Maybe I needed that. I was defeated by the food, and disgusted with myself for being in this position, and I mocked myself with a pompous phrase I'd heard a foodie use on a TV show: "I regret to say this dish is not fully achieved." But it was something in my stomach, and that was a victory in this hungry province.

Then I replayed my first glimpse of the bucket — the chicken, the flies, and the old woman asking "Which one?" It was the sort of choice you were faced with in Africa, but I had never seen it so stark, in the extravagant splashes of a florid sunset.

From the moment we arrived, this nameless place had seemed no more than a roadside clearing, the sort where locals might gather and linger because of its great sheltering tree. But we were alone. Only we entered the bar, which had perhaps started as a shop and run out of things to sell; it was a bar counter of warped planks, with beer bottles warming on a wooden shelf on the back wall. The man behind the counter sat with his chin resting on the planks and his arms wrapped around his head, cradling it.

What seemed vague and undefined in the failing light became distinct after sunset. In the dark, the kerosene lamp in the shed transformed the shed into a wide square lantern, sharpened its windows, casting bright shafts of light across the ground where a lame dog lay. The underside of the tree was brightened by the lamplight, and the road — which was a main road — was hidden in shadow. We were becalmed in the darkness of the bush, surrounded by chittering insects.

In the thin woods behind the shed there was a village, more audible than visible, for though I could see only the topmost licks of a high flaming bonfire, I could hear the rhythm of drumming, first as a patter and then what seemed a reply to the stuttering thud on a thick drumhead. The drums and not the fire made the village come alive.

The drumming was so insistent I needed only to jerk my thumb at its sound for the barman to reply, "*Cerimônia,*" and he smiled a little and caressed his head with his spidery fingers.

Though the word was plain enough, I did not speak more than a few words of Portuguese. This was a handicap, not merely because the country was generally Portuguese-speaking, but also because of its isolation from the world. Angola was an anomaly: apart from Portuguese, nothing else was spoken except for its many tribal languages, and these differed from province to province. Swahili and Chichewa, both of which I spoke, were usable in the western and northern provinces, but here I was linguistically lost.

Remembering that Cuban soldiers had fought all over Angola,

and especially in the south, I said, "*Habla Español?*" The barman smiled. I said, "English?" He smiled again and patted his head. As a joke, I said, "*Parla Italiano?*"

Behind me, I heard, "*Io parlo.*"

It was Gilberto, one of my fellow passengers. I said in Italian, "Really—you speak Italian?"

"*Sono stato in Italia per sei mese,*" he said. "*Anno passato.*" Six months, that was something. And his friends began to laugh because Gilberto was fairly drunk, and bare-chested, standing with his blue jeans tugged down so that his underwear showed. Whether this was street style or bush slovenliness I did not know. "A priest took me, with some other boys."

The priest was Italian, Gilberto said, a missionary in Angola, whose hometown was in Calabria, in the south of Italy, but whose friary was in Rome. Six boys went on the trip; Gilberto was about eighteen, and I assumed the others were the same age. They prayed at the Vatican, they visited the antique sights of Rome, they ate pasta, and they stayed at the friary.

I asked Gilberto whether the other priests talked to the Angolan boys.

"Yes. They were so nice to us! They took us to the beach"—to Ostia, the coast outside Rome. "They played football with us."

Sometimes a person tells you a story and you seem to hear it in stereo. The storyteller is enthusiastic and gives details and believes he is persuading you of its truth. But as the monologue continues, you hear a parallel story, translating the details differently, and in your imagining you see something else.

Gilberto's version was a jolly six months in Italy, paid for by the priest, a vacation from Angola. In my version, Gilberto was on a recruiting trip, the priest like a college coach showing football players around a campus, in order to dazzle them so they'd sign up for a place on the team. It is well known that parish priests are in short supply, and missionary priests even fewer, and that the next generation of Catholic vocations will not come from Europe or America but from Christian Kerala in south India, the Philippines, Latin America, and Africa.

After Rome, Gilberto and his friends traveled by train to southern Italy and stayed on a small farm, where they worked in the gardens, prayed, and went to church. They studied Italian most evenings, and were encouraged to speak it in the daytime.

"Lots of words in Italian are the same as Portuguese," Gilberto said, "so we didn't have a problem."

But Portuguese — notoriously nasal and slushy — lacks the crisp dentals and subtle labials of Italian, even if it shares an approximate Latinate vocabulary.

"You speak it well," I said. "Did the priest want you to join the missionaries?"

"He mentioned it a little. He said for us to think about it. Doing good work, helping Angola. God would tell us the rest." But Gilberto said this in passing. What he loved about Italy was the food, and he recounted the meals he'd eaten with such energy, describing the ingredients, that the others with us — João, Ronaldo, Camillo — listened with hungry, drunken impatience. I looked for Paulina but did not see her.

"What did you think about becoming a priest?"

"Angola is a Christian country. Most of the people are Catholic. We have so many churches!"

"Do you want to be a priest?"

He laughed. "I can't, because of this." He wagged his bottle of beer. "And I like women!" He repeated this in Portuguese for his friends, making them laugh.

We were standing outside, in the light that shot from the windows of the shed, the darkness all around us, the smell, which was a sharp hairiness of foul and turdy dirt. Cars had ceased to pass on the road as soon as night fell, though now and then someone wobbled by on a bicycle, the chain rattling in its sprockets.

"Ask that man where we are," I said, indicating the barman. "What town?"

He asked, the man explained. Gilberto said, "No town. We are near Uia. The big market and the petrol station are at Xangongo."

Camillo said, "*Zona verde.*"

I understood that, and liked it as a euphemism for the bush. *Zona verde* — everything that was not a city — summed up the Africa that I loved.

"What about the music?" I couldn't remember the Italian word for drumming, but he got the point when I imitated the sound: it was still loud. "Where is that coming from?"

"The village," Gilberto said, after conferring. "They are having a celebration. He told me what it is, but I don't know the word in Italian. It is *Efundula*" — and he spoke to the other boys. "Even in Portuguese we don't have the word *Efundula*. It is Oshikwanyama. These are Kwanyama people."

"Is it circumcision?"

"No. They don't do such things to girls here. *Efundula* is just for girls." He spoke again to the barman for guidance. "It goes on for four days. Yesterday was the last day, but they are still dancing. Sometimes they dance all night."

"Initiation?"

"Something like that."

The barman went on talking, and his explanation became elaborate, because he had unwrapped his hands and arms from his head and was gesturing, speaking in his own language and in Portuguese. Gilberto was smiling, the others were listening with interest, and then Gilberto put up his hand so he could tell me what the man had said.

"The dancing is strong because if a girl is pregnant, she won't be able to continue, and she will stop."

"They don't want pregnant girls?"

"Not for this *Efundula,* no."

"Ask him if we can go to the village and see it."

Gilberto didn't ask; he knew what the answer would be. "It is just for them. But you can listen."

We drank beer, we muttered, we listened, and then it occurred to me that if I didn't claim a place in the car I would have nowhere to sleep. While they were talking I went to the Land Cruiser. I cranked the seat back into a reclining position, covered myself with my jacket, and to the drumming in the distance and the muttering of the boys sitting on the steps of the shed I subsided into sleep. From time to time I awoke, and I was surprised by the gusto of the drumming, but in the darkest hours of the morning it ceased, and the silence, which was like apprehension, kept me awake until sunlight and heat filled the clearing.

In daylight the place was ugly, more littered and beat-up than it had seemed the day before. The boys had tossed their empty beer bottles aside and they lay scattered in the dust. Some grease-stained plastic wrappers were stuck to withered tufts of grass. And the tree that had seemed noble in its height and overhang looked vandalized — the lower trunk had been hacked at and carved with initials and numbers and names.

The look of Angola was not just the ugly little town and the slum of shacks but also the ruin of a brutalized landscape, of the stumps of deforestation and the fields littered with burned-out tanks, of rivers and streams that seemed poisoned — black and toxic. And not the slightest glimpse of any animal but a cow or a cringing dog. In most parts of the southern African bush you at least saw small antelopes or gazelles tittuping in the distance on slender legs. The impala was everywhere, and it was almost impossible to imagine a stretch of savanna without the movement of such creatures. And wherever there were villages, there were always scavengers, hyenas or intrusive baboons.

But no wild animals existed in the whole of Angola. One effect of the decades-long civil war here was that the animals that had not been eaten by starving people had been blown up by old land mines.

The extermination of wild game had been complete. Now and then cows in pastures were shredded by exploding mines, and so were children playing and people taking shortcuts through fields.

A country without wild animals seems inconceivable, because many animals in Africa, antelopes especially, are prolific, reproducing in such large numbers they are able to establish sustainable herds in the unlikeliest places. But the long war had wasted them, the hungry Angolans had eaten them, eaten the hippos, even the crocs, and if there were snakes, I did not see any. Oddly, the bird life was thin too. Even where the landscape was not picked apart, where some trees had been spared, the absence of animals — and the presence of squatting, oppressed, if not defeated-looking, humans — made these places in *zona verde* seem mournful, violated, with an After-the-Fall atmosphere. Something inexplicably deleted from them had sapped their vitality.

In the land without animals, humans were more conspicuous and seemed to exist in greater variety, many of them, in their destitution, taking the place of wildlife, living at the edges of settlements in low simple shelters that were like the twiggy brakes that some animals huddled against.

Walking around this compound in the early morning saddened me and made me impatient. With the sun striking from above the tall grass, the heat took hold, and I had the fugitive thought again: What am I doing here?

I heard the dull clink of metal against metal, and saw the old woman in the yellow turban approaching with her bucket and tongs. I welcomed the sight of her, and said good morning. She swung her bucket up and lifted her tongs over it with the panache of a magician producing a little miracle out of the container.

"*Frango.*" The two remaining pieces at the bottom were more flyblown than the day before, perhaps because I had eaten one of them and the flies, deprived of their meat, had settled on the other two pieces: less chicken, more flies.

I gave the women a dollar and clumsily asked her name.

"Ana Maria," she said.

Seeing that Gilberto was up and stumbling, I called him over to translate.

He greeted the woman politely and smiled at my brushing flies from the chicken leg in my hand.

"Gilberto, ask her if she knows about the ceremony in the village."

"She knows," he said, translating my question. "She says it is the *Efundula.*"

"Did she see the dancing and drumming?"

"She heard it. It is for the girls. But the important person is an old man. This old man comes from another village."

"What does *Efundula* mean?"

The old woman's explanation in Portuguese was lengthy, but Gilberto listened with recognition. He said, "We have this in my home village, but it has a different name. It means the girls become women — ready for marriage. They are decorated, they dance, they sing, sometimes they cook some food." Now I couldn't tell whether he was describing the ceremony at his village or the one here. "The girls wear special clothes, they rub them with a certain oil from a tree. They decorate their hair, they wear shells in the hair."

"Ask this woman how long the ceremony lasts."

"It is four days."

He hadn't asked the woman. He was speaking from his own experience, so I encouraged him to ask the woman for details.

"Four days," he said, after she explained. "Each day has a name. She tells me in Oshikwanyama, but I don't know the words." He conversed with her some more, nodding as she spoke, then he nodded and said to me, "Yes. The first day is 'the Sleeping of the Chickens.' Yesterday they call 'the Day of Love.' The music we heard was that."

To have arrived by accident in this remote and stricken place and to have discovered myself in the presence of a traditional initiation rite was just wonderful, the kind of luck I had always depended on in travel. I knew nothing of the region. I did not know then that the Kwanyama people were related to the Ovambo in Namibia, and that they dominated this province. All I knew was that the war had been fought here—the wrecked vehicles were everywhere; that the villagers had been routed and the towns destroyed; that South Africans, Cubans, and the guerrilla army of Jonas Savimbi, UNITA (the National Union for the Total Independence of Angola), had crept back and forth, torching villages, massacring and beheading civilians; and that this had gone on for almost thirty years.

How amazing after all that chaos and death to find, in the persistence of memory, this enduring ceremony with its particular names and purpose. A girl's initiation into womanhood was common all over sub-Saharan Africa. In Malawi, the ceremony for girls who had experienced their first menstruation (and thus were regarded as ready for childbearing) was called *Ndakula* ("I have grown up") and included a course of sexual instruction—how to please your man. As for Kenya, I was walking with a Masai man in the Masai Mara Reserve one September a few years ago, near the hot springs settlement in the Loita Hills called Maji Moto, and we came across a group of young girls out fetching water. They whooped when they saw us. One of them came boldly forward, laughing; she wore an ornate headpiece, partly a coronet that had a fringe of white beads that jiggled against her forehead. I remarked on this to the Masai spearman who was guiding me, and he told me that this headpiece advertised the fact that she had been *emuratare*—circumcised, he explained—the word was the same for both males and females. He said that the other girls with her were children, but that she was a woman. "She can be married now." He became indignant when I questioned the cutting, the purpose of which was to eliminate a woman's sexual pleasure.

But clitoridectomy, also known as female genital mutilation, widespread among the Masai and many other African peoples, was not a feature of the Kwanyama initiation ceremony in the nearby village. The practitioners of genital mutilation nearest to this settlement were the Himba people, who straddled the Angola-Namibia border, a hundred miles southwest of where we were squatting.

Gilberto was still talking to the old woman, and was so engrossed that he had stopped translating into Italian so I could follow it. I sat and made another small fire, trying to kill the germs on the piece of chicken, then I ate it slowly. Afterward I joined Gilberto and the old woman again. When I interrupted, Gilberto smiled and, seeming to remark on what the woman had been telling him, said, "Very interesting!"

Hardly eight o'clock and the day was already hot, and the sun-baked soil yielded a strong smell of decay. Camillo was yawning. He lifted the front of his shirt and wiped the sweat from his face, then he nodded at me, indicating hello. The red Land Cruiser sat immobilized in the center of the compound, dusty footprints on its doors. It was now part of the scene, the wrecked vehicle that seemed a feature of every Angolan settlement. I had no idea why it wouldn't start, but I did not notice any urgency in the others to fix it.

A few cars and motorcycles had begun to pass by on the road. I was tempted to hitchhike to Xangongo, and though on my map it seemed a sizable place, my maps had misled me many times before: a boldfaced name on the road map was often no more than a name. If I saw a bus, I could flag it down, and then I could continue on my way to Lubango.

But I was in no particular hurry. I felt sure that the nearby village, the one of the drums and the dancing, would have some food. And I was curious to know more about the ceremony, apparently having finished its last ritual the night before. My phone didn't work here; I had not bought an Angola SIM card or minutes. But even if it had worked, it would not have helped — it would only have reminded me of my predicament. Anyway, I knew that Camillo wanted to get his vehicle and the rest of the passengers to Lubango eventually; all

I had to do was stay with him. These people needed to eat too, so something was bound to turn up.

"I'm going for a walk," I said to Gilberto. "I'll be back in an hour."

"We won't leave without you," he said.

Needing to rouse myself, and seeing that there was a small river marked on my map (and with a name: Techiua), I walked north along the road to see whether I could find it. My bag was in the car, but I carried my small briefcase with my passport, my important papers, and my money. If someone stole my bag with my clothes inside, I could easily buy more. Some children tagged along ("*Senhor! Senhor!*"), and when I asked them about the river, they ran ahead, urging me to follow.

It wasn't far, and it ran under a bridge on the road. Hardly a river, it was more like a stream, about as wide as a two-lane road. Several things interested me about it. The first was that women were washing clothes at the edge of it, slapping and twisting them and cramming them into plastic basins. Another was that some children were bathing in it. And midstream, a man was standing in a dugout canoe, poling it along, seemingly on a fishing trip. It was a scene from old Africa — not the Africa of rappers and cell phoners, but the idyllic-seeming Africa of rural serenity.

But of course it was not idyllic at all. It was the Angola of hardship and penury. More than half the country's population of twenty-three million lived below the poverty line, and I was looking at about thirty of those people. If there were any edible fish of a good size in the river, I would have been surprised, and the river itself was so muddy that laundering and bathing seemed pointless activities. The smell of the river, the pong of stagnation, penetrated the air and clouded the bridge with stink. Yet the sunlight was beautiful, scattering the surface of the water with gold flakes.

"*Senhor!*" The children wanted me to go down the embankment with them. They saw that I was studying it closely, and when I got there they'd demand money for having guided me.

But I'd seen enough—and the dugout canoe looked like the sort of tribal artifact you'd find in a museum. If anyone boasted of Angola's oil-rich prosperity, I could say that I'd seen this: hungry, half-naked people on the stinking banks of a muddy river.

The children stopped following me when I returned to the clearing, to the log where I'd been sitting to eat the chicken leg. Camillo had opened the hood of the Land Cruiser and was picking distastefully at greasy wires. Now that I had something to write, I took out my notebook. I continued my abbreviated narrative, picking up from where I'd left off, describing the hotel on the Namibian side of the border at Ondangwa and the business of the crossing, the harassment, and the shakedowns. As usually happens when I am writing, several hours passed without my noticing it, and while I worked some children approached me with baskets of bananas.

I was still writing when Gilberto came over and said, "You have a camera?"

Not a real camera, just the one in the iPhone I'd brought on the trip. But I could not access the Internet or make a call. I had the $20 phone I'd bought from Mr. Khan in Otjiwarongo, and had hopes of using it sometime when I'd fitted it with an Angola connection card. In the meantime, I occasionally played music that I'd stored on my iPhone. I seldom took pictures, but I often paged sadly through photos of my loved ones, feeling like an astronaut reminding himself of Earth.

"Yes," I said, and thought: Why do I so seldom take pictures? I was glad he had reminded me.

Behind him, a man in a red soccer jersey and brown trousers, wearing stylish glasses, was looking at me. He was young, probably in his twenties, and would have seemed very tough except for his hopeful smile. An older, fleshier woman in a black dress, with tightly braided hair and a necklace of blue beads, stood near him, and she seemed to have an imploring expression too.

I noted the way they were dressed because of what I saw next:

three skinny girls, bare from the waist up, but childlike, almost boyish. Their most striking feature was an extravagant coiffure of beads and shells; it was as though they did not have hair at all but thick multiple strings and loops of beads hanging from their heads, cascades of tiny white shell-like beads, woven into their hair so densely their hair was invisible. They wore knee-length wraparound skirts of brightly patterned cloth, and necklaces too, thick clusters of strands.

They pressed in close, the way kittens sidle up to you and rub against your legs, with an obliging head movement. They laughed with the boldness that costumed people often have, the finery or the disguise giving them confidence. They were like children at a fancy dress party, even if all the beads made them seem pharaonic, gotten up in an ancient style. They were admired by the much-younger girls, the urchins who surrounded these compliant and unlettered nymphs.

The man said something to Gilberto, who relayed it to me, this time in English: "Take photo."

Children at a fancy dress party—that's exactly what they were. They were the girls—so the man in the sunglasses said—who had been initiated in the village over the past four days, and for some weeks before that. None looked older than thirteen, but it was their fate to have menstruated—it is said to happen earlier to girls in the bush—so they had been selected for the ceremony.

"What's that word for the ceremony, Gilberto?"

"*Efundula*," he said.

The others heard, and laughed. Now a crowd had gathered—people from the village, older women and men, and the much younger girls looking adoringly at these decorated initiates, as if proudly at big sisters.

I used my iPhone camera to get close to them, so I could examine the beaded coiffures, and I showed the pictures to the man in the soccer jersey, who smiled at them approvingly. Then I touched the beads, with a querying expression.

"*Elende*," the man said, giving me the word for the decorated hair.

Their alikeness was a thrill: three nymphs, the Three Graces, a trio of skinny girls standing side by side, their arms around one another, representing beauty, charm, sweetness. The ordeal of their initiation was over, and now they were in the world, pleased with themselves, approved of by their elders. The smallest of the three — she seemed a mere child, an androgynous one; she could have been a skinny boy — had loops of green and blue beads in her hair and a yellow necklace.

I asked their ages. Gilberto translated — "Fourteen or fifteen" — yet none of them seemed that age. They had to be younger. I pressed him again, and he talked to the older people.

"They want to be married," Gilberto said. He spoke in Portuguese, to the crowd. The people laughed and pointed at me. Gilberto said, "You can take one!"

Seeing my expression, the people laughed harder.

"I have some questions," I said. I asked Gilberto to relay them to the man who'd requested photos. He didn't want copies of the photos; he merely wished to formalize the event in pictures — and the girls were gloating over the pictures as I put my questions to him. "Can I visit the village?"

He said yes, and we filed past the shed and through the trees on a narrow path that led across hacked-open furrows that seemed like gardens in preparation. I smelled the dead embers of the fire and saw the first row of huts, most of them woven in a latticework of intertwined sticks and stripped boughs, some of them with tin roofs and others thatched with hay bundles. This was the traditional fenced compound known as a *kuimbo*, which I'd seen from a distance farther south. I looked for a place to sit, because I wanted to write, and when I found a tree stump, the three ornamented girls pressed against me again, laughing, and a woman brought me a bunch of bananas.

"What will happen to the girls now?" I asked Gilberto, who repeated the question.

"They will look for a husband. They will have children. They are women now."

Nevertheless, they looked like children to me — young children, three schoolgirls. I asked if the ceremony was over.

"No," the man said. There was more, but it was for fun, not a test, not the all-night dancing to exhaust them. They would rub themselves with powdered ash to whiten their skin. And this, part of the masquerade, would allow them privileges. He implied that with their freshly coated faces they could assert themselves. I tried to imagine these three girls whitened with ash, with their coiffure of beads and their heavy necklaces and short skirts, and it seemed a vision in tribal maquillage of pretty painted coquettes — which was in fact the whole intention. Beautify them, get them dancing, give them approval and some instruction, and send them flashing out of the village to snare a husband. But a husband was merely a means to an end. As in much of the region, the object of womanhood was to bear a child: a woman without a child was not really a woman, and had no status. A man could get rid of her, send her back to her parents, if she proved to be barren.

In Angola, as in many societies I knew, you were not an adult until you got married, but the marriage was only speculative; it became real when you gave birth to a child. Maybe this sort of thinking was an underlying factor in teen pregnancies in the United States, which were often seen as accidental. Perhaps there was something calculated in it, a wish to have a place in the world, in the sense it was regarded here in Angola: the fast track to adulthood was finding a likely man and having a child. The anthropologist Merran McCulloch put it nicely, writing of a related Angolan people, the

Ovimbundu: "A child or an adolescent is only a 'potential' person (*omunu*)" (*The Ovimbundu of Angola*). Motherhood and fatherhood made them whole. But there was an unintended consequence: complications associated with childbirth were the leading cause of death ("maternal death") among girls thirteen to sixteen years old in this part of Africa (World Health Organization report, March 2012).

I sat and nibbled bananas while a woman boiled water in a blackened pot and put some dry leaves in it and pronounced it tea. Gilberto had wandered away, so it was impossible for me to communicate except in gestures. Instead, I hauled out my iPhone and we went through the photos again, and the Three Graces smiled at themselves and twiddled their beaded locks with slender fingers and seemed to me birdlike and beautiful.

The cliché for them was nubile. And nubile was exactly what they were: in their case it was not a cliché at all but a precise description, because nubility denotes adulthood; "nubile" means marriageable. The word comes from the Latin *nubere,* to marry, and this rite of passage, the *Efundula,* was a nubility ceremony that recognized their capacity to bear children and made them eligible for marriage. The event itself, more than a coming-of-age ritual, was a sort of marriage initiation. But the taking of a husband, an inevitable consequence, involved much less drama. That could happen any time now, and the sooner the better, because these girls had achieved the desired condition. Our word "nuptial," which people tend to smile at as pretentious, is derived from the same glowing word "nubile."

Some details I discovered afterward, in books on kinship of the Kwanyama and related tribal groups, such as the nearby Kwamatwi, who hold a similar ceremony in which a ranking woman cries out "*Wafukala!*" — "You became nubile!" That in one of the rituals on the second day ("the Day of the Little Jackal") the girls drink beer mixed with the semen of the man presiding over the ceremony. That the profusion of beads has a purpose beyond ornament, because beads are seen to promote fertility. That, as an elaboration of the whitening of the skin, the initiates repeat a saying: "To a white person" — that is, one powdered with ashes — "nothing is prohibited."

They'd find husbands soon enough. They were very pretty, and being young, they were strong; they'd be useful working in the gardens and raising children, and this being sub-Saharan Africa, they'd be doing both at the same time. The fiancé would pay a dowry, of money or a cow, and for this he'd have his own field hand for life. Once this transaction is settled, the wedding is understood; the man takes her home.

"There is no solemn nuptial procession," Carlos Estermann writes in his definitive study of the Kwanyama people, *The Ethnography of Southwestern Angola*, which was first published in Portuguese in 1956. Estermann was an Alsatian priest, linguist, photographer, and anthropologist who sailed from Lisbon to Angola in 1923, did fieldwork in the southern provinces, became a full-time ethnographer in 1951, lived for nine years among the Kwanyama, and, undaunted by the civil war, remained in Angola. He noted that in the Kwanyama court the royal jester or buffoon was always a tiny Bushman. As late as 1976, Estermann was studying spirit possession in the region, his anthropological investigations far exceeding his missionary zeal.

Estermann goes on: "That night she shares the bed of her betrothed, who is now considered to be her husband. The consummation of the marriage is not accompanied by any ritual, nor is it made known, unless very discreetly. In this connection it may be said that the Kwanyama do not concern themselves with the bride's virginity. It is a thing that is not spoken of, and there is no word in their language to express that quality or the physiological sign of it."

I found that informative book later, and it clarified some aspects of the ritual, but at the time I was content with what I'd seen. The man in the red soccer jersey, whose name was João, brought me a chair, and in comfort I stayed in the village until early afternoon. I was happy. I wasn't hungry anymore. I was just tired enough to be relaxed. Seeing that I was fascinated, the three girls stayed teasingly, almost flirtatiously, in my orbit. It seemed that this was my purpose in coming to Africa, to spend a night and day like this, and I would have been delighted to stay longer. I liked being in a village; they had food here, and shade, and places to rest. I knew enough of the scavenging and precarious life of the road to hate it.

In the heat of the afternoon, around two o'clock, Gilberto called out to me, "*Andiamo!*" His speaking Italian made the villagers laugh.

I said goodbye, thanked the elders, and quietly gave each of the girls some dollars.

Leaving the perimeter of the village, I saw blue-black smoke blowing from the exhaust pipes of the Land Cruiser, Camillo revving the engine.

Nearby, staring at me, the old woman Ana Maria stood with her bucket, and I knew what was in it. Out of politeness, I looked in, and now the mass of flies covered the remaining piece of chicken, which was familiar to me in all its contours, but more dark-specked and bitten by the flies, which were familiar too.

"*Frango*," Ana Maria said in her hungry juicy way, swallowing a little.

She was gaunt. She looked hungry and tired. I gave her a dollar. I took her tongs and ceremonially removed the last piece of chicken from the bucket. I made a formal business of waving it around and brushing the flies from it. Then I gestured with it to her, as though flourishing a scepter, and put it back in the bucket. She understood: this would be her next meal. She smiled with gratitude and touched her heart with her skinny fingers.

Camillo blew his horn, calling me from this happy little chicken interlude: back to the road.

13

Volunteering in Lubango

THAT AMBIGUOUS, SOMEWHAT startling, stumbled-into occasion of the *Efundula* ceremony of the Kwanyama stayed with me, for its unexpectedness and its vitality — for its ritual aspects too, because so much that I saw in Angola was improvised or imported or crooked. Angola's rich — the few — were greedy walled-in plutocrats and dandies, while its poor — the many — were exhausted and cynical and living in squalor. But in the Angolan bush I had found remnants of traditional life radiating energy, even if (as in the case of the Kwanyama people) that energy consumed its maidens, turning young girls into coquettes so that they might attain a life of domestic drudgery and a brood of malnourished children.

Back on the road — but not really a road at all — we made a succession of detours, the usual Angolan snakes-and-ladders route along arbitrary tracks, many of them deep troughs of muck, flooded in this mud season of sudden rains. The zigzagging did not take us quickly, but it was all a revelation to me. We coursed through villages mostly. We were seldom near the notional road, part of which was being graded by enormous loud chewing-and-rolling machines, and the rest abandoned or nonexistent, a waste motion (creation, destruction) that was brought to perverse perfection in many areas of Angolan life. It was as if this mechanism imitated Portuguese colonial futility, for surely no colonial power was ever so politically arrogant and culturally insufficient — Portugal's obsolescence, bumbling, and antique mind-set producing a rarefied and conceited cruelty that was Angola's inheritance.

And it was strange in this vehicle to be traveling so intimately with village people, passing at times in a ten-foot space between a mud hut and a clothesline, and just missing the big yellow woven mats on which fat red peppers were drying in the sun, arrayed like firecrackers, a surprised face in the hut window or a scowling one from a man with his pants at his ankles, squatting at the trench edge of his open-sided latrine.

A different Camillo emerged on this stretch of the trip, a kindlier one. At a village remote from the road he slowed down, recognizing a familiar figure ahead, and it had to have been someone he knew: a crippled man, one leg missing, possibly a land mine victim, who swayed under a tree. Rolling to a stop, Camillo gave him some crushed kwanza notes and a handful of mangled bread slices — the first indication I'd had that he had squirreled away food in the car. It happened again some miles later, another mutilated man, this one wearing a red smock, Camillo pausing in the drive to hand over bread crusts.

Deeper in the bush at a cluster of huts, a boy approached with a bird, a green parrot he wanted to sell. Camillo took it and examined it closely, wiggled one of the parrot's legs, demonstrating that it was broken (probably in the boy's snare), and gave it back as unacceptable. Soon Camillo reverted to his old crapulous self, becoming a loud, red-eyed drunk.

On the slabs of torn-up mud and the deep, water-filled potholes and wallows of these bush tracks, we traveled slowly, to my relief.

And a new song was playing in the car, this one sweeter than "Take Over Control." The words were "Marry me," sung in an Angolan accent: *Meddy me, meddy me, I love you . . .*

And so we went bouncing and swerving, cross-country, through the villages of Huíla province, music blaring. At intervals of twenty miles or so Camillo stopped, I thought so that we could find food — some villagers ran toward us with bananas — but it was for him to buy more beer. Camillo drank steadily, and fifty miles into the trip he was drunk, drooling, shouting to the music.

At several stops the villagers appeared with small bags of fried potatoes, slick with grease in the tight dirty plastic. I said no, but was hungry, and like the pieces of chicken that had turned my stomach the day before, the slimy potatoes began to look appetizing. So I gave in and ate, and disgusted myself, and surrendered to the noise, the bad driving, and the heat.

New passengers had gotten on, the vehicle was overloaded, and in the back a crying baby and a screaming woman — the baby's mother, I assumed — were quarreling with two shouting boys. You naturally wonder at such a time whether this trip was necessary, and answering my own question, I concluded, Yes. I had vowed not to take a plane, vowed to travel overland, and although it was uncomfortable in this beat-up Land Rover, and the fighting among the passengers was annoying (and made worse by Camillo's drunken swerving), I was passing through the hinterland of Angola, which I had always longed to see because so little had been written about it — nothing, really, except out-of-date war stories.

Beyond the town of Cahama, where the road improved, we were at a higher altitude — cooler, greener, taller trees, hills in the distance that were lumpy and flat-topped, some like anvils, others like plump loaves of bread, some with green skirts. Bellied-out spinnakers of clouds blew along, high in the blue sky. The great surprise to me were the few signs of colonial buildings — a scattering of ruined shops, an occasional abandoned farmhouse, the thick walls and tile roofs of the sort of rustic peasant construction you might see in the cottagey countryside of northern Portugal. In a way, that was the whole story of the Angolan hinterland: Portugal had exported its brutalized criminals and illiterate peasants and made them into *colonos,* first to enslave and deport Africans and then to lord it over the Africans who remained. The walls of the small farmhouses were broken, the roofs fallen in, and the tiles smashed. Yet there were only a handful of such buildings in fifty or seventy-five miles of travel — this in a country that had been a colony for more than four hundred years.

Some of the houses were smashed to pieces because their occupants had bolted, or had been driven away, as independence approached in the 1970s. But also, like the whole of southern Angola, this had been a war zone for decades. Here, between Cahama and Xangongo, the South African army, in a major offensive in 1983 (Operation Askari), had battled Namibian SWAPO guerrillas who were massing, intending to push south across the border to liberate their own country, South-West Africa. And many of these houses had been booby-trapped, and the fields strewn with land mines. It is estimated that twenty million mines were planted in Angola by all sides during the long conflict.

But white settlement in Angola had never been great, and in the bush, white *colonos* had always been thin on the ground. Almost from the beginning, its first landfall by the great Portuguese navigator Diogo Cão, in 1482, Angola was viewed as nasty, unhealthy, and violent, filled with poisonous air and savage people — "the white man's grave" of the cliché. What the Portuguese wanted from Angola was what nearly all colonialists wished for: gold and slave labor. The weirdness of Portuguese settlement is well described by Gerald Bender in *Angola Under the Portuguese: The Myth and the Reality* (1978). Angola began as a penal colony. From the late fifteenth century to the 1920s, Angola was a dumping ground for Portuguese criminals, convicts known as *degredados* — exiles. These men were Angola's civilizers and colonists.

It is impossible to understand Angola without knowing something of the Portuguese character. Like Ireland, Portugal was for centuries an exporter of its peasants, a maker of exiles — fugitives from the mother country and so oppressive in its colonies that it turned Africans into exiles too. Portugal has been described by the English traveler and literary critic V. S. Pritchett as "practical, stoical, shifty, its pride in its great past, its pride in pride itself raging inside like an unquenchable sadness." To that list of qualities I would add archaic and obsolete. As for Portugal being practical, it should also be said that Angola was the only African country that began its colonial existence as a penal settlement, Angola being Portugal's own version of Siberia, a jail.

Bullying and predatory criminals are natural despots, and many of the exiled Portuguese convicts became important slave traders. They were well suited to the diabolical task, since they had been schooled in Portugal (and its other colonies) as thieves, con men, and murderers, efficient as persecutors and intimidators. The convicts were not a mere ragtag oppressed element who had been (like the exiles in early Australia) persecuted in their poverty and convicted of petty crimes. They were ruthless villains, all male (a third of the exiles to Australia were female), who formed the core group of Angola's colonists, promoted, after the long voyage, from the criminal class to the ruling class. The crooks had to be the colonizers of Angola because so few other Portuguese wanted to live there. They served as slave traders until Portugal outlawed slavery in 1878, and then they transitioned as exploiters by engaging in the forced labor system (bamboozling Africans, burdening them with indebtedness), which was in most cases more abusive than slavery.

Since slaves could not be exported abroad, where slavery was illegal, other forms of slavery or imposed servitude remained in place within the colony. Forced labor in Angola continued until 1961 (a year of uprising in Angola for that very reason), and it was then that devastating reports were published about the punitive labor conditions. "'I need to be given Blacks' is a phrase which I frequently heard from *colonos*," Marcelo Caetano (later to be Portugal's prime minister) wrote in 1946. "As if the Blacks were something to be given!" None of this is ancient history. In the early 1960s, around the time I became a teacher in soon-to-be-independent Nyasaland, a colonial high inspector in Angola, Henrique Galvão, wrote with passionate contempt, "Only the dead [in Angola] are really exempt from forced labor."

Before 1900 virtually all Portuguese settlers remained in the coastal towns, decrying the interior as dangerous for its wild animals and hostile Africans. As late as 1950 there were fewer than three thousand Portuguese farmers in the entire country, some of them upcountry in smallholdings. But they were unproductive and demoralized, dependent on Portuguese government assistance and African forced labor.

Although over many years Portugal tried numerous rural settlement plans to encourage *colonos* to take up farming, nearly all the attempts ended in failure, and only the (foreign-operated) diamond mines, and later (foreign-operated) oil production, allowed Angola to be viable. The white population, predominantly male and coastal, aspired to petty trade, shop owning, and barkeeping. The Portuguese had tried to create a capital, Nova Lisboa (now Huambo), in the center of the country, but that too had not amounted to much. The proof that the Angolan interior was largely unsettled by *colonos* was obvious here on the main road in Huíla province — empty, undeveloped, the few colonial houses (none dating from earlier than 1950) tumbled to the ground or bombed out.

The upside of neglect, indifference, contempt, and underdevelopment was a landscape that was green and practically empty of villages — great swaths of grassland, wooded hills, and stretches of bush that had once been battlefields but had become overgrown and depopulated. Amazing that the centuries of colonization and the decades of war had left no mark; and if you did not take the mood of people and the traumas of their history into account, you could almost be uplifted by the sight of lovely green hills and the apparent purity of the place.

We stopped for beer and hard-boiled eggs at Chibia. Some local traders were heading home from the improvised market. They were cattle-raising Mwila people who lived outside of Chibia, less than thirty miles from Lubango, and still smeared themselves with animal fat, coated their hair with mud and cow dung, creating dreadlocks, and wore necklaces of shells and of hardened mud. Of course there were no wild animals, and the road was a horror, but seen from the green bosom of this huge province, it was all like picture-postcard southern Africa, an Eden.

That was before we climbed the *planalto* — the chilly high plateau of the southern highlands — and rolled into the distant outskirts of Lubango, the shantytowns and cinderblock huts, the shacks and roadside market vendors, the squatter areas that were scoured of all greenery and — fuel-deprived — deforested for firewood. Only slums surrounded this southern city. The word in Angola for slum, or shantytown, or "informal settlement," is *musseque* — meaning "red earth," the sandy soil on which the shacks were usually built, a word suggesting an infertile and blighted place, a wasteland. Not a bush or a blade of grass remained among the *musseques* of Lubango, but for miles it was heaving with people.

I thought: I have been here before.

Another African city, another horror, more chaos — glary light, people crowding the roads, the stinking dust and diesel fumes, the broken fences, the vandalized shop fronts, the iron bars on all the display windows, the children fighting, the women heavily laden, and no relief in sight.

By now Camillo was helplessly drunk, legless and incoherent, and I was glad to get out of the car and away from the quarreling passengers and the hideous music. He began to pick a fight with me as I left him, claiming that I owed him money. He screamed at me on a Lubango back street, but his drunkenness made him distractible, and I simply slipped away down the shattered sidewalks of this cold and overripe-smelling city.

The following day, the Lubango streets were empty. It was a national holiday, Dia de Finados, or Dia de Defuntos — Day of the Deceased, Day of the Defunct. In the socialist revolutionary republic of Angola, holy All Souls' Day of the Catholic liturgical calendar was a feast day, equal to Easter and Christmas, observed with the same solemnity as Colonial Repression Martyrs' Day (January 4) or Day of the Armed Struggle (February 4). Every shop was closed. The restaurants were shut. No one worked.

"This is a very Christian country," an Angolan explained to me that day. "Even during our war the churches were not attacked. People sheltered in them and they knew they would be safe."

Where am I?, I thought. Nothing to do on the Day of the Defunct except walk around this high sloping city, reflecting on my trip. What am I doing here?

Lubango lay sprawled across a plateau at almost six thousand feet. The weather was pleasant now, in November, but in the Angolan winter of July and August — so the locals complained — it was cold enough in this region for people to wear heavy coats, and some days frost crystals had to be scraped from windows and windshields.

Until independence, the town was called Sá da Bandeira, named for a Portuguese nobleman, Bernardo de Sá Nogueira de Figueiredo, the first marquess of Sá da Bandeira, who in the 1830s became an idealistic (that is, anti-slavery) prime minister. And then the town reverted to its traditional name, Lubango. Toward the end of the colonial period, Sá da Bandeira had attracted emigrants from Madeira (they didn't know the colony was doomed), another hurried project and instant failure of Angolan settlement.

Ten miles south, at Humpata, Boer trekkers had put down stakes in the late nineteenth century and farmed, and some were buried there, in a little fenced-in cemetery I found one day in the middle of a cornfield. The *colonos* hated the interior for its remoteness and for the arduous work necessary to grow crops. It was a long, slow trip from the coast. Lubango's only attraction — and it is still the iconic picture associated with the place — is the precipitous valley, formed of a volcanic fissure, the sheer rock cliffs and the chasm called Tunda-Vale, the view west across the plains: a scenic spot with a lovely panorama that was outside town, on a bad road that was being improved.

My hotel was a pretty good example of the state of the nation. Newly built, it was a walled-in compound of gardens, terraces, and low, elegant-seeming buildings. But half the lights in my room did not work, I could not open any windows, the bathroom stank. In the public areas, some foreign guests conferred in whispers — all businessmen (briefcases, cell phones, brisk mannerisms, hand-shakes). The restaurant was good, the rooms were expensive, and I was eager to leave after one night. I moved to the rundown, seedy Grand Hotel da Huíla, in the center of town, which was less than half the price of the new hotel.

Only its name was grand. The food was terrible and the hotel was practically empty, even a bit ghostly, but the Grand was friendly and clean, and I could sit on the veranda by the big cracked waterless swimming pool and write undisturbed.

Nothing had been written about travel in the interior of Angola, nothing I had read that described what I had seen on the back roads. The Angola story that reached the world was a condemnation of Portuguese colonial abuses, or a history of the long civil war, or amazement at the phenomenal oil profits. This alone made me glad I was here. The business visitors to Angola were efficient, tactful, and noncommittal, and many of them were rather tight-faced and (so they intimated to me) anxious to leave. They did not describe the country except to their companies back home. Angola had no other travelers, no backpackers, no birdwatchers, no anthropologists or political scientists, no casual visitors, no idle wanderers like me — none that I could see.

Books about Angola were typically accounts of warfare and crisis, most of them outdated. The best-known one in English, Ryszard Kapuściński's *Another Day of Life,* is a breathless narrative of the capital, Luanda, and some desperate excursions into the bush, during the war in the mid-1970s. It is harrowing, very short, partisan, and vague on details. *Bay of Tigers* by Pedro Rosa Mendes recounts a 1997 trans-Angola (and trans-Africa) trip; it is eloquent, impressionistic, surreal in places, but even vaguer on details than Kapuściński. Most books about Angola are relentlessly political, because its history is a chronicle of violent crises, interspersed with long periods of colonial torpor or brutality. The lengthy civil war was extensively reported by journalists at the time. But I found that it was seldom discussed now. Most Angolans are too young to have experienced the worst of the war and too distracted by their poverty to care. The subject on the minds of most Angolans I met was money — how to get it, where to spend it, and please could they have some of mine?

In this country without foreign travelers, without foreign tourists, I had penetrated to the small city of Lubango and was sitting on the veranda of its old hotel, becalmed by the Day of the Defunct. What now?

I'm beginning to think that this sort of travel experience is mainly fantasy, I wrote in my notebook that day. *Many travelers are essentially fantasists. Tourists are timid fantasists, the others — risk takers — are bolder fantasists. The tourists at Etosha conjure up a fantastic Africa after their nightly dinner by walking to the fence at the hotel-managed waterhole to stare at the rhinos and lions and eland coming to drink: a glimpse of wild nature with overhead floodlights. They have been bused to the hotel to see it, and it is very beautiful, but it is no effort.*

My only boast in travel is my effort . . .

It was such a slog, such a lot of trouble to have gotten here, a kind of stumbling and uncertainty, begun at the border, where I was the only distinguishable foreigner—a magnet for the pesterers and touts. I'm conspicuous and solitary, and after two bone-shaking days I make it to the provincial city—a sort of victory if you value that kind of trudging through misery, realizing the fantasy of having seemed to blaze a trail all by myself.

I was lucky, I made it, I saw the initiated girls, I perversely enjoyed the three-pieces-of-chicken metaphor that to me was like a short story. I was fascinated by the rusted tanks and war wreckage along the road, by the ruined huts of vanished colonials, by the nonexistent road and the washerwomen at the river and the still serviceable dugout canoes. But what did all this add up to except a traveler's tale, something to report, the I-did-it boast, newsworthy to those who don't travel? And it's expensive, uncertain, physically difficult, and lonely.

I have always felt that the value of a travel narrative, especially one that detours down back roads, is that it becomes a record of details of how people lived at a particular time and place: how they spoke, what they said, what they ate, how they behaved. The Soviet Union I saw and wrote about in the 1960s doesn't exist anymore, nor does the South America I saw in the 1970s, nor the China I traveled through in the 1980s. The way of life on many Pacific islands has changed since I paddled around them in 1990, and as I was witnessing on this trip, the Africa of 2001 had undergone significant alterations—a few improvements, many degradations. To console myself, I think: Maybe the incidental details in these narratives will someday be useful for historians. Preserving the texture of life in a chronicle of travel could help inform the future, just as the diaries of foreign travelers like Smollett or Montaigne helped us understand old Europe.

The French historian Fernand Braudel frequently cites humble diarists and bold travelers in *The Structures of Everyday Life,* his encyclopedic account of how we have come to live the way we do on earth. On November 2, 1492, in Cuba, Christopher Columbus saw an Arawak man puffing on rolled tobacco leaves, a European's first glimpse of smoking. Tea arrived in England from Holland in about 1657, and Samuel Pepys drank his first cup of tea on September 25, 1660, so he wrote in his diary. The use of the individual fork at a meal dates from the mid-sixteenth century. Until then, all Europeans ate with their hands from a common trencher. Of his manner of eating, Montaigne wrote, "I sometimes bite my fingers in my haste." Around 1609, an English traveler—one Thomas Coryate, who ate with his hands—saw diners in Italy using forks and ridiculed them. The villagers I saw in January 1964 in southern Malawi, scooping stew into their mouths from a common bowl using hand-shaped lumps of steamed *nsima* dough, now employ spoons and forks.

This argument for the importance of trivial observation is obviously self-justifying, but if you're alone on the road, you need to be bucked up somehow, and even if the observations are illusions, they are illusions necessary to your existence. And if you aren't vitalized by fantasies—here I am in this old car speeding through the bush, here I am among tribal people engrossed in a ritual—the experience would be demoralizing. But the implied vanity bothered me, because being a fantasist in travel is simply self-regarding, and much is lost in translation.

I am looking for something to write about, because that's the nature of this travel, and perhaps of most travel: to see something new —a stimulus; to satisfy curiosity—a pleasure; to follow an itinerary —a narrative. But behind it all, and especially fueling the fantasy, is the need for the traveler to be at large in an exotic setting, to be far away, to act out a narrative of discovery and risk, to mimic the modes of the old travelers, to find similarities and differences.

My ideal traveler is the person who goes the old, laborious way into the unknown, and it is this belief that lies behind my travel, and drives me. I want to see things as they are, to see myself as I am. And look: I am a seventy-year-old man traveling like a backpacker in the middle of Angola, and the only other foreigners I see — six or eight of them — are businessmen hustling to make a profit off the country's resources. Maybe that's me too, another sort of business-man, another sort of huckster, someone hoping to make a living by being here and noting down what I see.

I need to be realistic, I wrote as the veranda lights came on, so dim that I could hardly see the page of my notebook, *because I have never been more keenly aware of the sadness in wasted time. Angola is perhaps a lesson in wasted time.*

When the fierce immigration official at the Angola border post had bared his teeth, scowled at me, and said, "*Você é professor?*" and I had replied, "Yes. *Sou professor,*" I was not lying. My letter of invita-tion stated that I would be traveling in Angola to teach in various schools. Since tourists were not welcome — and what would they do if they did visit? — I needed a reason to be here, and lecturing to English-language students was a persuasive one. It was not a ploy.

I was in Lubango to teach a few classes at the Instituto Superior de Ciências da Educação, a set of buildings and a campus within walking distance of the Grand Hotel. My contact and nominal host was an American woman, Akisha Pearman, whom I met soon after I arrived.

Akisha had lived alone in Lubango, teaching as a senior English language fellow at the institute, for almost two years. She lived in a few small rooms in the center of town. She was one of the people who had told me of the frosty July days ("I had to order winter clothes from the States"), and that nearly every day in the city the electricity went out for three to five hours, that there was a shortage of running water or a similar nuisance. Akisha laughed these off as minor annoyances. Uncomplaining, patient, dedicated, and hard-working, she had been prepared for this life by her two years as a Peace Corps teacher in Mozambique and by her ten years of teaching in the United States, Spain, Korea, and Madagascar. Her Angolan students and colleagues told me they loved her. Akisha had earned that love.

In my what-am-I-doing-here? mood, Akisha was a timely lesson. She made a point of staying positive, didn't grumble, never gossiped, and she expected the best from her students. She was also a passionate photographer, and though her talk was always upbeat, her photographs were a record of all she had seen. She did not judge or talk idly, but her photographs showed that she noticed everything — the disparities in wealth, the vandalized buildings, the contradictions, the humor, the goodwill, the scheming, and the violence in Angola as well as the joy.

When I said that I needed to adapt my cell phone to Angola and buy minutes, Akisha said, "We'll go to the mall — we actually do have a mall in Lubango!"

The Millennium, as the mall was called, had been plunked down next to a desolate parking lot in Plaça João Paulo II (named for the pope), a large yellow-painted structure with a high vaulted ceiling that mimicked a night sky picked out in dimly lit stars, the whole interior kept in deliberate semidarkness. In dazzling sunlit Angola such darkness was a novelty. The shadowy stores were built to resemble old Portuguese shops and cafés, with bow windows, antique lamps, and Euro-kitsch fittings, and at the mall's center was a rudimentary fountain and a pool — no water. A single-screen theater occupied one corner, and the shops sold phones, pizza, shoes, clothes. In another zone of the ridiculous place, a nail salon, three banks, and two boutiques selling hair extensions and wigs, which were desired by many women but (as my friend Kalunga Lima was to tell me later) mocked by Angolan men, who euphemistically laughed them off as *tetos falsos* — fake roofs.

"Let me show you how expensive these things are," Akisha said. She took me to a men's clothing shop. A simple polo shirt that would have cost $20 in the States was priced in Lubango at $120. Men's suits had price tags in the many hundreds of dollars, and pointy-toed shoes were $500 or more. All the merchandise was imported from China.

Business was good, the stylishly dressed (tight black jeans, stiletto heels, frilly blouse, false roof) clerk claimed when I asked. But the store was empty, there were no more than thirty people in the mall itself, and no one was buying a ticket to the movie. The mall had not yet become a hangout, and the only shop that was busy was the one selling cell phones.

For a few dollars, the woman in the cell phone shop got my cheap phone working. The Internet was unreliable in Angola, it was not much use in Namibia either, nor had it been available where I found myself in the Okavango. Perhaps Africa was going to bypass the email and Internet generation, and communication would be, as in Japan and some other countries, based on smart phone technology — texting, social networking, and not much else.

As we walked around the Lubango Millennium — which was an eyesore, already falling apart — Akisha told me a bit about herself. She was the eldest of five children. Her father, a former professional football player, was a successful coach in North Carolina, and both of her brothers were standout college players — one of them a former NFL running back. Akisha was an athletic presence too, radiating health and strength along with her good sense and optimism. Most of all she was independent. She had liberated herself by joining the Peace Corps a year after graduation from college, and as a teacher in Mozambique had become fluent in Portuguese.

Akisha's example reminded me of how much I admired people who worked humbly in Africa. Like the best of them, Akisha saw herself as more a student than a teacher, looking to be enriched by the experience. And though she never alluded to it, she could not have found it easy to be the only American in Lubango, a young single woman living on her own in this remote and, from what I could see, inhospitable place.

But she had lived and worked for two years in Inhambane, a sleepy seaside town—long ago an important port—in southern Mozambique, so she had come to Lubango with an understanding of isolation and a knowledge of the damaging absurdities of Portuguese colonialism.

Probably more nonsense has been talked about, and more myths have been created around, Portugal's imperial adventures than any other nation's. The most ludicrous was "Lusotropicalism," a cock-amamie theory and mystique of racial harmony proposed in the 1930s, which posited that because of their unique temperament and culture the Portuguese were the Europeans best suited to adapting to other lands and dealing with equatorial natives—finding (so it was argued) common ground in sympathy and like-mindedness. "We understand the natives better than you do" was the Portuguese boast. This implies not only that Portuguese imperialism had been a triumph, but also that Angolans had colluded in their own en-slavement and willingly offered up their diamonds and gold.

But the reality is that Angola's history has been a colonial tragedy, and sometimes a farce, rife with racism, resistance, rebellion, and death. And the briefest glimpse of any Portuguese overseas terri-tory is proof of the mess they made of their colonies. A dramatic fact, pointed out by a historian of Angola, Douglas Wheeler, is that in the four hundred years from 1579 until 1974 there had never been a five-year period in the colony without at least one punitive Portuguese military campaign. The glory of the Portuguese was their great navigators and discoverers, but they were incompetent administrators, ruthless bosses, and greedy exploiters. The crooked aristocrats and desperate peasants who planted themselves far from home, and finally fled, left nothing behind but derelict slave quarters, empty vinho verde bottles, and gloomy churches.

In Malawi in the 1960s, I met middle-aged Portuguese men across the border, in Vila Cabral, in Mozambique (then a sleepy, underfunded colony popularly known as "Portuguese East"), who had emigrated from poverty-stricken villages in rural Portugal to become carpenters, stonemasons, and barbers in the African bush. Their wives were idle and cranky, screaming at the first servants they'd ever had in their lives. Few of the *colonos* were able to speak the local language, and it was no surprise when revolutionary movements began to harry them, to hasten their departure. Because of the character of the colonizers, this process was inevitable, as Douglas Wheeler also described, noting that the settler from "an archaic rural society, semi-feudal in some provinces, often tries to cheat the African because he is weaker, and because he himself is used to being humiliated in his poverty back home and has come here to get rich." The settlers got along well enough with the Africans in villages sustained by their traditional ways. The somewhat Westernized Africans were another story: the new settlers resented the ones who could read, who had ambitions and political ideas. Those Africans were despised and belittled as *calcinhas*—wearers of trousers.

When I mentioned that the bumbling and often cruel nature of the colonial Portuguese became clearer only after one had actually traveled through a former Portuguese colony, Akisha said, "I have a great story."

While working in Inhambane, Mozambique, she had become acquainted with a Portuguese husband and wife who, like the ones I had met as a Peace Corps volunteer long ago in Vila Cabral (Niassa province), had immigrated to Mozambique in the 1960s. This was a period when the Portuguese government, under the tenacious, long-ruling dictator Antonio Salazar, created incentives for its poorest citizens to seek their fortunes in the colonies. They were given free passage on ships, lessons in husbandry, and seed money to begin new lives. And of course one of the great incentives was the promise of cheap workers, under the forced labor regime then in place that browbeat village Africans into plowing the fields and serving white farmers.

Akisha, during her first stint in Africa, was impressed that forty years earlier these Europeans had left their modern, native land to start a life in humble, distant Mozambique.

"It must have been a great adjustment to travel all that way from Portugal to Africa," Akisha had said.

"Yes, in a way" was the response of a Portuguese man.

"So different!" Akisha said. "How did you manage?"

"It was easy, really," the man said.

"How so?" Akisha asked.

"We came from a poor village in Portugal," the man said. "In Mozambique we had electricity and running water for the first time in our lives."

Over the following days I became a part-time teacher at the Instituto Superior de Ciências da Educação in Lubango. My students were Akisha's English-language group, all of them teachers themselves, improving their skills, many of them intending to return to their own schools, or to use their proficiency in English to study abroad for a further degree—two of them wanted to study law elsewhere.

Nothing is more satisfying in travel than to land in a place and assume an occupation, even a temporary one, as a teacher; to cease being a voyeur and have a purpose and a routine, especially one that involved interacting with intelligent students. I had once been a contented teacher in Africa, so I happily slipped into the role and was comforted with a sense of belonging.

"Many of them want to write stories and poems," Akisha told me.

Without frankly discouraging them from imaginative writing, I extolled the importance of being an eyewitness, of dealing with verifiable facts and the recent visitable past. I mentioned that foreign journalists seldom came to Angola (but did not mention the reason: the Angolan government hated foreign journalists). A number of the students were older — in their thirties. Some of them had seen war. The town of Lubango had changed hands several times during the civil war, so they had experienced occupation and divided loyalties and the hardships of sieges — shelling, shortages, survival, death, the intrusion of soldiers into their lives. And as a result they had known suspense and uncertainty and fear. This was something to write about.

I suggested structures, I told them stories, and I encouraged them to tell me stories, all of them related to the theme of the eyewitness: something they had seen and experienced, perhaps a vivid childhood memory. And so we talked about early memories, to practice English and to rehearse the stories.

"My mother wanted me to go to school," Miguel said. "She talked about it all the time, and after a while I was eager to go to school. I had no idea what was in store for me." He described his apprehension — his mother's urging, his father's passivity, his utter ignorance of what school entailed. And then came the day for school, which was a long walk from his village in a remote part of Huíla province. "I sat there in the classroom," he said, the memory of it making him falter a bit, "and I realized I was trapped. I couldn't go home. I was afraid. I was captive there."

"I was with my friends some distance outside my village, walking along a path," Gomes said, standing and gesturing with his expressive hands. "We were about ten or eleven. We saw a woman approaching us. She rushed to us and said, 'A house is burning in the village. You must do something!'"

The small boys asked what they should do. "First, take off your shoes," she said. "And please accept this money." She gave them each a few kwanzas. They were dazzled to have the money, even though it was a pittance. "Now go to the village and help put out the fire." Taking her for a witch with special powers, they hurried to the village, but found there was no fire. When they returned to look for the woman, they discovered she'd made off with their shoes.

"My earliest memory goes back a long way," a woman, Dinorah, said in a solemn voice. "I was two years old and lying in my mother's arms. She held me tight, and I knew she was upset about something, but I didn't know what. She whispered to me, 'Kiss your father.' But I didn't know where he was. She led me to him and I saw his face. I thought he was sleeping. I kissed him." She paused for dramatic effect. "He was dead, lying in a coffin."

In another class I described the use of dialogue. One of the students, Delcio Tweuhanda, had an idea for a novel. Jumas Chipondo had written a series of essays about his life; he was a Lunda-Chokwe, one of Angola's most artistic people, and had lived as a refugee in Zambia and Botswana for a decade during the war years. Several others wanted to form a group and write a book together, perhaps an oral history. They asked questions and spoke about their plans, and whenever I was with them I was hopeful, for them and for myself.

I made a point of asking them where in the world they wanted to go. Not Portugal, they said. Not Cuba. Not any of their bordering countries, the easiest ones to get to — not Namibia, not the Republic of the Congo, not Zambia. South Africa, perhaps. And, with unanimity, America.

Now the Grand Hotel no longer seemed seedy or abandoned or a place of funereal gloom, as it had when I first moved in; it was my refuge, a peaceful place. Akisha had stayed there for months on her arrival. "It's like that hotel in *The Shining*!" I saw her point: a large empty hotel with sinister echoes and ambiguous odors. But I could write there, and so it suited me.

Every morning at breakfast, I sat before a large painting that covered one wall of the Grand's dining room like a mural. At first glance, it was a European landscape, rich in picturesque details, showing a village of stucco houses with russet tiled roofs, a white steepled church at the center, and a cluster of dignified municipal offices — all these buildings looking solid and indestructible. A ridge of magnificent mountains rose in the distance, and a sky of fluffy clouds, and in the foreground two peaceful cows grazed in a lush meadow.

The only human I saw in the picture was a Portuguese man in a frock coat strolling on a path near the cows. The whole painting, with its soft contours, spoke of peace, serenity, abundance, fertility, permanence, even holiness — the shafts of sunlight like a blessing from above.

The Algarve? No, it was of course a painting of Lubango in its previous incarnation as the colonial town of Sá da Bandeira. Though in style and substance it was a nineteenth-century panorama of a European pastoral, it had been painted (very small date and name in the right corner) by Rolla Tze (perhaps Chinese from Macau?) in 1945, the year of the Grand Hotel's opening. Nothing of it smacked of Africa — no Africans, no thatched huts, no exotic animals or flowers. At least none was apparent. But standing very close to it one morning — it loomed over me — I found a small black man sitting in tall grass in the deep left-hand corner.

This was how Portugal idealized Sá da Bandeira, hoping that colonials might see it that way too, as Portugal-across-the-sea, awaiting the settler's ax and plow, beckoning to a pious congregation for the church, which was the present-day Cathedral de São José. Sá da Bandeira was advertised as the sort of market town that existed in rural Portugal.

Although it had never found prosperity, Sá da Bandeira lasted as a colonial fantasy right up to the year of independence. Here is the experience of an American traveler, Mrs. Alzada Carlisle

Kistner, arriving with her entomologist husband, David, at the Grand Hotel on their beetle-collecting trip through Angola in 1972 (as she recalled it in *An Affair with Africa*, published in 1998): "A liveried doorman bowed a welcome; the receptionist, dressed in a cutaway coat, was coolly efficient; servants carried our bags. The flower-filled tiled courtyard had a gorgeous swimming pool and a hedgehog curled up like a ball on the lawn. Our suite had parquet floors and a marble bathroom, where we bathed and dressed for an elegant dinner. Surrounded by hovering waiters, we ate as a trio played 'I Left My Heart in San Francisco.'"

Two years after that, all hell broke loose, and the city was today still suffering the effects of the war. It had grown, it sprawled, it was now a city of a million and a half. Nearly all those people lived in hovels — some in a dense shantytown in the heart of the city, which anyone on foot — it was my usual route — had to traverse in order to get to the Millennium Mall, and that meant passing among the shacks, the raucous boys, the beer joints, the mud puddles, and the latrines — and stepping over a dead dog, which was not moved the entire time I was in Lubango.

Looking for ways to spend the time when I was not teaching or writing, I found the ethnographic museum, housed in a small whitewashed villa on a side street. I visited twice, and on both occasions I was the only person in the place. I hoped to find slit-eyed Chokwe *pwo* masks used in boys' initiations or a Chokwe body suit of woven fiber. But what I found were objects that I had seen along the way from the border: wooden staffs that the Kwanyama elders had used in the *Efundula* village; baskets and wooden bowls like trenchers I'd seen; and finger harps, marimbas, fetishes, and carvings that were still being used in the Angolan bush. The centerpiece at the ethnographic museum was exactly the sort of dugout canoe I'd seen a man paddling and fishing from on the Techiua River south of Cahama a week before — revered here in Lubango as an ancient artifact. So both ways of life persisted in parallel, and it seemed that the old way was, if not the more reliable, then the more common, because it was a necessity.

I asked Akisha about the Chinese who'd come to Lubango. She said there were many—hundreds here, thousands on the coast, but they kept to themselves. Like their counterparts in Namibia, they had all arrived within the last few years from the People's Republic. They ran small businesses, they were engaged in construction, some were farmers, and three of them owned a restaurant in a corner of Lubango.

For our farewell meal, Akisha took me to a Chinese restaurant, which was on a sloping potholed dead-end road. Like many of the other shops, it had a red-painted façade and a wooden porch. But inside, it was China, with sticky plastic tablecloths, a pinkish calendar showing a colorful pagoda, porcelain animal figures, and a small shrine of a gilded, potbellied immortal flanked by a dish of burning joss sticks.

Eight chain-smoking Chinese men sat at one of the round tables, shouting and drinking beer. They were the sort of tough manual laborers I'd once seen in China lashing bamboo scaffolds or digging ditches—hard-eyed and suspicious, and these were wheezy and red-faced from the alcohol. They yelled for food, they yelled at each other, they yelled for the bill. Outside, in Angola, they had to be deferential or circumspect, but inside, in this version of China, they could howl. "Heaven is high and the emperor is far away."

Like us, they were served by a young woman, Mei, from Tsingtao, and the food was cooked by Zhou, a middle-aged man in an apron. The manager was a woman I took to be about thirty-five, Wang Lin, from Yantai, who called herself Irma; but she told me she had a nineteen-year-old son, so she must have been more like forty-five. Akisha and I had spicy *mapo dofu* with rice and got acquainted with the owners.

Mei, in her mid-twenties, was a recent arrival. Wang Lin had been in Lubango for a year; she said it was okay — not bad, a little quiet perhaps. But she didn't miss home.

"I might go back to China for a visit," Wang Lin said in Portuguese to Akisha, "but not to stay. I am staying here."

Mei said, "I want to go to Spain for a holiday."

Zhou said, "This is where I live now."

Angolans never came to the restaurant, they said, but that was all right. There were enough Chinese and Europeans and Cubans in Lubango to keep the place busy.

Every time I encountered Chinese in the hinterland I felt I was seeing the future of Africa — not a happy future, and not a distant one, but the foreseeable future. They were a new breed of settler, practical, unsentimental, mainly construction workers and do-it-yourselfers and small businessmen, hard to please but willing to put up with tougher conditions than any Portuguese.

Some Africa watchers and Western economists have observed that the Chinese presence in Africa — a sudden intrusion — is salutary and will result in greater development and more opportunities for Africans. Seeing Chinese digging into Africa, isolated in their enterprises, offhand with Africans to the point of rudeness, and deaf to any suggestion that they moderate their self-serving ways, I tend to regard this positive view as a crock. My own feeling is that like the other adventurers in Africa, the Chinese are exploiters. They have no compact or agreement or involvement with the African people; theirs is an alliance with the dictators and bureaucrats whom they pay off and allow to govern abusively — a conspiracy. Theirs is a racket like those of all the previous colonizers, and it will end badly — maybe worse, because the Chinese are tenacious, richer, and heavily invested, and for them there is no going back and no surrender. As they walked into Tibet and took over (with not a voice of protest raised by anyone in the West), they are walking into the continent and, outspending any other adventurer, subverting Africans, with a mission to plunder.

Over the Chinese meal, I mentioned this to Akisha, but she simply said, "We'll see."

When I asked her for horror stories about Lubango, she just smiled her kindly schoolteacher smile and gave nothing away. She missed her family, she said, but she was committed to her students and to being self-sufficient. She was a marvel of serenity and dedication, much stronger perhaps than she realized. But that is the way of the teacher in Africa: you get stronger or you go home. She'd become interested in the Portuguese language and wanted to study it more deeply, perhaps in Brazil. Her contract was soon coming to an end, but with friends in Namibia and some in Cape Town she had no immediate plans to return to the United States.

She made me feel small and superfluous, and though that was the nature of the sort of traveler I was, I had begun to accommodate myself to Lubango. After all, I had something useful to do here, so for a time I was not merely a voyeur — or at least, with this effort, I could justify my voyeurism.

I returned each day to the Grand, as if home from a job, and during this time I rejoiced in having gainful employment, both a distraction and a relief, which gave me a greater understanding of the country. If there was any hope here, it lay in these students and teachers, but it was clear that they were underpaid. Some teachers in rural schools, as I read in their essays, were not paid their salaries for months, and had to be supported by donations from the parents of their students. The teachers in Angola, as in much of Africa, were ignored and used badly by their government, which earned billions from its oil and gold exports. Probably many of these teachers would look elsewhere for a future. And this is why foreign teachers are always welcome in Africa — someone else foots the bill.

The routine of teaching in Lubango suited me, and surprised me too, because I had come to like the predictable day. I had spent my life on the road, waking in a pleasant or not so pleasant hotel, and setting off every morning after breakfast hoping to discover something new and repeatable, something worth writing about. I think other serious travelers do the same, looking for a story, facing the world, tramping out a book with their feet. The traveler physically enacts the narrative, chases the story, often becomes part of the story. This is the way most travel narratives happen.

I had for a happy period suspended my travel. That made uprooting myself from Lubango all the harder. The best of travel involves short, intense periods of residence. I had enjoyed the routine of being a teacher. But there is no routine in travel, only early starts and insults, and if there is a rhythm, it is a rhythm of disruptions and shocks and uncertainty — and in Africa the godawfulness of dark, early morning starts and filthy buses.

14

The Slave Yards of Benguela

O NCE, LONG AGO, when Lubango was a country town named Sá da Bandeira, a railway regularly served it, clattering around steep valleys and rolling hundreds of miles from the high plateau to the arid coastal settlement of Moçâmedes, now named Namibe. No longer. The train fell into disuse, and the tracks were sabotaged in the post-independence war. Buses have replaced the train, Namibe is off the map, and Benguela is the main destination on the coast now, retaining its old notorious name.

Benguela was once among the grimmest slave ports on earth. This swampy, low-lying little town helped populate the Americas with its exports of humans sentenced for life to captivity and hard labor. Consider the description of Benguela in *The South African Year Book and Guide* for 1923: "Straggling town . . . formerly a busy place . . . Many of the old houses are substantially built and provided with large encircled compounds, formerly used for slaves awaiting shipment." It is estimated that as many as four million slaves were shipped out of Angola or died in raids, on marches to the coast, or at sea. Slaves captured from the interior were kept in Luanda's and

Benguela's holding pens, where they were fattened for the Middle Passage.

Does any aspect of the Angola slave trade resonate today? Yes, and sometimes in peculiar ways. I was at a café with an Angolan man who said, "Let's have some peanuts," and then to the waiter, "*Queremos alguns jinguba*," and I caught the word *jinguba*.

The Kimbundu word had been brought by Angolan slaves to America, where it persists as "goober." ("Goodness how delicious / Eating goober peas.") I was later to learn a Kikongo word from the north of Angola that is even nearer, the word *nguba*, as in the Kikongo proverb urging discretion: *Ku kuni nguba va meso ma nkewa ko*, "Don't plant peanuts while the monkeys are watching."

I was headed to Benguela, but it was not a simple matter. In Africa and around the world, trains leave from the city center, and the bus station is generally on the outskirts, in the poorest and dirtiest part of town. The passenger bus business needs an expanse of cheap space — for parking the oversized vehicles, for maneuvering them and turning them around, and especially for providing them leeway for the mobs that mill about and wait with their bundles so they can board these notoriously unpunctual things. You find that kind of space adjacent to the slums. A bus station in sub-Saharan Africa is not really a station; it is a glorified parking lot, and it is one of the unpleasant inevitabilities of overland travel, not just unpredictable but offensive and rowdy, and haunted by stray dogs snarling over the scraps of garbage discarded by the passengers waiting to board.

It was not yet six in the morning, and a fight was in progress at the Lubango bus station, a bus having just drawn in, rocking in the wide potholes like a ship in a gale: a number of drunks trying to board a bus were resisting their being thrown off by two of the toughs hired to control the crowd.

The noise had woken the dozing passengers, who, with red eyes and wild hair and creased, sleepy faces gaped from the windows, and then, aroused by the brawl, they began screaming abuse. They had come from another town, south of Lubango. Their mockery was not aimed at the rabble or at the struggling drunks but instead at the heavies who were dragging them to the ground, the easier to kick them senseless.

A man yelled from a window in Portuguese, "So Lubango is a place where a drunk can't get on a bus!"

That owlish observation caused cackling laughter, more abuse, and more of this unrhyming dirty poetry of early morning, but the rest of it was lost in the louder rap music that blared from an amplifier at the ticket office.

I had risen in the darkness of the hotel. I waited in the darkness and stink of the bus station parking lot. A feeble rubious hint of morning light bled sideways into the sky, each puddling bit of brightness making the place look uglier with sharpened details of its decrepitude, and the shouting made it worse. *What am I doing here?*

Broken signs, slumping power cables, burst-open boxes of garbage, a tidemark of muddy litter, a muttonish smell in the air as of goat breath and decayed meat. Added to that were the overburdened women with swollen cloth bundles bound in string and two or three small well-behaved children, the usual Angolan rapper crowd of oafish boys with baseball caps and earphones, and pretty girls standing daintily in the morning-moistened dust. The sight of these girls made me think that a whole study could be made of hairstyles in Angola — not just the extravagant hair extensions and fluffy wigs, but hair strung with beads or woven into cornrows or twisted into snaky locks, and some women's heads were beautifully shaved to a shining baldness like polished mahogany finials on Victorian staircases.

The Benguela bus arrived as the sun rose over the low tin rooftops, the noise and the heat rising at the same time. So the urgency to board was combined with the sweat of pushing, and I was part of that same pushing — odd and obnoxious for me, elbows out, to be part of the scrimmage, but necessary or I wouldn't get a seat.

And when we set off I saw that the habitable part of Lubango, the orbit of my teaching duties, was really very small, that the city was a set of small Portuguese plazas surrounded by shanty settlements, just like every other town of any size in Angola. And if you didn't know any better, you'd never think it was a country floating on a sea of oil. You'd think, as some sentimental people do: Poor little beat-up place — we should do something to help. We should send money, maybe lots of money; Angola (with annual revenues in the billions) seems to need money.

Outside of town we passed the now familiar roadside rusted and burned-out tanks and military trucks near the fallen-down Olde Worlde Portuguese farmhouses, their tile roofs shattered. This was at a place called Viamba, as we approached the edge of the Serra de Quilengues escarpment. Whose tanks, whose trucks, whose houses? Impossible to tell. Time moves on, no one cares, the scrap yard grows; no one mourns the dead in these rural tableaus of abandonment.

An hour into the trip, at Cacula, we stopped at a small market where hawkers — pleading women and dusty, spaniel-eyed children mostly — offered food on trays, fat tomatoes, stacks of small bananas, discs of sliced pineapple, loaves of bread, piles of bread rolls, and plastic bags with squished and greasy potato fries. Several women balanced bunches of onions on their heads, and one with a basin of chicken pieces spotted with flies approached me and asked, "*Qual?*"

Again the existential question: Which of these old, dark, fly-blown, and inedible chicken legs do you desire, *senhor?*

After that, everyone was eating on the bus and arguing in a jeering and companionable way. We traveled under jacaranda trees that were shedding their violet blossoms, the blooms bursting and crackling under our wheels, and we slowed for the cows that crowded the road.

At greater intervals a general cry was raised from the back of the bus, and then the driver shouted what sounded like an order and bumped to a stop. Fifteen or so people got out to piss. They did not go far. All pissed in full view of the bus and its seated passengers. There was no indecency in this, no urgency either. Perhaps their staying close to the roadside was not laziness but a result of the land mines that, everyone knew, had been laid—and never deactivated —just off Angolan roads, especially here in the southern provinces. The men stood, feet apart, and hosed the tall grass. The women lowered their tracksuit bottoms, squatted, and spattered; some used a shawl, shrouding themselves a few feet from the bus and dripping like leaky tents. As on the trip with Camillo, it was more like a pissing contest than a call of nature, and it was accompanied by continual chatter—the pissers cheerfully calling out to one another, holding conversations as they casually whizzed, laughing and teasing.

The paved road was too good to last. It gave way to gravel and sent us sideways. And then, two hours into the journey, we left the gravel road for a detour through woods and bush and clusters of hot, exposed mud huts of poor villages. In some places the road was under construction, in others it had washed out in the recent rains. The delay didn't matter much. We had left the escarpment and were tipped downhill into the heat. Bumping over bony tree roots, near a ramshackle hut on one of these bush tracks, a small, misshapen, paralytic boy struggled forward, hanging on to his stick, stabbing it into the dust and hobbling. The bus driver slowed down —as Camillo had done a week before. He handed over a package of bread, thrusting it through the window, and the skinny boy touched his heart in thanks.

Whatever inconvenience it was to be riding this way, slowly and uncomfortably, at least I was privileged to witness this impulsive act of human kindness toward a crippled and abandoned soul, propped up on a stick in the middle of the bush.

Traveling overland, as I had from the border, I saw that Portuguese Angola had been a colony not of towns but of outposts, most of them failures. And independent Angola was not much better — still a country of isolated outposts, but bigger ones, and just as hungry. Around noon, five hours into the trip and not even halfway to the coast, we came to Quilengues, which was a haunted little town, frozen in its period, perhaps the assisted-immigrant 1950s. Quilengues had a church, colonial houses, and shops beside the road. It seemed a whole intact place, but two of the student teachers I'd known in Lubango had taught in a school here, and told me they often were not paid for months — eleven months in one year — and when finally some money did come in, it was apportioned in small installments. So the teachers were held hostage: they could either stay and wait or leave and forfeit everything they were owed. A pretty place, Quilengues, but the inner story was of cheated teachers, underfunded schools, and severe water shortages. Again, this in a country immensely rich in oil revenue.

In most African travel along bush tracks of this sort you'd expect to see animals. As I had noticed earlier, not in Angola. Not a gazelle, not a monkey. It was as though, from the conspicuous absence of game, its soul had been stolen. There was plenty of room for animals to range, enough habitat and fodder, and many waterholes. On the way to the coast we rode through distinct landscapes and climates, descending from the cool highlands to great sloping bush to grassy plains. But they were landscapes without any animals except a cow or a goat, only the occasional village of thatch and mud.

The day growing hotter, we entered a belt of bush areas that had seen violent fighting, based on the evidence of half-buried, rusted, and blown-up tanks. Many represented old battles, but one at Chongoroi, which we rolled through, had taken place only a dozen years before. In March 1998, a hundred armed men from Jonas Savimbi's UNITA forces descended on Chongoroi, burning the vehicles of UN monitors and the vans of the World Food Program, killed two people and injured three, before making their escape. Instead of a memorial marking the dead and wounded, there were overturned trucks with shell holes in their sides.

Nearer the coast, the villages were larger, and one town, Catengue, a former Portuguese settlement, had been rebuilt — the first rural town I'd seen that looked habitable, with old, smooth-sided buildings and mended roofs. One reason for this might have been that it had become a railway town again, the train from Benguela passing through twice a week, but not today.

More food stops, piss stops, fuel stops, roadside markets with chickens, oranges, bananas, and greasy fries, with more angry yelling from the back of the bus, the driver responding by yelling back and laughing. The man next to me shrugged at the shouts, and explained, "*Muito lento,*" which, like a tempo indication on a musical score, was easy enough to understand. The bus was going too slowly for the impatient passengers.

At one of the food stops, as I searched for a cup of coffee, a man from the bus asked me in English, "*Senhor,* can I help you?" I was the only *branco* on the bus, and perhaps also the oldest. When I told him I was looking to buy coffee, he said, giggling a little, "No coffee here."

"But Angola grows coffee."

"Yes, but," and he laughed again, shrugging, "this is . . ." His gesture meant: We are nowhere, we are in the bush, there is nothing here. Then, "What is your country?"

I told him what he wanted to know.

"What you think about Angola?"

I said, "Angola very nice."

And at that moment I waved away a woman who held out a basin holding some sticky, shapeless mess, as if showing me a sample of stagnant pond life.

The man translated my compliment for his friend beside him, who practically gagged on the banana he was eating—two Angolans by the roadside, sharing the Americano's hilarious joke. *He said Angola very nice!*

They were Miguel and Delfino—Miguel was the English-speaker. They had been at a wedding in Lubango and were headed to Benguela to catch another bus to Lobito, where they lived. They too complained that our bus was slow. We should have been in Benguela by now, Miguel said. And he shrugged.

"In Angola we have bad situation," he said. "Nothing is right. Nothing is justice. You see the road? Bad. You see the food? It's . . ." He made a sour face. "Lobito is good. My home is good. But we have slow business. Everyone want"—he fidgeted his fingers, making the money sign.

I said, "Angola has oil. Angola has gold and diamonds. Angola has money."

"Big people has money," Miguel said. "Big people has too much of money. But not"—he nodded at the market activity, the women with trays on their heads and infants on their backs, the children with buckets of plastic water bottles or baskets of oranges, pleading for customers, the girls swinging bags of fries, the basins brimming with shapeless, sticky pond creatures, everyone jostling to sell their wares, smilingly destitute, competing and elbowing forward before the bus left and a great sunlit silence descended on their market once more—"not leetle people."

"But you're a big person, Miguel," I said. And he was—physically imposing, fat-faced, with a potbelly, perspiring in a blue-striped sweater-vest that he'd probably put on that morning in chilly

Lubango and hadn't yet taken off. Delfino was smaller, dapper in a black leather waistcoat and pointy-toed shoes, listening attentively, watching me with close-set eyes.

"Me, I am big" — and Miguel clapped a hand to his belly — "but I has no money." He leaned toward me and said, "Government people has money — and their friend, and their family. Politician people has money." He was whispering now. "They keep. They don't geeve."

I made a sympathetic noise in my sinuses.

"Is bad," Miguel said, and after explaining in Portuguese to his friend, Delfino muttered something Miguel agreed with: "Is trouble."

"Big trouble?"

He nodded and, sticking out his lower lip for emphasis, said, "Big trouble. Leetle people not happy."

I wasn't that happy myself. I was thinking: I have heard this before. I have seen this before. The unending echo of underdevelopment, but with a difference — more people, more squalor, a greater disconnect between the governing rich and their parasitic friends, and the poor who live without hope.

We came to a weird plain of bush, with maybe a thousand baobab trees, more than I had ever seen in one place, no other trees near them to diminish the power of their swollen bagginess, their fat bulgy trunks and stubby, wrinkled, rootlike branches. Because baobabs are a favorite of elephants, for the water stored in the pith of their trunks and branches, they are often stripped, splintered, and gored by the great beasts' powerful tusks. But in the absence of elephants this baobab forest remained intact.

The long straight road down sandy slopes to the coast, the last twenty miles of this ten-hour trip, offered a panorama of the scoops of shoreline bristling with palm trees, the Bay of Benguela, and the South Atlantic Ocean, an expanse of shimmering blue silk on this sunny day. And then we were in honking, screeching traffic on narrow tropical streets.

Hot, flat, coastal Benguela was the opposite of cool, hilly, high Lubango. But both were ramshackle and disorderly, praised by people who lived in them by saying, "You should have seen this place ten years ago!" — the sort of backhanded compliment you hear in Calcutta. But they had reason to say so. The American journalist Karl Maier, in *Angola: Promises and Lies,* described how in 1992 pro-government forces shelled the Benguela headquarters of the occupying UNITA army, which had dynamited the central market. "Both sides carried out summary executions," Maier wrote. "Bulldozers were brought in to scoop up hundreds of bodies that had been left rotting in the streets."

The bloodshed in Benguela had been horrific and relatively recent. But I had come for a reason. I had agreed to teach English classes here, too.

"Benguela of the slave yards," the Angolan novelist Pepetela writes in his family saga, *Yaka.* Pepetela, which means "eyelash" in Kimbundu, is his nom de plume; his real name is Artur Carlos Maurício Pestana dos Santos. This novel is a good introduction to the town, an account of the immigrant Semedo family over four generations, beginning in the nineteenth century, the family growing as Benguela grows, first with the slave trade, then in commerce and shopkeeping and farming, but always exploiting African labor. *Yaka* opens with two vivid memories of young Alexandre Semedo: the first, his fear of the slave yards, "monotonous songs and mysterious drumming mingled with the sound of chains," and the second, the sound of lions roaring at night. "Lions never frightened me, they were my first lullaby."

Fiction gives life to places in expressive ways that no history book can begin to suggest. Characters in novels admit us to intimacies — not true of scholarly chronicles, no matter how detailed. We know the people in novels better than we know our friends. Without underlining the racial complexity of colonial Angola, Pepetela takes for granted the various strata of white society; in *Yaka,* Alexandre's mother refers to herself as belonging to "the lowest class of whites" because she has no servants or slaves, and says, "I'm a second-class white because I was born here." This sort of coloration gives Angolan fiction an odd texture and emphasis—neither Zimbabwean nor South African fiction, which is often full of white settler families, strays into such racial classifications, or describes whites as so poor they work as menials and don't have servants.

In the Benguela of *Yaka,* Alexandre reflects on how "his mother died with a complex about being a second-class white; she had wanted a first-class white [to marry] her son." Status is everything in the remote colony—exiled criminals looking for respectability are "offended when their rotten past is recalled." But no one plays by the rules, only thieves win, and physical passion dominates characters' lives: Father Costa, a rural priest, has defiantly fathered fifteen mulatto children.

Since Angola is so seldom written about, and fiction is always so revealing, I made a point of boning up on Angolan authors. The Angolan novel is unusual; it is unlike the typical African novel of tribal life, of the yearning for freedom and an awakening political identity and the coming of independence. The Angolan novel is an anarchic and multicultural hodgepodge, as self-referential, incestuous, and homegrown an artifact as everything else in isolated and xenophobic Angola. Its theme is often disappointed expectations.

Such novels are not for the literary critic or the connoisseur of fiction. They aren't much fun, and it's tedious work to finish them. But I wasn't interested in whether these books were well or poorly written. I only wanted to know if they gave any clue to the inner life of the country, and even badly written or clumsily translated books often manage that. The Angola of Angolan fiction (of Pepetela, of José Luandino Vieira, of Arnaldo Santos and Sousa Jamba) encompasses the lives of black Africans, usually Kimbundu-speaking people, but also of white peasants and white slum dwellers, many of whom speak a shantytown slang of mixed Kimbundu and Portuguese words.

Yaka portrays a Benguela of rednecks, rich landowners, racism, family secrets, impartial cruelty, casualties of war, family strife, litigious yokels, brutal sex, hard drinking, and the long shadow of the past hanging over all of this fictional hothouse. It sounds like Faulkner, down to the Southern Gothic sweep and scope, but it is not so felicitous as Faulkner, and like many African novels it is sententious and lacking in humor. Yet the book gives access to Benguela. *Yaka* is a chronicle of the country seen through the eyes of a large multigenerational family whose first ancestor, Oscar, is a convict sent to Angola in 1880 for killing his wife — ten years in Angola is his punishment, as well as banishment to the colony for life.

The strict chronology of the novel is helpful, like a flesh-and-blood history book: the early settlement, the slavery and forced labor, the growing family, the fierce wars, the tribal battles, the uprising of 1961 that led to clandestine networks of rebels, the departure in 1975 of the Portuguese from Lobito, the port "cluttered up with crates of every possible size . . . All of Angola is going in those crates, the lieutenant said. Dismantled machinery, diamonds in the petrol tanks of cars, textiles, appliances of every kind, the most incredible things . . . even things not thought to be valuable, wooden statues and masks, everything sells in Europe, leopard skins and mats, ivory and baskets, it's a case of plunder."

The last section of *Yaka* concerns the shaky independence and the subsequent war, when Alexandre Semedo's great-grandson (adopted by some Cuvale people from southwest Angola) fights in the guerrilla war "that will be famous, behind the enemy troops, and the occupation of Benguela will only last a hundred days, one hundred dark days."

The reference is not to occupation by the Portuguese, but after independence by the South Africans, whose soldiers commandeered the city, intimidated its people, and handed it over to the government opposition after a major battle in 1975, which took place in the area I traveled through, from Lubango to Benguela. Most of Pepetela's fictional locations (among them Dombe Grande, and Capangombo on the plateau, near Humpata) can be found on a map—where the characters moved, where they farmed and owned shops, where they looked for wives, where (near the coast road and the Caporolo River, which I had crossed late in the day) the Portuguese in the 1940s set off in hunting parties to provoke Africans and massacre them after they'd managed to engage them.

The first place I saw in Benguela, because I had rushed to the seafront for relief and a breeze, was the central slave quarters. It's one of the city's landmarks, an old, low prisonlike fortress, a stockade in stone, facing the ocean. Because it is so near the water, the slave quarters is a popular place for youths to gather, and though some of them were selling ice cream and candy and chewing gum, all of them looked hungry.

Benguela was not a natural place for the Portuguese to settle, yet it was identified as a prime site for development in 1615 by Manuel Cerveira Pereira, who named it São Filipe de Benguela after his patron, King Philip II of Spain and Portugal. But it was swampy, unhealthy, and inhospitable. As the novel *Yaka* dramatizes, it was for centuries a town of petty shopkeepers and slave traders, nearly all of them, of course, exiled convicts.

From its beginnings as a small slave port in the late 1600s, Benguela would a hundred years later rival Luanda in importance. It never had an extensive settler population. Even into the twentieth century the number of whites in Benguela and Lobito was still tiny (the "native town" of the 1920s guidebooks). But then the white population of Angola was relatively modest. Until 1940 ethnic Portuguese constituted less than 1 percent of Angola's inhabitants, and it was not until 1950 that their proportion approached 2 percent.

The government of Portugal, attempting to stabilize the white population, tried to create an agricultural colony near Benguela in 1885. It failed because it was run by ex-convicts who hated farming and were tyrannical toward their workers. The failed farmers were pressed into the army, but they failed at soldiery too, because of their mindless brutality or their simple desertion. The historian of Angola Gerald Bender noted that by 1907 the majority of crimes in Benguela were committed by these ex-convicts.

All eyewitness accounts of Benguela through the years describe a small miserable town supported by the slave trade. After slavery ended, forced labor was instituted. The practice was the same; it was just a change of name, from slave (*esclava*) to servant (*serviçal*). Like the slaves, the servants were bartered for guns and cloth, marched to Benguela and Lobito, and sent to other Portuguese colonies that needed labor, among them São Tomé and Principe. An average of three thousand people a year were shipped out in the 1920s. Some Portuguese observers objected, and in the 1940s one of the harshest critics, Captain Henrique Galvão, a long-serving government official, compiled a report of abuses committed against the Africans who had been forced into servitude. The Salazar government responded by arresting Galvão for treason and banning his report. Despite the introduction of some labor reforms in the late 1940s through the late 1950s, as I learned in Lubango, forced labor continued into the 1960s. So you could say that until just the other day, Benguela had been no more than a depot for human trafficking.

Wandering the city one day, I happened upon a church built in 1748 and dedicated to the city's patron saint, São Filipe de Benguela. It was a weekday, but even so, a dozen people were earnestly praying inside, a group of women near the altar loudly declaiming a service together as a sort of chorus. The church was cool, shadowy, a refuge from the heat and noise and dust, and the eight praying women — black, white, brown — seemed to assert a continuity of belief that had survived the centuries, because in addition to their search for rubber and copper and gold and slaves, the Portuguese had also wanted to find souls to convert. Along with fattening them, the colonizers ritually baptized every slave and forced laborer in kneeling groups before being chained and rowed out to the ships.

Another place I saw soon after I got to Benguela was an area in the southern part of town where Chinese developers and laborers were putting up six big, ugly multistory buildings, some of them pale pink, others canary yellow, still others pastel blue. Chinese industry, Chinese people, Chinese effort, Chinese paint, and Chinese investment are evident everywhere in the port cities of Benguela and Lobito.

The first Chinese workers to arrive in Angola were criminals, prisoners of the Chinese justice system — thieves, rapists, dissidents, deserters, and worse, an echo of the earliest immigration from Portugal. Characters in *Yaka* speak of being exiled to Angola to work off ten-year sentences. The first workers the Chinese sent were convicts shipped in chains, to work off their sentences in forced labor. Angola, having begun as a penal colony of the Portuguese, became just recently a penal colony for the Chinese. These Chinese convicts were the labor force for China-Angola development projects — the ugly oversized pastel buildings, the coastal roads, the dredging of the deep-water port of Lobito — and after they had served their sentences, the agreement was that they would remain in Angola. Presumably, like the Portuguese *degredados,* they would elevate themselves to the bourgeoisie or a higher class of parvenu.

Possibly, again like the Portuguese convicts, the Chinese would become the loudest racists, and for the same reason. "The inferiority complex of the uneducated criminal settler population contributed to a virulent form of white racism among the Portuguese, which affected all classes from top to bottom," the political historian Lawrence Henderson wrote of the early settlers. The Portuguese convicts became the most brutal employers and the laziest farmers, and a sizable number turned furiously respectable, in the way atoning whores become sermonizing and pitiless nuns.

After the first wave of Chinese convicts ("We started seeing them around 2006," a man in Luanda was later to tell me), more shiploads of semiskilled Chinese workers arrived. As with the early Portuguese convicts, they were all men. Then, a few years later, women were allowed to work in Angola, like Wang Lin and Mei, whom I had met in Lubango. Now there were Chinese marriages, Chinese children with Angolan nationality, Chinese shopkeepers, and Chinese stonemasons, plumbers, carpenters, and heavy-machinery operators up and down the country.

How many Chinese were there in Benguela and Lobito? Everyone I spoke to had a different figure, but always a high one. One estimate — wrong, it turned out — was a quarter of a million. I put these high figures down to fear. As in Namibia, Chinese businessmen were at the low end of the construction industry — for example, manufacturing cinderblocks to sell to Africans to make slum houses.

One of the newest buildings I saw in Benguela was the railway station, a fenced-off, flat-roofed, one-story building; it had been designed and put up by the Chinese in 2011 to replace the old bombed-out one. The Benguela Railway, Caminho de Ferro de Benguela, had been formed over a century ago to create an 835-mile link to the town of Luau, at the eastern edge of Angola, near the Congo border and the copper mines in Congolese Katanga. An Englishman, Robert Williams (after whom a rural station is named), had been the moving force behind the railway, a concession granted by the Portuguese. Work on the tracks began in 1903, at a time when there were fewer than 10,000 whites in the whole of Angola, most of them *degredados* — convicts, deserters, dissidents. But the railway was not in full operation until 1928, when the Portuguese boasted that it was a money-earning transcontinental line, taking Congolese minerals to the Atlantic coast and part of the overland route to Mozambique, on the other side of Africa.

Over the years, the Benguela Railway became a target for sabo-teurs, until it was totally destroyed during the long civil war. One challenge to rebuilding was that land mines had been laid up and down the line. Over a recent ten-year period, 2,000 mines had been found in the rail corridor and removed by a British charity called the HALO Trust. (In all, 68,000 mines in Angola have been cleared by this gallant organization, which is still uncovering land mines in the country.) The Chinese, loaning $300 million to the Angolan government and providing both skilled and convict labor, helped with some of the mine removal, relaid the track, put up new sta-tions, and rebuilt the infrastructure as far inland as Huambo, with the intention of reaching the Congo border.

The word was that the line was working. But the new, glass-fronted Benguela station was shut, and no one knew when it would open. No schedule was posted, nor did anyone know when the next train to Huambo would be leaving.

"What's Huambo like?" I asked.

"It's like Lubango, but not as nice."

I have been known for saying that I never saw a train without wishing to board it. I could have tried harder to find information about the Benguela line, and I might have managed to buy a ticket to Huambo. But having just arrived from the central plateau, where some of the same towns were linked by the line, I had an intimation of the trip. I already knew the railway towns of Catengue and Binga, and I had a pretty good idea of what Huambo would be like. So — almost unknown in my experience — I shocked myself by saying, "I don't think I'll take that train."

"I thought you'd jump at it," the American woman who'd brought me there said.

"I'm not jumping."

"I've heard you love trains."

Yes — what happened? Why was this trip going flat? Was it be-cause I always had to fight for a seat, and kept seeing the same dreary sights, the same bad roads, the same sorry market women, the same slums? In Africa every rural village is different, but every city is the same, and a perfect fright.

The American woman was Nancy Gottlieb. She had lived in Angola, mostly in Benguela, off and on for seventeen years, and she swore that the city was improving. One of her several projects was running an English-language school. I taught a few classes for her and also gave classes at the Instituto Superior de Ciências da Educação in the center of town.

The institute's name was grand, and the students and teachers were attentive. They spoke English fairly well — English was their subject, and half of them were employed as teachers in schools in and around Benguela. They were fond of books, they said, but when I pressed them, none could tell me the difference between fiction and nonfiction; a novel, a history book, a memoir of family life, a short story about an atrocity, an animal fable — they were all pretty much the same ("stories"). This slender grasp of definition and form seemed something of a handicap in teachers of literature, like a chef having no sense of smell.

"Books are so expensive," Sylvia volunteered when I urged them to read a bit more. Sylvia was stylishly dressed and a college teacher. True, everything was expensive in Angola except bananas, but the people were scholars. The rest of the class agreed: books were unaffordable.

"What do you read?" I asked.

They named some decades-old Nigerian paperbacks they'd been given. They were unfamiliar with the Angolan novelists I'd been reading.

Domingo said, "Can you give us some of the books you wrote?"

"I didn't bring any with me," I said. "Why don't you ask the Ministry of Education, or one of your billionaires!"

My lessons were mainly an effort to encourage them to write about events they had witnessed, economic changes, the progress of a wedding or a funeral, the novelty of Chinese settlers, even (I delicately suggested) political repression and intimidation—because the government reacted violently to any rallies, demonstrations, or protests, beating and arresting people, deploying dog squads and water cannons.

The great irony, if not outright farce, of human rights in Angola was that one of the first prisoners of conscience selected by Amnesty International, at its founding in 1961, was Dr. Agostinho Neto, who was named "political prisoner of the year" because he'd been locked up by the Portuguese. After he was released from prison, Neto went on to become the first president of Angola, and soon he began jailing *his* opponents, who themselves became prisoners of conscience. So Amnesty was in the paradoxical position of appealing for justice for the victims of the very man they had successfully championed. I mentioned this to the students at the institute, who weren't impressed, responding blandly and probably with some truth that worse things happened in Angola.

After I got to know them better, I asked them where they had been in their country. Apart from visits to Luanda and Lubango, they had not traveled much, and none had been south of Lubango. They had no desire to see Angola's rural areas, nor any African country. Where in the world did they wish to go, I asked. Like the students in Lubango, they were unanimous in choosing the United States. They were specific about places—New York, Chicago, Florida, California. On the rare days when the Internet worked in Benguela, these students trawled it for images of America. They were certain about what they'd find there.

"And Texas," Francisco said.

"Why Texas?"

"Because everything is bigger in Texas." This caused laughter, but after class, when I asked him if he was serious, Francisco said confidentially, as though giving me a travel tip, "Austin, Texas, is the best place for parties. Lots of bars, lots of music and women. You can have fun there."

"Can't you have fun in Benguela?"

"Not that kind of fun."

Money was on their minds. Money was on mine, too, because only cash, preferably U.S. dollars, was acceptable in Angola. No hotel or restaurant would accept a credit card. Not having enough cash was not an excuse — an ATM machine would be pointed out. "Use that." And it was in Benguela that I used my card with the highest credit limit and found that it was repeatedly turned down. This was the card that had been hacked in Namibia, my identity stolen. The card was unusable, so I depended on the dwindling stock of dollars in my bag. I had not known about the credit card fraud; I assumed that there was something wrong with the Angolan ATM machines, since there was so much wrong with everything else in Angola.

My money worry added to the melancholy of Benguela, the complacencies and longueurs of hot afternoons, stifling even next to the ocean, the turbid greeny-brown sea and the yellowish froth from its short breaking chop, the ruined pier to which the fattened and baptized slaves had been marched before being taken out to the slave ships.

Added to this was news of unrest in the Congo and the continuing Boko Haram massacres in Nigeria — the killings by fanatical Muslims of anyone who looked Christian or Westernized or foreign. I had thought I might head that way. But hundreds of Nigerians had been killed in the north of their country, and every week brought another bloody attack.

I was restless, and that made me curious about Nancy Gottlieb, who had stayed in Benguela and ran the English school. I asked her bluntly how it was that she had landed here. She said she had a degree in business, but had become disenchanted with the companies

she'd worked for in the States. She had learned of a Danish charitable organization with a "people-to-people" philosophy. She joined
it and was sent to Benguela in 1994 to help run a school. In the
following years she had lived through a rough period; for instance,
in 2001 the school was attacked and some of the students were kidnapped by anti-government soldiers. The uncertainty, deprivation,
and occasional violence lasted until the end of the war.

I asked what kept her—a slight, single woman—for so long in
a provincial town in Angola. She said that after spending time in
India doing Vipassana meditation, she'd had an insight. "I sort of
said to myself, 'If I don't find the man qualified to be the father of
my children, I think I would rather spend my time helping children
in Africa.' You know, a kind of thought that you just have and keep
to yourself, but you know that you had it."

And after seventeen years she still found her life here rewarding,
and felt safer than in many cities she'd known in the States.

"Everyone I meet has problems that are so much bigger than
mine," she said. "And yet for the most part they're almost always
happy, laughing, energetic, smiling."

I was told there was a man in Lobito whom I should meet. Lobito
was only sixteen miles up the coast, and on the way I stopped at
a ruined fort on a high mound outside the town of Catumbela,
just above its namesake river. Nearby, but at a greater height, on
a hilltop, the luxury Riomar Hotel was being finished by Chinese
laborers—one of the many projects of the president's billionaire
daughter, Isabel. The mansion of the governor of Benguela—it, too,
looked like a hotel—was also a feature of the hilltop.

The old fort, on the flat-topped Catumbela mound of yellow clay,
had dense stone walls, with interior cells and apartments, square
and squat, commanding a view of the surrounding countryside.
The mansion and the hotel were exceptional. All the other dwellings along the river were slum huts or shanties.

A notice on the fort gave its name as Reducto de São Pedro, *reducto* indicating a redoubt or a stronghold. The text in Portuguese ran as follows: "This [fort] was made at the cost of the inhabitants of Benguela, in honor of the municipal administration [because of] the continual insults made to the white people by the indigenous people of the district" — *os continuous insultos feitos aos brancos pelos indigenas deste districto.* "First stone placed on 5 October 1846."

It was quite an indictment. Because of your threats and insults, we had to build and pay for this fort. Look what you made us do!

I discovered afterward that in 1836 a settlement of free whites had been founded nearby on the river, but it had failed. Still, a handful of Portuguese remained, and punished the upstart locals. Later in the 1800s, a trader named António da Silva Porto lived on the river near here. He was a *sertanejo*, or backwoodsman, a trader who circulated from the coast to the interior. Polygamous, with a number of African wives and many *mestiço* children, and with an uncertain business, Silva Porto was a Portuguese Mr. Kurtz, but jollier, less successful, and, judging from one of his diary entries, realistic about his residence in Angola. Porto wrote, "In the land of the blind, the one-eyed are king. As poor as I am now, if I retired to Portugal today, I would amount to nothing; on the other hand, I am who I am around here as long as I possess one piece of trade cloth."

That neatly sums up the entire Portuguese adventure in Angola — hopeless, shiftless, horny Europeans exploiting Africans who they believed to be more hopeless and more shiftless. And it was a legacy, the corrupt Angolan president, Eduardo dos Santos, still in power after thirty-two years, continuing to exploit the people and accusing his critics of spreading *confusão* — chaos.

Lobito, just across the Catumbela River and up the road, was the brightest place I had seen so far in Angola — a deep-water port that was being improved by the Chinese, a large oil depot, a town center that was only mildly vandalized, and an older restored hotel, the Terminus, which had once been connected to the Benguela Railway.

The hotel and this somewhat salubrious part of Lobito was on a narrow spit of land called the Restinga, a Portuguese word for sandbar, which it much resembled. This finger-shaped peninsula protruding from Lobito was an upscale ghetto, with beaches on both sides, lined with palm trees and grand villas, modest bungalows and two-story apartment houses. A few of these buildings dated from the 1920s, but most of them had been put up in the 1950s, the time when Portuguese immigration to the colony had been encouraged with generous subsidies. And you could see that on this piece of land a *colono* might feel safe, since it gave the impression of being an offshore island.

The person I'd come to see was a tall, handsome man of about sixty with the sonorous name of Rui da Câmara e Sousa. It turned out that he had read some of my books and was happy to sit and tell me about his distinguished family. He was a descendant of a well-known governor of Benguela, and was himself a college professor and a real estate entrepreneur. His villa, built in 1954, was a pretty place, but as with all the homes on the Restinga, there was a continual clamor of shouts and music from boom boxes of the people picnicking on the beach just across the narrow road, some of them swimming, others eating or dancing under the palms and ironwood trees, many of them screaming at each other. Rui said he was used to it. He'd been born in Angola.

His earliest ancestors, having sailed from Madeira to Moçâmedes, down the coast, had been pioneers on the Huíla Plateau — in Sá da Bandeira, still fresh in my mind as Lubango — and Humpata. When I had hiked around Humpata one day, and seen the Boer graves from the 1920s, I had been struck by how hilly, cool, and fertile the land had been, how like a farming community in Portugal, the very qualities that had attracted the Boers and the Portuguese. Madeira at the time was poverty-stricken, like many of the places (the province of Bragança in Portugal, the Azores) from which Portuguese peasants emigrated. In Angola these people were largely subsistence farmers, most of whom cultivated sweet potatoes.

"It took about two months to travel from the coast to Humpata," Rui said, meaning a journey by ox cart. "But it was a good place to settle — the Portuguese there called themselves 'the white tribe of Angola.'"

Rui ran through the rest of his pedigree, not boastfully but rounding out the family portrait. His great-grandfather Captain António Barrada de Câmara had been military governor in 1900, and he died in a hunting accident. Rui's grandfather Hortensio de Sousa, governor of the province, had not been forgotten; a bridge and a park in Benguela had been named for him. Hortensio had been very poor in Portugal, a law student, and then a lowly employee in a Lisbon bank in 1914. When the First World War started he became involved with a dubious man in Luanda.

"The crooked man was Alves do Reyes," Rui said. "He wanted to be like Cecil Rhodes but was more like Bernie Madoff in his scheme to make counterfeit notes. His business was good, of course. When Reyes was arrested for fraud, my grandfather became prosperous."

Though the province was in constant turmoil in the 1920s, Hortensio flourished in Benguela. He was one of the few men in the small white population who was not a criminal exile and who did not become a shopkeeper or a trader. As an administrator, he rose to be governor and had lived in that huge mansion I had seen on the heights of Catumbela.

"It took a long time for the Portuguese to have continuity here," Rui said. "It is a recorded fact that it was not until 1906 that the first Portuguese person was born in Angola, and survived. All the other babies died."

I said, "But very few women came to Angola."

"No women came!" Rui said. "That's why I say that the greatest contribution Portugal made to Angola were the *pombeiros*."

The word was new to me.

"They were the indigenous people who wore shoes," Rui explained —agents, free men of color, all of them mulattos. "*Pombeiros* made the country. They were the ones who contacted the Europeans and facilitated the commerce. They supplied the slave traders with captives. They traveled into the interior. In some cases they traveled deep into Africa. Long before Livingstone made his famous trip to Angola, the Portuguese traveled on foot to Mozambique."

David Livingstone not only traversed the continent, walking 1,500 miles in six months, arriving in Luanda in 1854, but he also refused to abandon his men, the Makololos who'd been his porters and guides. His unstated reason was that he still needed the men as guides and porters, and so instead of accepting passage on a ship, he turned around and walked back, eastward, to the coast of Mozambique, describing and mapping and naming Victoria Falls on the way.

Rui was hospitable, and as a builder, speculator, and Angolan citizen he was optimistic about the country's future. Nonetheless, it was baffling to hear him extol the influence of the *pombeiros*. In his eagerness to explain one of the permanent institutions that the Portuguese had created in Angola, he settled on these *mestiços,* these *pombeiros,* who'd made their living as slave traders, commission agents, and middlemen, swapping cloth and beads, copper wire and rifles, for humans, who were rounded up, handed over to the slave master, then shipped out in chains.

We talked a little about the word *pombeiro.* I wondered if it came from the Swahili word *pombe,* for alcoholic liquor; someone who sold *pombe* might be called a *pombeiro.* The Portuguese adopted many Swahili words, and there are Portuguese words in Swahili: *meza* for table, *sapatu* for slipper, and the word *gereza* — prison — is derived from *igreja,* church. Later in my trip, an Angolan of my acquaintance said that *pombe* meant "pigeon roost" — a euphemism for slave quarters. But Fernand Braudel writes, "The word *pombeiro* may come from *pumbo*, the busy market in what is now Stanley Pool" — today called Malebo Pool, on the Congo River. Whatever the origin of the name, Braudel added, *pombeiros* "exploited their African brothers even more cruelly than the whites had."

My black Angolan friend didn't agree with Rui, and said that the *mestiços* were disliked by blacks and regarded as collaborators.

Still, it was a novelty to be sitting in a pleasant house on a sunny day in Lobito, hearing the family history of a man whose ancestors had settled the country. Arrayed on tables and on shelves were African artifacts — household objects, masks, stools, fetishes, and baskets — created by the masters of Angolan carving, the Lunda-Chokwe and the Yaka people. Even the most mundane wooden implement, such as a stirring spoon or a headrest or a pestle, was finely made, chip-carved and ornamented, and Rui handled them with a connoisseurship that suggested inner knowledge. There was no pretense to this Angolan-born white man, who considered himself a member of the white tribe. He was full of plans, too, for business deals and local opportunities. He was an optimist, he said. The country had a great future and he saw himself sharing in the coming prosperity.

The conversation came to a sudden halt, though, when Rui's cell phone rang, and he raised his hand to me and showed his palm in a wait-just-a-minute gesture.

Then he began speaking efficiently and rapidly, and the voice on the other end was a near-hysterical weeping, easily audible, though I was six feet from the phone.

"*Filipa*," Rui said, trying to interrupt. "*Filipa . . . Filipa . . . Calma, por favor, ouça, Filipa . .*"

He soothed the disturbed voice, spoke a little more, and hung up. Then he said, "That was my daughter. She has just had a bad automobile accident on the road from Luanda. I think she's all right, but she is very upset and her car is destroyed. They happen very frequently on that road — terrible car crashes. I must go to her now. You will excuse me?"

On the Restinga in Lobito, at an outdoor seaside café, I was given a celebratory meal, because I would be leaving in a few days for Luanda. The others at the table were American expatriates, with whom I had spent the day.

It was a beautiful evening, festive with strolling lovers holding hands, diners, Angolan families, youths on cell phones or tapping out text messages, all well dressed, their big cars and SUVs parked nearby.

At our table we were talking about a man we'd met, Jim, a Texan, who worked for Exxon Mobil in the design and manufacture of steel platform legs for offshore oil rigs.

"There's more oil in Cabinda than in Nigeria," he'd said.

Jim did nothing but work — ninety days straight was normal, and on his few days off he drank beer. His wife and six children were in Houston. For safety reasons, his company did not allow him to travel after dark even the short distance to Benguela, and he was accompanied by bodyguards whenever he went out in the evening in Lobito. An odd working life, but he'd seen odd places before — "oil countries are always the weirdest" — Algeria, Pakistan, the Persian Gulf states. Jim didn't complain. This was one of the wealthiest countries he'd ever been in, though not many Angolans did the work; his employees were British, Filipino, and Bangladeshi. He'd be leaving Angola soon. Jim said without much interest that he had never traveled the sixteen miles from Lobito to its sister city of Benguela.

"The oil people are subjected to strict travel rules," one of my expatriate friends said. "They can't cross the Catumbela Bridge after dark."

We had pizza, drank beer, and talked about how pleasant this meal was, how like a café on the Mediterranean, a light breeze from the ocean, the laughter, the fragrance of the food, the lovers, the drinkers.

And that was when I saw the children sidling near. At first I thought they were polishing the luxury cars — one was flicking a rag at a new Mercedes parked five feet away. But it was a ruse: the boy with the rag seemed to be busying himself so that he could have a plausible reason to approach us.

He was about nine or ten, extremely thin, barefoot, in a torn T-shirt and ragged trousers. He had the large bright eyes of someone either very sick or very hungry. The boy inched forward as we finished the meal, a third of a pizza still remaining on one plate, an unfinished crêpe on another.

The boy remained watching, the others behind him, all of them looking hopeful. Then the boy dared the question in a whisper, a word that sounded like *termina*, easily translated, and the woman who spoke Portuguese said we were indeed finished, and pushed the plates of scraps nearer to him.

He took the food from the plates into his skinny fingers and walked a few feet, and there, in the happiest and wealthiest enclave I had seen so far in Angola — the stylish Restinga — I saw the boy wolf down the food and then stumble away, and in this desperate expression of hunger, gasping from the effort of it.

Rui's daughter Filipa survived the crash. Rui was not so lucky. Nine months later, alone in his house — his wife and children were on vacation in Portugal — he was found by his maid, murdered in his bed, "his head smashed to pieces," it was reported in *Correio da Manhã*. "A trail of blood." There was no sign of forced entry, "which leads police to believe that the entrepreneur had opened the door to acquaintances." The police also speculated that the motive might have been robbery. "It was a house with many valuables but all that could be said for sure to be missing were a television, a computer, and a mobile phone."

"My father had no enemies," his son Ricardo told the newspaper *Sol*. "He will be buried here in Lobito. He was born here, like his father and grandfather. This is his land and where he wanted to be."

The person who had introduced me to Rui told me one gruesome detail that resonated. "He was bludgeoned to death by a big stick, the kind used to pound corn to flour—it was in his house." The stick was one of the finely made, heavy village pestles he had shown me in his collection of African artifacts, which he had held lovingly, as though they were family heirlooms.

15

Luanda: The Improvised City

R OLLING NORTH ALONG the coast, past the twisted wrecks of car crashes (I stopped counting at forty), and churning through towns clogged with yellow sludge washed from the sand cliffs by the rains, the roadside itself a tidemark brimming with litter, I seemed to be traveling into greater misery. Not my misery — as a flitting bird of passage, I had nothing to complain about — but the misery of Africa, the awful, poisoned, populous Africa; the Africa of cheated, despised, unaccommodated people; of seemingly unfixable blight: so hideous, really, it is unrecognizable as Africa at all. But it is, of course — the new Africa.

Angolans lived among garbage heaps — plastic bottles, soda cans, torn bags, broken chairs, dead dogs, rotting food, indefinable slop, their own scattered twists of excrement — and in one town a stack of dead cows, bloated from putrefaction, looking like a forgotten freightload of discarded Victorian furniture, with the sort of straight stiffened legs you see fixed to old uncomfortable chairs. This blight was not "darkness," the demeaning African epithet, but a gleaming vacancy, the hollow of abandonment lit by the pitiless tropical sun, appalling in its naked detail. Nothing is sadder than squalor in daylight.

Never mind, there is more squalor down the road in the next town, looking exactly the same, yet in spite of its familiarity just as frightening. The point beyond which you cannot find any more words for the squalor is the point at which you think: Why go any farther? It is like the futile feeling of describing a vastation, the ultimate ruination, a bomb crater, an earthquake, a war, or a massacre: your sigh echoes the despair you've just witnessed. Some of the South African townships I'd seen inspired this feeling and perhaps could have prepared me for what I was seeing now. But a nightmare does not prepare you for the next one. Each new nightmare is singular in its own ghastly way. And so it is with African cities.

For some weeks now I had been thinking that, in the overcrowded cities of Africa, I learned nothing except that people who had come to those places endured the dirt and discomfort because they were buoyed by their hopes of leaving and felt safer in the dense anonymity of a slum. A sense of temporariness made the squalor bearable. It was the same rationale that travelers had in the bus stations, which were merely filthy, oil-soaked parking lots: "Yes, dreadful. But, *senhor*, a bus will come to take us away!" No one conceived of living for any length of time in an African slum—without light or water it wasn't possible—only of going away, and the ultimate wish was to be delivered to another, less pestilential country.

"Where do you want to go?" I always asked the students.

"Away from here" was the inevitable answer.

An Angolan was not someone working, but someone waiting. You couldn't blame them for wishing to flee, though some were remarkably conceited in one respect. When Angolan students were awarded a scholarship to study in the United States, or were offered a three-month, get-acquainted, five-city tour there, they often insisted on flying first class—so I was assured by the officials who processed these travel grants. And when the demand for a first-class ticket was turned down (for even the American ambassador flew economy), the student applied to the Angolan government for an upgrade, which was routinely approved. After all, the Angolans in power traveled first class.

When I confided to the few foreigners I met on the road that I found all this dreary and unpromising, they either disagreed with me or were noncommittal. Some said they had hopes. I felt they couldn't bear to look hard, or perhaps were more idealistic than me. Or maybe they saw something I had missed. Some argued convincingly that Angolans had been brutalized by their past, or had seen much worse in their colonial history and in their wars—this part of the coast had been a chain of battlefields in the fight for Luanda. My own hopes were dwindling, and I thought the slow, wearisome trip might be making me delusional. Maybe I was wrong. Maybe I expected too much.

In that inquiring mood I met Kalunga Lima, an Angolan, younger than me, whose sentiments echoed my own—but he knew much more about the country than I did. In my relief, and in this spirit of agreement, he became my friend. He articulated what I felt.

"Something is coming here, something I fear," Kalunga said. "This is a country of young people, and very few of them have jobs. All were born after Dos Santos took power. They don't know any other government. They don't know their history. They have no idea of what happened in the war."

He glanced down at me writing this in my notebook. I said, "Can I quote you?"

"Someone has to say it." He went on talking. "These young people will show their anger—at prices, at corruption, at injustices. This is an intensely corrupt country. Everyone in power gets a commission."

I asked him for examples.

"You can't get a diploma or a certificate at any school without bribing or paying off the teachers. Everyone in the government takes bribes. The whole country is based on bribery. It will end badly."

He was talking fast. I was still writing, and looked up for more.

"I think the tide will turn," he said. "Look at all these idle youths. They sit around in the slums, but they see what's happening. The government lets the Chinese put up their buildings. They let the foreign oil workers earn their income and pay their bills. These youths are not involved. All they do is watch from the *musseques*" — the slums. "They are getting angrier."

"Yes?"

"Paul, listen. The infant mortality rate here is among the highest in Africa.* The roads are terrible, the housing is awful, the schools are useless. People don't have water. And it's a government of multi-millionaires. Profits from oil alone are forty billion dollars a year!"

Kalunga said everything that was on my mind, and was thoughtful and eloquent. In his indignation he had the authority that came of living and working in the country. He shrugged when I pointed out a nearby group of tough-looking policemen, and said that maybe they'd arrest him for sedition, or spreading alarm and despondency.

"Those cops?" We were at a sidewalk café. It was nine at night and the traffic was heavy; the street, Rua da Missão, was one of the -city's busiest. "They're waiting to stop a car so they can get a bribe. They call it a *gaseosa*. 'Give me a soda.'"

Within five minutes they had pulled over a van and were huddled with the driver, demanding the payoff Kalunga had predicted.

An Angolan in his mid-forties, Kalunga was heavyset, balding, and physically powerful. He had an intense gaze and the sort of face that seemed lit from within, suggesting high intelligence. He was a scuba diver, a professional photographer, and a filmmaker. He usu-

---

* And in the world: 215th out of 224 countries, according to the *CIA World Factbook* for 2012. There are 84 infant deaths per 1,000 live births in Angola.

ally rode a big Kawasaki motorcycle. One of the first things he told me was that he often traveled on this bike from Luanda to Lubango, stopping only for food and fuel — almost six hundred miles on bad roads and bush tracks. He was unlike anyone I had met in Angola, and I could not remember having encountered an African of his insight and objectivity, who spoke so freely and with such candor.

That was in Luanda, a few days after I had arrived from the road. The trip north from Benguela had started at five on a dark morning, at the bus station, as usual a bleak oily field. As we swung north toward Lobito, I noticed things I'd missed before: a huge new (Chinese-built) soccer stadium, a vanity project for a Pan-African tournament and a reminder of how many schools could have been built or improved with the money; a new (Chinese-built) airport, not yet opened; a new (Chinese-built) bridge over the Catumbela River; and the deepening of Lobito's port, Chinese workers doing the dredging.

Farther on, the garbage and the sight of wrecked lives, people existing like castaways at Xilip, Cangulo, Sumbe, and Porto Amboim: the slum dwellers crowded and immobile like their own trash heaps. Why did they fling away all this garbage, fouling the very places they lived? Between the towns, the river valleys were green, still wooded, and most of the beaches empty, glittering scoops of looping bays and headlands, no fishing boats onshore, no boats at all, just the running carpet of yellow sand next to the glare of water.

The main road was narrow but straight and paved, and this symmetry created a greater danger than rutted, potholed gravel because it emboldened drivers to speed. The consequences littered the roadside — burned-out trucks, minivans, and crashed cars the whole way to Luanda. One of the most recent wrecks, I now knew, belonged to Rui's daughter, Filipa.

Nine hours of this, with cows, goats, and dogs to steer around, and with stops. But a stop would be fifteen minutes in a muddy courtyard of a coastal town, yellow sludge up to my ankles as I sloshed to the shack selling—what? Greasy bags of poxy fries and piles of flyspecked *frango* ("Which one, *senhor?*") and no bananas. And a chat with Agostinho.

"What your country?" was a question I could answer, but "You tourist?" was a hard one.

I said, "I don't know."

"You business?"

"No business."

"You teacher?"

"Sometimes."

He poked me in the chest with a big blunt finger and laughed, saying, "Why you come here?"

"To see this," I said. I pointed to the heaps of garbage, the market women squatting against their baskets of bruised fruit and fanning away flies, the children whining for food, the rapper boys, the beaten dogs, the bullet-scarred shop fronts, the stacks of pirated DVDs, the strangely overdressed girls in tight slacks and curly gleaming hair extensions, eyeing me with disapproving pouty faces.

And Agostinho welcomed me in the national language.

I was surprised to see the wide empty beaches. Perhaps close-up they would look as befouled as the towns, but at this distance, seen from the higher coast road, they appeared wave-washed and clean and desolate. In Luanda I was to meet a young, athletic Portuguese diplomat who told me that on most weekends he drove down the coast to surf the waves here at Cabo Ledo and Cabo de São Bráz. He surfed alone, he never saw other surfers.

From the coast, some inland stretches were green, villages showing through the trees, some of them clusters of small thatched huts, others tracts of one-room cinderblock houses with tin roofs. Areas of the landscape had been burned out or deeply eroded, and looked blasted by time and the elements (and artillery shells), but no matter what lay inland, the seashore beneath the sloping hills was lovely

—remained lovely, probably, because it was uninhabitable. No one could live on or near the beach. Nothing would grow in the sand. The water was undrinkable. The traditional knack for small-scale sea fishing had apparently been lost.

In the afternoon we crossed the Kwanza, a wide river for which the Angolan unit of currency is named (*kwanza,* a Kimbundu word, should not be confused with the Swahili word *kwanzaa,* meaning "first"). The bridge over the Kwanza had been blown up many times and was being improved again—Chinese design, Chinese laborers, Chinese money.

Though I didn't know it at the time, this was a significant boundary, the river somewhat mystical for Angolans, a setting of myths and folktales and many battles. The land surrounding the Kwanza seemed almost idyllic. But not long after we passed it—thirty miles from the capital—the Luanda blight began. Soon there were no trees, only shacks and people and bare soil. The blight was not simply the small shacks, cement-block houses, roadside dumps, and stricken villages sitting in a sea of mud; blight was also evident in the new, larger cement structures, unfinished or abandoned or vandalized and sitting in seas of mud.

What appeared to be a modest building boom was in reality cutthroat opportunism, random and shoddily put-together real estate ventures—ugly houses and grotesque skeletal structures projected to be hotels. Why would anyone stay in these hideous buildings surrounded by slum huts? The building boom had been outstripped by the growth of squatter camps, hillsides of shacks. Buildings were rising, but slums were also growing—the buildings vertically, the slums horizontally. Like the South African pattern of migration, people from rural areas kept coming—the burgeoning shantytowns outstripping any slum improvements, the low mean city of new arrivals visibly sprawling.

In a bus that stopped in traffic for twenty minutes at a time, and with the continual dropping off of passengers, I thought I must be near the center of Luanda, so I got off with some other riders. The place was called Benfica, a district of heavy traffic and ugly buildings, stinking of dust and diesel fumes. Africa, yes, but it was also a version of Chechnya and North Korea and coastal derelict Brazil, places without a single redeeming feature, places to escape from.

As I stood at the roadside, tasting the grit, a small car intending to avoid the clogged traffic sped past, banged into a road divider, flew sideways, and, deformed by the crash, swerved off the road. A man with a bloody face and hands pushed the driver's side door open and, seeing him, bystanders laughed. The bloody-faced man staggered, his arms limp, his mouth agape, like a zombie released from a coffin. He was barefoot. No one went to his aid. He dropped to his knees and howled.

"*Idiota*," a man next to me said, and spat in the dust.

I became conscious of entering a zone of irrationality. Going deeper into Luanda meant traveling into madness. Everything looked crooked or improvisational, with a vibration of doomsday looming. I would have been happy to get on a bus going in the opposite direction, but I had a dutiful sense of needing to follow through on my plans, continuing north into the insanity.

Many places I'd been in the bush — Tsumkwe or Grootfontein or Springbok — had been described as "nowhere." Yet that was not how I saw them. They were distinctly themselves, isolated though they might be, settlements with a peculiar look — the look of home. But this Benfica was the very embodiment of nowhere, and on the way to nowhere, the twitching decrepitude of urban Africa. Standing next to the sheet-metal shop, the blowing dust, the big trucks and fumes, the noise and the heat, I thought how this was in microcosm the whole of the city experience in most of Africa, though up to now I had avoided facing the fact. And at that point I hadn't yet seen the full extent of Luanda's awfulness.

From the immensity of the slums, the disrepair of the roads, and the randomness of the building, I could tell that the government was corrupt, predatory, tyrannical, unjust, and utterly uninterested in its people — fearing them for what they saw, hating them for what they said or wrote. Though the regime was guilty of numerous human rights violations, it was not outwardly a politically oppressive place. The police were corrupt, but casually so — Angola was too busy with its commercial extortions to be a police state. It was a government of greed and thievery, determined to exclude anyone else from sharing, and Angolan officialdom had an obsession with controlling information.

I knew of many instances when investigative journalists were arrested for doing their jobs — two of them around the time I was in Luanda. In one case, a print journalist, Koqui Mukuta, was beaten and locked up for reporting on a peaceful demonstration, and twenty of the activists were also arrested. In another example, a radio journalist, Adão Tiago, was jailed for reporting episodes of "mass fainting," possibly caused by the release of toxic industrial fumes. But the Angolan government does not actively persecute the majority of its people; it is a bureaucracy that impoverishes them by ignoring them, and is indifferent to their destitution and inhuman living conditions.

A society of shakedowns and opportunism is inevitably a society of improvisation. That came across vividly in Luanda: the improvised bridge or road, the improvised hut or shelter, the improvised government, the improvised excuse. Angola was a country without a plan, a free-for-all driven by greed. It was hard to travel through the country and not feel that the place was cursed — not cursed by its history, as observers often said, but cursed by its immense wealth.

A sense of hopelessness had weighed me down like a fever since I'd stepped across the border weeks before. And with this fever came a vision that had sharpened, coming into greater focus, as if inviting me to look closer. My first reaction was a laugh of disgust at the ugliness around me, like the reek of a latrine that makes you howl or the sight of a dirty bucket of chicken pieces covered with flies. After the moment of helpless hilarity passed, what remained was the vow that I never wanted to see another place like this.

The xenophobia that characterizes Angolan officialdom in the remote provinces, small towns, and coastal cities is the prevailing mood in the capital, where hatred of outsiders seemed intense. Individually Luandans were friendly enough, sometimes crazily so, screeching their meaningless hellos. Nancy Gottlieb, in Benguela, saw this as "happy, laughing, energetic, smiling," but it seemed to me nearer to frenzy. In crowds they pushed and jostled with the mercilessness of a mob, and anyone with a uniform or a badge or any scrap of authority was unambiguously rude or downright menacing.

Friendliness is helpful to a stranger, yet I could manage without it. Being frowned upon or belittled is unpleasant, but not a serious inconvenience — no writer or traveler is a stranger to hostile or unwarranted criticism. But xenophobia of the sort I found in Luanda, and on an official scale, institutionalized alien-hating, was something new to me. It seemed odd to be disliked for being a stranger, and while the foreigners I met in the capital had their own explanations for this behavior (slavery, colonialism, civil war, the class system, tribalism, poverty, the cold-hearted oil companies) and had ways to cope with it, I found it inconvenient to be so conspicuous and developed a general aversion to being despised.

Luanda was a surprise because it had been to me, like much of Angola, a foreign land without a face. The reason for this silence or absence of description was that the Angolan government severely restricts the entry of foreign journalists, pretending to be contemptuous, accusing them, in their favorite buzzword of paranoia, of spreading *confusão;* outsiders disrupting the smooth back-and-forth of bureaucratic thievery. But contempt was the wrong word — contempt is inspired by superiority. A truer word was fear; politicians and businessmen alike were terrified of being found out, of anyone telling the truth about this corrupt country.

When Luanda does get into the news, it is usually a hooting headline to the effect that the city is practically unaffordable to foreigners: "The most expensive city in Africa!" The *Economist,* the BBC, and other media outlets have run such stories, with grotesquely colorful details, about the unreasonable sums you had to pay to get very little, which caused expatriates to complain. The people who suffered most from Luanda's high cost of living were not the expatriates but, of course, the urban poor, the people huddled in the *musseques.* They were mainly a silent class. Not a sullen class, though; Luanda's slums were characterized by blaring music and high spirits bordering on hysteria.

And when I heard of the foreign expatriate couple who paid many thousands of dollars for a tiny room in which the electricity often failed, or hundreds of dollars for a modest restaurant meal, I suspected that they were obliquely boasting, because what kept them in Luanda were their huge salaries. "My rent is seven thousand dollars a month," an expatriate in the oil industry told me. "And there are people who pay eight thousand a month who don't have water half the time." The only reason foreigners came to the city was to make money, and they stayed because their salaries kept growing as oil profits increased. Oil production figures had just been revised upward, output approaching two million barrels a day, at $100 a barrel: a billion dollars of gross revenue every five days, an almost unimaginable cash flow.

Luanda was a hardship post — it had been that way throughout its history — but it had become a boomtown based on oil. No traveler had ever praised Luanda in its poor days of the past, but it was much the worse more recently for its wealth: the bad restaurants where it was impossible to get a table, the stinking bars where it was hard to order a drink, the expensive neighborhoods with potholed streets, the traffic jams in which people sat for hours in their unmoving BMWs, Mercedes, or Hummers — I saw more bulky, over-priced Hummers in an average day in Luanda than I saw in a month in the States. Or the bad hotels where locals said I'd be lucky to get a room.

I found my way to the city center, and at the reception desk of a newish but already seedy hotel I was told they might be able to fit me in for three nights. I thanked the clerk for her hospitality.

Unsmiling, being busy, looking away from me, she said, "Pay in advance. Three nights. That will be eleven hundred dollars. Cash please. No credit cards."

"And you might not have hot water," came a teasing voice behind me.

I had no alternative. The whole of Luanda was a convergence of oil and mining interests, vying for the city's few hotels and restaurants (and prostitutes). The guests at my hotel were foreign workers in the national industries — some rough types in old clothes, especially rowdy in the evening, and the slicker, nastier-looking operators of all nationalities in their new suits, making deals in oil, diamonds, and gold. The words "oil, diamonds, and gold" have such allure, and suggest glitter and wealth in a fabled city fattening on its profits. But this was not the case. The city was joyless, as improvisational as its slums — hot and chaotic, inhospitable and expensive, grotesque and poor.

It had always been a city of desperation and exile. No one went to Luanda for pleasure. Criminal exiles were succeeded by slavers, and later by traders in rubber and ivory, like King Leopold's Belgians next door in the Congo. When the rubber and ivory trades declined, Angola returned to slavery and then forced labor. But these cruel roles were never mentioned. Ask any Portuguese to explain his country's relationship to Angola and you'll be given a version of Lusotropicalism, how the Portuguese had a natural affinity for the dusky people in these warm, sun-kissed lands. But the reality was that Portugal, having imposed itself on the land, was completely out of touch, socially and culturally, with Angola. One small example: Angolan music was not allowed to be played on the national radio station — the only radio station in the country — until 1968.

The city had never elicited any praise. A traveler in Luanda in 1860, quoted by the historian Gerald Bender, reported a town "ankle-deep in sand . . . Oxen are stalled in the college of Jesuits." You might say, "But it was 1860!" That's true, but it was the premier city in the colony, and the colony had existed for more than two centuries. Later in the nineteenth century another traveler reported Luanda as "a burning furnace [with a] cohort of mosquitoes, spiders, lizards, and cockroaches — an infernal scourge." In the mid-1920s, "Luanda was described by a Portuguese commentator as *cidade porca* — 'pig city'" (Douglas Wheeler and René Pélissier, *Angola*). At that time, only two places in Angola, Luanda and Benguela, could claim a skilled, working populace of "trousered blacks" — *caminhos*, as they were known in Angola. No Africans wore trousers elsewhere. Not that it really mattered, but the Portuguese boast — largely a self-flattering fiction — was that, as inspired imperialists, they had created a whole class of *assimilados* — indoctrinated, educated, assimilated Angolans.

Even in the 1940s Luanda was small, with a mere 61,000 inhabitants. The population increased rapidly in the 1950s and '60s. Most Portuguese were happy to get away from the mother country then, a time when only 30 percent of households in Portugal had electricity and less than half had running water. Migration was a step up, and continued into the mid-seventies, when whites numbered well over 300,000. We know that figure because just before independence there was a frantic scramble of Portuguese to flee Angola, and that was the number that left — virtually all of them. One vivid urban myth still making the rounds of Luanda describes the fate of a young Portuguese girl abandoned by her parents in their urgency to escape the country. The girl was raised by the family's former maid in a *musseque,* the solitary white waif in a black slum.

In 1974, the year of freedom and bolting *colonos,* the serious fighting began, bitter warfare that had never been seen in the history of this embattled country, as two main factions and their foreign supporters (Cuba on one side, South Africa on the other) skirmished to possess the land. The nearly thirty-year war finally ended in 2002 with the killing of the opposition commander, Jonas Savimbi, with an Israeli-made rocket (Israelis were said to be complicit in the assassination). Angola was the embodiment of Rebecca West's dictum in *Black Lamb and Grey Falcon:* "It is sometimes very hard to tell the difference between history and the smell of a skunk."

A country that has been so besieged, battle weary, and burned out, subjected to decades of fighting and uncertainty, can perhaps be forgiven for being half mad and dysfunctional. The Luanda of 1991 and '92, which seems to me like only yesterday, is described in Karl Maier's *Angola: Promises and Lies* as a city under attack, a ghost town of artillery damage and corpse-strewn streets, its population of refugees supported by food drops from the UN's World Food Program. Without calling attention to his own bravery, Maier reports intimidation, persecution, massacres, and *limpeza* (murder under the name of "cleansing"). In Luanda, Maier finds evidence of mass executions and hidden graves: "I detect movement, a scurrying among the graves we pass. Closer inspection reveals small tunnels the width of a beer can. There are tiny passageways everywhere among the tombs — rats are burrowing into the graves."

This, then, was the heritage of Luanda. Without oil wealth, it would have remained just another rotting African city by the sea, like Freetown or Monrovia or Abidjan, the horror capitals of West Africa. But it was floating, bobbing, buoyant on a lake of oil, and so it was busy. More than busy: it was out of its mind.

Don't listen to me. Listen to José, a man of thirty-five or so, a middle-level functionary in the oil industry, born in the province of Cabinda — site of the oil wells, most of them offshore. A serious, slightly flustered, and candid soul, José confided his doubts to me. He didn't know me, I didn't know him; we had met casually in a Luanda bar over a Cuca beer, and my direct questions provoked him.

"There is something wrong with this country," he said. "I have been to the U.S. on oil business. I was in Texas. I could see how different it was from this."

"Weren't you tempted to stay in Texas?"

"Yes. Because it was so nice. But how could I stay? It's not home. Your country is not my country."

"Where exactly do you live?"

"You wouldn't know the name. My town is in Cabinda — I love this town. But it's hard to get to. For one thing, I can't go by road to Cabinda, because that means passing through the Congo, and that is not possible."

One of the geographical anomalies of Angola is that oil-rich Cabinda is a separate, isolated province surrounded by the Democratic Republic of the Congo, a weird result of Portuguese colonial expansion. But it has proven valuable only recently. When John Gunther traveled in Angola for his *Inside Africa* (1955), he was unimpressed by anything in the country, and he dismissed Cabinda entirely, as a remote area without any resources. "One geographical curiosity is Cabinda," Gunther wrote, "an enclave of Portuguese territory separated from the rest of Angola by the mouth of the Congo. Not much is known — or is worth knowing — about Cabinda." Cabinda is the source of virtually all (95 percent of the national revenue in 2011) of Angola's immense wealth. Being prosperous and cut off, with some educated people, the province even has its own secessionist movement, which now and then sets off a bomb or sabotages a building.

José didn't want to talk about that, and I couldn't blame him — after all, I was a foreigner with perhaps too many questions. And I was a noncommittal American. The CIA had a long history of meddling, its covert operations designed to further Angola's instability, as I knew from reading *In Search of Enemies* by a former CIA operative in Angola, John Stockwell. Yet José seemed eager to unburden himself.

"Angola," he said, shaking his head. "There's something wrong. You can't treat people like this!" He sighed in exasperation and looked at me closely.

"You have traveled here?"

"A bit."

"You see how poor are the people? But others are so rich. Some people in big cars, just sitting, expensive watch, jewels, suits from Lisbon. And outside the car, the women on the street, no shoes. You see them, they carry things on their head."

"And they live in the *musseques*."

"Yes. This city is so dirty! I am here for a business meeting, but if my company asks me to come here and live, I will have to pay three or four thousand dollars a month for a little room. It's a problem for me. I can't do it. I would go anywhere but here."

"So what do you think is the problem, José?"

"The government is the problem," he said without hesitating. "They don't care. They are just stealing money from the oil business."

"Like Nigeria."

"Worse! Much worse — and Nigeria is terrible," he said. "We need a change — the whole government should just go away. We should get a new one that will use the money better."

A bit breathless from having spoken his mind, he seemed to have surprised himself with his own candor. He asked me what I was doing in the country.

I said, "I'm just visiting."

He said, "I'm sorry it looks like this."

No foreign newspaper reported the weirdness of Luanda, though the writer Pepetela had published a hallucinatory novel about the city. Perhaps to avoid censorship, his 1995 book *The Return of the Water Spirit* is oblique, depending for its effect on the strange collapse, week by week, of tall modern buildings in Luanda, as if from the effects of a curse. The manner of destruction is a mystery, seemingly bound up with the violation of the serene habitat of a resident spirit — possibly the disturbance of "the old African identity." But the curse is simple enough to understand: it is the blight of incomplete and misdirected modernity. Urbanization has so upset the natural order of things that the land itself has become seismic and unstable.

This fanciful fiction is penetrated by occasional glimpses of reality, as when Pepetela describes daily life in wartime Luanda: "'How much lower can we sink?' people asked while standing in the queue, either for the bus, or in front of the store with goods that few of them could afford to buy, or at the hospitals that had neither medicine, cotton nor gauze, or in the schools that had no books and no desks. Luanda was filling up with people fleeing from the war and hunger — at a rate that was as fast as it was suicidal. Thousands of homeless children loitered in the streets, thousands of youths sold and resold things to those that drove past in their cars, countless numbers of war amputees begged for alms at the market. At the same time, important people had luxury cars with smoked glass. No one saw their faces. They drove past us and perhaps they didn't even look so as not to have their consciences made uneasy by the spectacle of all that misery."

This description of Luanda in the early 1990s can easily stand for the Luanda I saw almost twenty years later. So, for all its obliqueness, the novel is prescient. And two characters who make cameo appearances in the narrative are other living Angolan writers, Arnaldo Santos and José Luandino Vieira. Vieira, who was born in Sambizanga, the same slum where the current president, Dos Santos, first saw the light of day, celebrates the slum as a vortex of energy. Santos is a minimalist poet, Vieira one of the first novelists of the revolution and himself an early political prisoner.

All three writers — Pepetela, Santos, Vieira — are white, but identify themselves as fully Angolan. White writers in South Africa also identify themselves as South African, and they are, but they come from a privileged, or at least an educated, class, whereas these Angolans are from the poorest level of society, slum born and bred. Another important Angolan writer, but much younger, is Sousa Jamba, born in a rural village near Huambo in 1966. Jamba spent much of his youth as a war refugee in Zambia, then shuttled between Britain and the United States, where he was educated. After publishing three novels, Jamba returned to his home village in 2004 and reported to the BBC that the place was in much worse shape than it had been when he left it decades before, during the war years: "The school has fallen apart . . . [The students] have to bring their own chairs, the windows are completely broken. They have no pens or pencils. I find it very sad that one of the wealthiest countries in Africa can have kids who don't have pencils."

I'd previously met Jamba in London, and Vieira in Portugal, where he had rusticated himself to a small village. Both men were likable and intelligent but had the stunned and rather solitary air of exiles: a look of lostness. Born in a slum in Luanda in 1935 and raised in poverty, José Vieira was an early target of the Portuguese, arrested by the colonial authorities as a dissident when he was twenty-four. Two of his novels, *The Real Life of Domingos Xavier* and *The Loves of João Vêncio*, and his short story collection *Luuanda*, are expressive, written in an almost untranslatable patois (so the translators attest; I read them in English), a combination of Kimbundu and Portuguese peculiar to the Luanda shantytowns, the ghetto idiom Vieira had learned, a "literary eloquence founded on slang, patois, and pimp terminology."

Over coffee in the Portuguese town of Matosinhos, Vieira told me that he was still routinely turned down for a U.S. visa because of his old political beliefs, his imprisonment by the Portuguese, and his former militancy. Since Pepetela and Santos still lived and wrote in Luanda, I made an attempt, through an intermediary, to meet them. And I said that if they were interested, I would be happy to speak at the Angola Writers' Union or meet them there for a cup of coffee.

This quaintly named organization, a bureaucratic collection of like-minded (that is, approved) writers, was a cultural throwback to the Soviet Union's adoption in the 1960s of Angola's liberation struggle. The Agostinho Neto Mausoleum in central Luanda was another Soviet throwback, inspired by the mummification in Lenin's tomb. Because of the avowed Marxism of one faction, many Angolans in the sixties and seventies were more inclined to study in the Soviet Union than anywhere else, and were offered Soviet scholarships. President Dos Santos was a Russian-speaker who had been educated as an engineer in Baku, Azerbaijan, and whose first wife had been Russian. (It was their daughter, Isabel, who had become a billionaire investor in Angola, and was touted as one of Africa's five richest women.)

"They don't want to meet you," my intermediary said of my proposal of a cup of coffee with the Angolan writers at the writers' union.

"What about my giving a talk? Did you mention it?"

"They had a problem with that."

"What sort of problem?"

"They don't see the point of it."

"Of my speaking to them?"

"Of listening to other writers. They're funny that way."

"Writers like me?"

"Any foreign writers."

"So what did they say?"

"That they didn't think there was anything you could tell them that they didn't already know."

"Probably true! But maybe they could tell me something," I said. "And what about literary curiosity—or any curiosity?"

"I guess they don't have it."

What they had—their chief trait, the affliction of Angolan officialdom—was xenophobia, a bit awkward in any writer and rather a burden. It made much of their writing humorless, self-righteous, and provincial, which was another reason their writers' union was necessary to them, because it legitimized them as writers. They had an engraved certificate they could frame and hang on the wall, the way dentists and massage therapists did. And, precious in that politically protected way, they could go on writing their fantasies, and be rewarded by the dictatorship, while the whole country was falling to pieces before their eyes.

Yes, they probably would not have wanted to hear me say this sort of thing to them.

In the meantime, I rattled around the city. The traffic was unmoving, the gridlock incessant. "It takes hours to go a few miles!" people said. "I have a two-hour commute!" The sidewalks were broken and obstructive. Blue-and-white jitneys called *candongueiros,* which followed no fixed route, roamed from street to street picking up fares. Some streets were named in the solemn way of political dogmatists—Rua Friedrich Engels, Boulevard Comandante Che Guevara, and even Rua Eça de Queiroz—honoring the author of, among other novels, *Cousin Basilio,* for which he is sometimes referred to as the Portuguese Flaubert.

One Luanda street I happened upon in the course of an evening walk was Rua de Almeida Garrett (off Avenida Ho Chi Minh). It was named for João Baptista da Silva Leitão de Almeida Garrett, a nineteenth-century Portuguese writer and politician, little known in the United States and perhaps even lesser known in Angola. I knew of him only from an epigraph quoted in a novel by José

Saramago, an assertion that resonated in Luanda: "I ask the political economists and the moralists if they have ever calculated the number of individuals who must be condemned to misery, overwork, demoralization, childhood, rank ignorance, overwhelming misfortune and utter penury in order to produce one rich man."

Many streets in the city had no name, a topic of satire among people from whom I solicited directions, a sort of you-can't-get-there-from-here paradox. But Luandans—the working ones, the foreigners, the businessmen—lived with all this inconvenience, and laughed about it, because enduring it meant they could make money. The weak went home, the poor died, the strong stayed and got rich.

Billions of dollars were routinely embezzled by Angolan politicians and oil executives. Martin Meredith devotes an enlightening chapter in *The Fate of Africa* (2006) to the gross cheating by Angolan officials, which is an extensive catalogue of klepto schemes. Some businessmen engaged in a mechanism known as "trade mispricing." This funny-money ploy was explained by Ed Stoddard in a 2011 Reuters report on corruption in Angola. "In this case, the way it typically works is that Angolan importers pretend to pay foreigners more for imports than they actually spend. The difference provides cash that can be discreetly put into banks or other assets abroad." It worked best with oil, but also with simple import transactions. "An Angolan importer overpays the exporter, say in the United States, and asks the exporter to deposit the excess payment in the importer's offshore account or a Swiss bank," said Dev Kar, a senior economist at the International Monetary Fund. Through this trade mispricing many billions vanished in an average year.

You'd expect such a place to be moribund, yet Luanda was abuzz. A current throbbed through it like a rapid pulse—a blare of car horns, *zungeiros* (street vendors), hawkers selling lottery tickets, shouting women with baskets of fruit on their heads, children and amputees loudly calling out—more demanding than beseeching. The days were also very hot—low-lying Luanda is noted for its enervating humidity. There was not enough space in the city for all the cars and impromptu markets, and the constant spillover of people, crowding the streets and sidewalks, made it a jammed and harassed place.

Because only cash was accepted, banks were besieged by people withdrawing money, and most high-end shops or businesses of any size had an ATM machine on the premises—my hotel had two in the lobby, and they were in constant use. The fact that so many people walked around with stacks of kwanza notes made it a city of muggers and thieves. An American woman told me that in order to make arrangements for her family of four to fly back to the States, she'd had to bring a bag filled with $4,000 in cash to the airline office to buy the tickets.

Because Luanda was dysfunctional and subject to sudden power cuts and water shortages, people with money—Angolans and foreigners alike—created small hermetic settlements, walled compounds, where they had their own generators, water sources, and amenities: tennis courts, swimming pools, golf and social clubs, and of course armed sentries and guard dogs.

The International School of Luanda was one of these salubrious compounds, an oasis behind a wall, catering to the children of expatriates, diplomats, oil people, and wealthy Angolans. Unwelcome at the state schools and rejected by the writers' union, I visited the school out of curiosity, to observe a sealed community in action. In return for their hospitality, I gave a talk to the students.

After a long and far-from-simple drive to the south of the city, through the improvised neighborhoods, the grim precincts of poverty, the International School was something of a surprise: orderly, well planned, spacious, clean, and surrounded by flower gardens. Healthy children of all races were gathered in congenial groups— 630 students, 91 teachers—and what was singular about the school was the presence of books. Apart from Akisha Pearman's department in the Instituto Superior in Lubango, books had not figured much in any of the schools I'd visited. *Please send us books from America,* I was implored, and my routine reply was to refer them to the billionaires in their government.

The newly built library at the International School was worthy of a small college. And the students were bright sparks, with the confident air that comes of being well taught, taken seriously, and — it must be said — wealthy, sheltered from the hideosities of Luanda. I gave my talk and answered questions and was shown around the school by the teachers, who were earnest and upbeat. It all seemed marvelous and almost unbelievable that such a place could exist amid the encircling gloom.

"So," I asked casually, "what's the tuition here?"

"Forty-seven thousand dollars a year," I was told by a teacher, who gulped as she managed to utter the words.

At the time, this was roughly the cost of tuition at Harvard University. Because many of the students were the children of oil industry employees, the existence of such a good school was an incentive for foreign workers to stay with their families in Luanda. An oil executive was later to tell me that Angolans simply did no work, and he added, "Forty thousand workers in the oil industry support twenty-three million Angolans."

The residential compounds and other amenities were the foreigners' way of turning their backs on the reality of the place, of shutting out the chaos, of being secure. In many respects this pattern was no different from the urban planning in Palm Springs or the gated communities around Phoenix and elsewhere, but in Luanda what lay outside the compounds were slums of extreme danger and pure horror.

16

"This Is What the World Will Look Like When It Ends"

THE INTENSITY OF A TRIP — bad food, hard travel, slow buses, hot weather, jeering locals — can induce a mood of isolation, provoking episodes of alienation that resemble out-of-body experiences. I think: Am I imagining this? And I have no answer, because no one hears the question. But then I found someone to ask.

Dazed with Luanda and dispirited by my trip, I was fortunate around this time to have met the clear-sighted Angolan Kalunga Lima, who had told me many things I needed to know — and most of all that my sense of Angola, and Luanda in particular, was not the consequence of travel fatigue. I was first introduced to Kalunga at a photographic exhibition one evening in Luanda. He assured me that I was not overdramatizing the situation. He was impressive, intelligent, and straight-talking, and his gift for satire was a relief to me.

I said, "A man in Namibia told me, 'Angola's a nightmare!'"

Kalunga said, "Namibians have a gift for understatement."

Perhaps a clue to his speaking his mind was his unusual history. The son of a politically passionate Angolan father and an adoring Portuguese mother, he had been born in Algeria, where his father, a committed revolutionary, was a soldier in exile. Kalunga had been educated in Canada and the United States, and later, on a whim, he taught on the Caribbean island of St. Lucia. He had traveled widely in Africa and Europe, was well read, responsive, funny, and hip. Seeing a Hummer stalled in traffic on a Luanda street, the African driver wearing thick gold chains around his neck, Kalunga said, "He got bling!" He was a maker of documentary films, and his latest project was chronicling the discovery of the "Angola Titan," a dinosaur whose fossil remains had been discovered in the southern desert near Namibe. He had also made a documentary about Angola's elusive and little-known giant sable antelope (*palanca negra gigante*), apparently its last living wild game.

I instantly took to Kalunga, for his warmth, his candor, his enthusiasm, and soon after we met, we made plans to travel in the Angolan bush, a safari on which he would be the photographer and I the writer. He wanted to show me the habitat of the endangered antelope.

"We'll collaborate! It'll be a major magazine piece!"

A major magazine piece was less of an incentive for me than delving deeper into rural areas. What convinced me that we'd be a good team was that we seemed to share certain crucial ideas, as aid skeptics and as disbelievers in the current political process, with a curiosity about traditional tribal culture and a general feeling that any salvation, or simple hope, in Angola was likely to be found not in Luanda but in the landscapes of the distant countryside.

The sable antelope was an animal unique to Angola, and because of that was an icon in the country—the symbol of the national airline, the name of Angola's national football team. It had the longest horns of any antelope in the world, and existed nowhere else in the world except a place called Cangandala.

"I thought there were no wild animals left in Angola," I said.

"Just this one, and it's doomed," Kalunga said. "You have to see it soon, before it becomes extinct."

"Where is Cangandala?"

"East of here. Near Malanje."

"That's where I want to go. On the train."

"*Zona verde*," he said.

"I love that expression. I heard a guy use it when we got stuck on the way to Lubango. The green zone."

"The bush."

"Why is it I always feel hopeful in the bush?"

Thoreau had written in his essay "Walking": "I believe in the forest, and in the meadow, and in the night in which the corn grows." I too believed in those verities.

"Because they haven't made a mess of it," he said. And being Kalunga, and gray-eyed, he smiled and added, "Yet."

It was true, he said, that Luanda was a city of idle millions. Three quarters of the country's population was under the age of twenty-five, and very few had jobs. A quarter of Angolans lived in Luanda. Unemployment he estimated at about 90 percent. But these were wild guesses, since statistics were nonexistent. No one knew the size of the population. The last general census had been taken almost forty years ago, in 1974.

"The people from the countryside flock to Luanda — and what for?" he said. "There's no work. It's just one slum after another. They don't go to school, they don't have jobs. They have no idea of the war that ended just nine years ago."

It so happened that I was in Luanda on Angola's Independence Day. It was a national holiday, but for an unemployed and cynical populace, whom the government regarded as "the mutable and rank-scented many," this was meaningless. There was no celebration, no music, no flags flying; there were no parades. It was just a day off, an empty day.

Kalunga mentioned a great battle, the siege in 1994 of Cuito Cuanavale in the south, a town held by Angolan and Cuban soldiers that was attacked by armored columns of the South African army. In forty days of shelling, Soviet tanks against Mirage fighter planes, the result was the deaths of more than fifty thousand people and defeat on both sides, the whole bloody business fought to a stalemate. I had heard it called "Angola's Gettysburg" and "Angola's Stalingrad."

"It was the biggest conventional battle fought anywhere on earth since World War Two," Kalunga said, "and these Angolan kids you see have no idea that it happened. There are land mines in Caxito" — sixty miles north of Luanda — "that are still blowing up farmers, but no one seems to care. People just sit around. Other people clean them up — foreign agencies."

"But if there's work for the Chinese, why isn't there work for Angolans?" I asked. The day before, I had spoken with a man in the know who said that an accurate figure for the number of Chinese expatriates, businessmen, and settlers in Angola was about seventy thousand, and slowly growing.

"The Chinese are a separate workforce," Kalunga said. "They keep to themselves. We first began to see them in 2006. They were living on ships anchored in Luanda harbor. You know why?"

"I was told they were criminals, working off their sentences."

"Right. Slave labor. They worked on the buildings that are now starting to fall apart — there are cracks all over the Chinese buildings. They're still here. The first generation of Chinese-Angolan babies is starting to appear. You see them in the shantytowns of Luanda, these little half-Asian *mestiços*."

Some of these Chinese former prisoners had served out their sentences, gone into business, and become wealthy, or at least well-off. They ran factories making plastic goods and cinderblocks. Some had resumed their old criminal professions. Kalunga gave the example of a large counterfeiting ring that had made fake 2,000-kwanza notes. This was a shrewd move; though Angolans could easily spot counterfeit hundred-dollar bills, no one recognized fake kwanzas because no one had seen the point of faking them. These dud bills were used in the markets and shops, and many had been exchanged for real U.S. dollars, the most desirable currency in the country. But the Chinese had their adjustment problems. For one thing, they were ethnically, visibly alien, and Kalunga and others I had met in Luanda told me that the Chinese were targeted for harassment, disliked, jostled, picked on, seen as easy prey, and robbed. The week before I arrived in the city, two Chinese men were stabbed to death in a casual mugging.

"More recently, Chinese women and children have begun to arrive and settle," Kalunga said. "And I see rich Chinese in the restaurants and gambling casinos. They're part of the life here."

"So if it's as awful as you say, how do you manage to live in Luanda?"

"I don't live in Luanda!" he said. "And I travel a lot."

It was then that he'd described his film on the iconic symbol of Angola, the giant sable antelope. When I mentioned that I knew the sable antelope from its picture on the 10-kwanza note, Kalunga laughed. No, he said, that was yet another example of Angolans getting it wrong: the animal depicted on the money was not a sable antelope but another creature entirely, called a bush donkey. Angolans didn't know the difference, but in any case, there were only about forty of the animals left in the wild, because of the erosion of their habitat and their being poached for their meat and their splendid horns. They were doomed.

"And we're probably doomed," Kalunga said. "That's why I don't live in Luanda. I moved my family to Lubango so we can get out of the country if there's trouble. It's possible from there to get to Namibia by road. In a crisis we'd never get out of Luanda by road or air. We'd be stuck here, and that, my friend, would not be good."

His wife, Maria Manuela, whom he called Nela, was a medical doctor in the Angolan army, and they had three young children: Carlos, sixteen; Rafael, nine; and Luena, seven. But his wife was barely getting by; doctors in Angola had no status, he said. Most doctors earned "about three thousand dollars a month — and a clerk in a bank earns about eight hundred." The government hospital in Lubango was so poorly run his wife could not perform necessary operations — Nela was a plastic surgeon specializing in correcting disfigurements and war injuries — so she had joined the staff of a hospital funded by a Canadian charity.

"Imagine, a private hospital! Because this government, rolling in money, can't run a hospital itself — that's how desperate things are," Kalunga said. "And Angolans don't make anything. Everything is imported. There's a lot from Brazil. Food from South Africa. Everything you see in this country — every single thing — has been made somewhere else."

Meeting Kalunga Lima energized me, because he himself was energetic. He spoke his mind and I could speak mine, and I was free to ask him ignorant questions. He revealed a side of Luanda that had been hidden from me. He introduced me to his friends; some of them were as intense as he was, others were smooth operators — money men, importers of luxury cars, oil executives. Instead of going to the gourmet restaurants — the crowded, expensive places — we went to hole-in-the-wall places that from the outside did not look like restaurants at all — simple shop fronts that were mom-and-pop diners.

This was another aspect of the secret, improvisational city. One of these eateries — no name, no sign — served home-cooked Portuguese food, and a large-screen TV showed a live feed of the Portuguese parliament debating the meltdown of Portugal's economy. Kalunga said that — given the food, the checkered tablecloths, and the genial hosts, Mr. and Mrs. Coelho — we might be in Lisbon or Oporto. And by the way, he said, the Portuguese prime minister would be arriving in Luanda within the next few days, hoping to borrow money from the Angolans to save Portugal from declaring bankruptcy. (This happened, just as he'd predicted.)

Kalunga explained to me the origins of the independence struggle. His father, Manuel dos Santos Lima, had been the first MPLA (Popular Movement for the Liberation of Angola) military commander, based in Algeria in the 1960s, and had helped found the military wing of the party. Kalunga said with a rueful smile that of all the foreign soldiers, only the Cubans had been idealistic, but in time they too became disenchanted with the corruption and selfishness that had followed the revolution. He detailed the atrocities, the beheadings, the mass killings committed on both sides, and the competition among independence fighters, and described the funding of the war, the slaughter of elephants for their ivory, the sale of blood diamonds.

But corruption was nothing new in Angola, he said. In the late nineteenth century a megalomaniacal chief in Ovamboland, in the south, had impoverished his people, stolen their cows, and built himself a castle in the bush. Other chiefs mimicked the Portuguese and dressed in frock coats. Certain chiefs of the Kwanyama bought imported clothes, drank champagne, studied etiquette, and stuffed themselves with food at a time when their own people were dying in a famine. These extravagances were a distant echo of what was happening in Angola right now.

Speaking of distant echoes, it was Kalunga who had used the word *jinguba,* meaning "peanut," which reminded me of "goober." He said the Kimbundu word *mbanza,* a musical instrument, probably became "banjo." His name, Kalunga, bestowed on him by his proud father, meant "God," "supreme being," or "highly intelligent being," and he laughed when telling me this. He explained that in this dispirited place many evangelical preachers from Brazil had become successful, turning movie theaters into churches. God-bothering was one of the growth industries of Angola — churches run by flamboyant Brazilian preachers. They were shysters, sweet-talkers, and because they demanded money from new believers and brandished fake diplomas, they were known as sellers of *banha da cobra* — snake oil.

"You've heard the word *assimilado*?" Kalunga asked over coffee one day. I had heard the term and thought it indicated a mulatto with an education. But he said no. "They were indigenous people who held the status of citizen. There were three requirements. One, you had to speak Portuguese fluently. Two, you had to sleep in a bed, not on the floor. Three, you had to eat with utensils. What do you think?"

"Sounds reasonable."

"But what about reading and writing?" He laughed softly. "Literacy wasn't a requirement! And you know why? Because the Portuguese officials who checked them — many of *them* could not read or write. Ha!"

A habitual blogger, Kalunga often left posts on a documentary makers' website, Creative Cow. One had been a message to a young filmmaker: "So much of life happens in ways that we can not entirely predict, so having a variety of experiences opens up possibilities you may not have predicted. For example, taking a course in a formal environment will give you a chance to meet individuals with similar goals you would not meet on your own.

"Last piece of advice, set yourself up for the long haul. What ever you do, make sure it is sustainable, it invariably takes longer than you think to get anywhere in life."

Kalunga put me in touch with a well-traveled friend of his whom I asked about the Angolan president's personal history, and he said, "I have seen *favelas* in Brazil and slums in Latin America and

Africa. The slum where Dos Santos was born, Sambizanga, is by far the worst of them all. I have never seen anything to compare with it in squalor and poverty."

We talked about paying a visit there. Kalunga said, "What's the point?" And the friend agreed: "When Mandela became president, he made a point of fixing up the township where he'd been born, improving the housing and providing water and electricity. But Dos Santos, a multibillionaire and powerful, has done nothing. He has no wish to improve his town or do anything. He has no sentiment, no pity."

The country was ripe for satire. In 2012, the *New York Times Magazine* ran a multipage advertorial, paid for by the Angolan government (a government that until then had refused to allow any *New York Times* journalist to enter the country), that referred to the "maturity of [Angola's] young democracy." "Young democracy" is a curious way to describe a country with a president who appointed himself in 1980 and has been in power ever since. Dos Santos's portrait is on the money. When a politician's face is on all the banknotes, you can be sure he is planning to stay in office for life. Young democracy!

I was invited to give a talk at the Viking Club to the Angola Field Group, its membership composed of some Angolans and many expatriates, teachers, oil industry functionaries, aid workers, hangers-on, and hospitable beer drinkers. Though he was not present that evening, Kalunga was a member and had shown his documentary films there.

My talk was preceded by the singing of three diminutive Bakongo men in snap-brim hats, from Uige province in the distant north. They called themselves the Disciples and harmonized to "Go Down, Moses" and "When the Saints Go Marching In," which they had learned at the mission station in the remote town of Bungo.

Instead of giving a formal talk to the boozy group, I merely described my trip from the border — only 2 of the 250 members of the club, I learned, had been near the border. I said, "There is nothing I can tell you about Angola that you don't already know, but I'm sure there are many things you can tell me" — and I invited comments.

One of the men in the audience elaborated on the various euphemisms the officials used to ask for bribes. Another said, "Do you know about *Dia do Homem*? It's Men's Day all over Angola — every Friday is Men's Day. Men meet, get drunk, go out and prowl and chase women. There is no Women's Day."

"The motorcycle taxi has a funny name," a young man said. "It's called a *cumpapata* — literally, a 'grab-ass,' because that's how the person behind the driver holds on."

A woman said, "Cuca beer — I will tell you what *Cuca* stands for. *Com um coração Angolano* — with an Angolan heart."

It was a pleasant evening of congenial foreigners and Angolans who lived in Luanda as if besieged. Afterward they regaled me with stories of how expensive it was to live in the capital. Yet none complained. Simple survival in the city represented a sort of victory.

I met Kalunga the next day, at another restaurant.

"That's a river fish," he said, explicating the ingredients of my meal. "It's called *cuchuso* — they catch it in the Dande River north of here. We can go there. We can go so many places! Angola has land and water. All the fresh food is imported from South Africa, yet Angola could feed Africa. This country has not been written about at all!"

So we made plans: to look for more giant sable antelopes; to visit the site of the recently discovered dinosaur the Angola Titan, which he had documented; to go north to Zaire province to see the Bakongo people and the trackless forests of Uige; and to take the train to Malanje. And we would travel by boat along the western limit of Angola, down the Kwango River, which David Livingstone had written about.

"To *zona verde!*" he said, toasting, and as we pored over the map, he said that it was all doable.

We drank to our proposed trip, our venture, as Kalunga put it, to *as terras do fim do mundo* — to the lands at the end of the earth.

I had never envisioned traveling with someone else. I had always extolled the virtues of going alone, putting up with the hassles, taking the risks; that was how I had arrived in Luanda. But I realized I could not go farther on my own — at least not in this country — and I was flattered that Kalunga saw me in the way I saw him, as a good traveling companion, someone fit to take into the bush.

On the day the Portuguese prime minister arrived from Lisbon to ask Angola for money to bail out his failed and bankrupt economy, Kalunga took me on his motorcycle to the Luanda train station at a place called Viana. We made inquiries — the times of the trains to Malanje, the cost. Two trains a week, cheap tickets, an easy trip.

"Are you sure you want to do this?" he asked teasingly.

"No. I want to think about it."

"Maybe the last train to *zona verde*." He was still teasing. Teasing is often a sign of trust, of friendship, of a bond.

We were still in sight of the city, with its buildings under construction, its many tall cranes, and the sound of bulldozers and jackhammers. It looked plausible enough as a city on the rise. But it was an illusion. Luanda was a city in decay. We rode out of Bairro Viana to the edge of a dense and ramshackle *musseque*. Better not go in too deeply, Kalunga said; his Kawasaki was new and powerful, just the sort of machine a gang of boys would love to steal. The idle watchful boys were like the idle watchful boys I had seen all over Angola; they had been my first glimpse of the country, the rappers and pesterers on the border at Santa Clara. Pretty girls sidled up to us and admired the motorcycle and flirted with Kalunga. Some girls were dancing with each other in front of a makeshift stall selling Angolan music. This Luanda slum was dense and labyrinthine, so we stayed with the bike, on the perimeter. Still, I could see it was a lively place — loud music, lots of chatter, hurrying crowds, and shrill, shrieking, giddy laughter.

Foreigners I had met mentioned the laughter. "They are a joyful people" was a frequent remark. One Englishman told me, "You sometimes see them jumping and doing handstands on the sidewalks." The leaping and the laughter did not seem mirthful to me, but rather frantic, like the overstimulation I'd seen in African cities. It was closer to hysteria or that sorry chattering you hear from someone on the verge of panic. It was at times like frenzy. I thought: This is the laughter in the shadow of the gallows, the sound of people who know they are doomed; this is the look of a place that is going to hell. This same hysteria is found in Thucydides's description of the plague in Athens: "Oppressed with the violence of the calamity, and not knowing what to do, men grew careless . . . and the great licentiousness . . . began."

Like the Athenians, the Angolans of the *musseque* acted as if doomsday was upon them: a shrieking, chaotic, reckless society on the brink of extinction. Not people in despair, but people dancing — doing the *kiduru* and the *kizomba,* as Kalunga explained of the pirouetting girls at the shantytown, and sometimes breaking into a jig as they walked. The city was thick with prostitutes, many of them refugees from the Congo, snatching at men at the Pub Royal and the Zanzibar. Most people were giggling crazily because they knew their number was up. That was how Angolan laughter sounded to me — insane and chattering and agonic, like an amplified death rattle. With disaster or death hanging over them, like the Athenians, "they thought to enjoy some little part of their lives."

Kalunga climbed on his motorcycle, but he didn't start it. He sat and stared at the city and said, "This is what the world will look like when it ends."

Two weeks later, Kalunga Lima died of a heart attack at his home in Lubango.

He had been scuba diving off Angola's southern coast a few days before his death, and that may have caused it, an embolism produced by a hyperbaric event. He had been working on a documentary about the coastal waters for Angola's national exhibit at Expo 2012 in Korea.

By then I had withdrawn from overpriced Luanda, and, procrastinating, I began to reconsider my onward journey.

17

What Am I Doing Here?

ALL ITS LAMPS BLAZING, its windows alight, its larval contours illuminated, the last train to Malanje had a glowworm's gleam, trembling in the dusty half-dark and heat of Luanda's Viana station, when Kalunga Lima had gestured to it and said, "Are you sure you want to do this?"

He was teasing, because since I'd met him he had pegged me as a procrastinator. Normally I am anything but: a leap in the dark is my usual mode of travel, and by the time I met him I had been on the road for many weeks. *He* was the procrastinator, in my opinion, an Angolan and longtime resident of Luanda who'd moved with his family to the provinces. Angola was doomed, he said, because of the few cheating the many. Kalunga had relocated to distant Lubango, the easier to escape the country by the simpler southern route when the chaos he expected arrived. And it occurred to me that many people shared his fears, that the slums of Luanda, like many in African cities I'd seen, were no more than transit camps for people wishing to flee.

My hesitation was much more of a reversal than he knew. I

was the man bewitched by the Chattanooga Choo Choo and the Patagonian Express and the Trans-Siberian, who had written, "Ever since childhood, I have seldom heard a train go by and not wished I was on it" — yet here was the brand-new Chinese-made train, lit up, on a recently restored line that could bear me in relative comfort east on a safari for 265 miles into *zona verde* — the green zone of Angola's bush, the site of the last few wild animals in the country and of the sort of village life that always seemed a consolation. My lifelong idea of supreme happiness was being a passenger on a train rattling through the night to a distant place unknown to me.

But I thought, *Not this time.* I had no desire to board the train. And, thinking it, I was joyous — a great relief to conclude that this was the end of my trip. *No more.* The same joy I had always felt on setting off on a long trip now visited me on this decision not to go any farther. *Not here, not now.*

It was then that Kalunga had taken me to the desperate *musseque* beyond Viana and, frowning at the loud music and squinting at the scuffling crowds and the shacks — the poverty, the twitching excitement bordering on frenzy, the hopelessness of it — had uttered the devastating pronouncement that stayed with me: "This is what the world will look like when it ends."

Struck by this doomsday vision, and saddened by his own doom so soon after that, I was left to ponder my next move. I knew that Malanje, the last stop on the railway line, was a dead end: no road led north from there. I'd have to return to hateful Luanda and take the coast road to a place called N'zeto. From the map I could not discern any onward road. I probably could not travel north at all except by air, and even if I spent weeks struggling by back roads to the border, my prize would be the Congolese river town of Matadi, a well-known hellhole. Then I would board a bus to Kinshasa, a rotting city much like Luanda — and rotting for the same reasons: a corrupt government rich on diamonds, gold, and mineral wealth, and on rarefied techniques of embezzlement and trade mispricing.

Rigged elections at this time had provoked rioting in Kinshasa's streets and a fierce police presence. After that, Brazzaville, Pointe-Noire, and a transit of the squalid cities of the coast, because the Congolese interior was largely made up of no-go areas. Of course, I could put my head down and travel farther, but I knew what I would find: decaying cities, hungry crowds, predatory youths, and people abandoned by their governments, people who saw every foreigner as someone they could hit up for money, since it was apparent that only foreigners seemed to care about the welfare of Africans.

Because I was traveling overland, what lay before me was a grubby and unrewarding itinerary of West African cities — that is, West African shantytowns. No poverty on earth could match the poverty in an African shantytown, and no other place was so bereft of hope. In an African village, poverty was a relative term. I knew that from the humble villages I'd seen in Botswana and Namibia and the Angolan interior, places where people survived, as they always had, in a subsistence economy, growing what they needed, bartering extra food for what they couldn't grow or buy, living in mud huts, using a slit-trench latrine, practicing slash-and-burn agriculture. It was a life of fetching and carrying and making do: walking an hour for water, washing in the river, scavenging for firewood, killing the occasional chicken, living hand to mouth — not flourishing but eking out an existence in meagerly productive routines.

This hard life in a rural area could not compare with the dog's life in a shantytown, where gardening was impossible, water was scarce, and fuel — firewood or charcoal — usually unavailable; where there was no muddling through except by a menial job, casual labor, or whoring, or handouts, or crime. But, this being Angola, it was the rich, and only the rich, who appeared to me sluttish and criminal. In the bush there existed the possibility of renewal: a new season, a new crop, a new water source. This extreme rural poverty could be relieved by modes of survival, many of them traditional strategies. But in a city slum, survival was not guaranteed, traditions did not apply, and a cash economy made people peculiarly deprived and rapacious.

The thieving was a tendency that some Marxist economists forgave (Eric Hobsbawm for one, in his book *Bandits*), by explaining it as the reflex of wronged or oppressed peasants practicing "social banditry," the politicized poor redressing inequality by stealing from the rich. My experience of credit card fraud in Namibia might have been construed as the act of a social bandit using high technology instead of a machete, but that did not make me feel any better. It left me nearly broke and somewhat demoralized.

Yet the loss of money was nothing compared to the loss of friends. Three people I had gotten to know pretty well, three men I had admired in their passion for Africa, had died — young Nathan violently crushed by an elephant, Kalunga way before his time from a heart attack, and Rui da Câmara, whose skull had been smashed by an intruder. The deaths of others in a time and a landscape you yourself inhabited cannot but remind you of your own mortality.

Travel, especially solitary travel, is a morbid business. "In traveling one is always accompanied by the retinue of Death or his batman," Henry Miller writes in *Remember to Remember*. It is a passage well suited to a road trip through Africa. "The quiet village where the river flows so peacefully, the very spot where you choose to dream in, is usually the seat of ancient carnage. What stirs one to reverie is the blood that was spilled more copiously than wine . . . the historical recitative whistles through the whitened bones of somnolent ruins."

During my last few long trips I often thought that I might die. I was not alone in that fear; it is the rational conjecture of most travelers I know, especially the ones about my age. The fears of some of my traveling friends were justified: a number of them had died on the road or become terribly ill. "He died doing what he loved" is a sentiment that might console a survivor, but if the victim had been offered a choice beforehand, what would he or she have done?

I sometimes imagined myself dismembered in a car crash in the bush. Often, in an overcrowded bus in Africa, I thought of nothing but death, and hating the trip I let out a ghastly laugh when I thought of anyone saying over my battered corpse, "He died doing what he loved."

In Cape Town at the start of my journey—though I superstitiously avoided mentioning it to anyone—I had dreamed of ending it in Timbuktu. I was headed in that general direction. I had traced a provisional itinerary on my Africa map that led me northerly, zigzagging from Cape Town to Angola, and (somehow) from there, via the Congo and Gabon and Cameroon, through Nigeria and onward to the fabled city in Mali.

All maps are misleading, and Africa maps are more misleading than most. At one time they were alarming for the great empty areas labeled *Cannibals,* but these days they were inaccurate for the roads crisscrossing them. Many of the wide multicolored thoroughfares boldly shown on the map of Angola did not exist, and the *H* symbol designating a hotel was a fiction. It is well known that the Congo has very few usable roads; in spite of its wealth, it is a trackless country, and because of that an insecure one. Yet I had always held to the belief that with enough time you can go anywhere. You just travel slowly, picking your way along, taking detours, walking where necessary, bumming rides, living the stop-and-go life of a vagrant.

This method works in most places. It does not work in Africa—though it did once. The followers in the footsteps of H. M. Stanley through the Congo, of David Livingstone through Angola, and of Samuel Baker through Sudan quickly discover that the trip is impossible in the Africa of today. The hinterlands are now controlled by heavily armed warlords, mercenaries, rebel armies, hostile tribes, secessionists, and religious fanatics—hard-line Islamists (Boko Haram, Ansar Dine) or crazed Christians (the Lord's Resistance

Army). Tim Butcher, who in *Blood River* recounts trying to re-cre-ate Stanley's overland trans-Africa trip, from east to west, ended up flying.

I could have flown, but what's the point? You don't see anything from thirty thousand feet. And now I had an inkling of what I would find — cities that were indistinguishable from one another in their squalor and decrepitude. In the broken unspeakable cities of sub-Saharan Africa, the poor — the millions, the majority — ignored by their governments, live a scavenging existence in nearly iden-tical conditions, in shacks, amid a litter of Chinese-manufactured household junk — plastic basins and buckets — and wearing Chinese-made clothes. They might have a cell phone, but in most cases it is little more than a maddening toy. They all suffer from the same inadequacies — food shortages, no plumbing, no clinics, no schools, no security — and the same illnesses — cholera, malaria, TB, and HIV/AIDS. They wait without much hope for deliverance, if not transformation. Even small, sedate, house-proud Windhoek had Katutura and its squatter camps; lovely Cape Town had Langa, Lwandle, Gugs, and other townships, equally bleak.

Though I was discouraged by the obstacles and appalled by the deaths of Nathan, Kalunga, and Rui, I had clung to my secret dream of traveling onward from Angola and ending up in Timbuktu. But soon two events shattered that dream. A secessionist coup by a faction of low-level army officers in Mali, fueled by rants from Al Qaeda in the Maghreb, meant that Mali was divided into two coun-tries. Timbuktu in the north (a region as large as France) was now a stronghold of Islamic indignation and threats. Foreign travelers were being kidnapped and held for ransom. One had been killed. In time, this power struggle might be sorted out, I was told, but at the moment the fabled city was closed to the outside world.

Nigeria posed a more serious problem, but also a north-south divide. The Muslim-dominated states in the north — directly on my route — were tormented by the Boko Haram movement. The name in the Hausa language means "Western education is sinful." The group's official name is Jama'atu Ahlis Sunna Lidda'awati wal-Jihad, which in Arabic means "People Committed to the Propagation of the Prophet's Teachings and Jihad." In these northern states in Nigeria, ruled by *Sharia* law, the Boko Haram jihadis attacked Christians, Christian churches, non-Islamic schools, and just about anyone wearing Western clothes — trouser-wearing Nigerians and foreigners too.

I first heard about this hostile organization during my stay in Lubango, and had made notes to myself on its looming threat on the Day of the Dead, when I began seriously to wonder whether my trip was worth the trouble. Ever since I'd crossed the Angolan border, the question "What am I doing here?" had flashed in my mind. It was not a lament; it was a puzzled inquiry — most thoughtful people on earth ask themselves this question on a regular basis.* I had kept going, as this narrative shows, hoping for an answer. But around the time I was making my decision to put my head down and take the road north, Boko Haram became active again.

A tortuously argued op-ed in the *New York Times* by the historian and Africanist Jean Herskovits, "In Nigeria, Boko Haram Is Not the Problem," explained that Boko Haram was "a peaceful Islamic splinter group" that had been exploited "for electoral purposes." Video footage of the violent death in Nigerian police custody in 2009 of a Muslim cleric had radicalized the movement, though Herskovits pointed out that the "root cause of violence and anger in both the north and south of Nigeria is endemic poverty and hopelessness."

She warned that, not mullahs and zealots, but criminal syndicates claiming to represent Boko Haram were terrorizing Christians, setting fire to their homes, and bombing hotels and markets, all to

---

* It was Arthur Rimbaud's in Aden, in 1884, unemployed, writing home and lamenting in the heat. "What a deplorable existence I lead in this absurd climate and under what frightful conditions! How boring! How stupid life is! What am I doing here?" (quoted in Jean Marie Carré, *A Season in Hell*, 1931).

destabilize the country. We should not be too quick to label this Islamic terrorism, she wrote, or to hasten into "a rush to judgment that obscures Nigeria's complex reality." The complex reality was a narrow-minded president named Goodluck Jonathan, a southerner and a Christian, his corrupt politicians, and the Nigerian people, growing poorer and more numerous daily.

A rush to judgment was the last thing on my mind. But what about the reported violence? After I read the piece, which smacked of special pleading, I kept close track of Boko Haram outrages. Six days after the op-ed piece appeared, 20 people were killed by jihadis claiming to be Boko Haram–related. A week later, 174 murders, and two weeks after that a dozen more, all sectarian. Nigerian troops became involved, killing 20 Boko Haramists. And then, at weekly intervals for the next three months, there were suicide bombs, arson attacks on schools and churches, and targeted killings — the murder of Christians in Maiduguri and Jos. Thousands of deaths by now in the cities and on the bus routes of my proposed trip.

Professor Herskovits had argued for patience but perhaps had not anticipated the multiple massacres that followed her strangely mollifying piece. More recently, a number of scholars have warned the U.S. government against branding Boko Haram a terrorist organization because doing so would "internationalize the sect" and raise its profile, making it bolder. As a Nigerian terrorist group (or a collection of criminal gangs), the thinking went, it was dangerous only to Nigerians.

But, it seemed, dangerous to Western travelers too. The scholars' line of reasoning (they wanted, among other things, to be in close touch with the Boko Haramists) seemed to me tendentious, self-serving, and unhelpful. If the root cause of the killings was not Islamic jihadism but "poverty and hopelessness," there would be many more murders, because Nigeria was poor and hopeless. And for a traveler like me who had no choice but to pass overland through northern Nigeria, it hardly mattered whether I was threatened by a Western-hating jihadi or the armed members of a criminal syndicate, both of whom used the name Boko Haram.

Travelers often become celebrated for risking trips through dangerous places. I had taken risks in my time, and endured my own version of the anthropophagi, and the men whose heads do grow beneath their shoulders. And so I was faced with the ruined Congolese cities and the fanaticism of northern Nigeria. It struck me that if I proceeded on my way, it would have been a travel stunt, like riding a pogo stick through the desert. A daredevil effort, and to what end?

"Is it worth it?" Apsley Cherry-Garrard asks at the end of *The Worst Journey in the World,* in talking about the doomed polar trek by Robert Falcon Scott in the Antarctic. Is life worth risking for a feat, or losing for your country? To face a thing because it was a feat, and only a feat, was not very attractive to Scott; it had to contain an additional object — knowledge.

Traveling north through chaos — what would I find that I had not already learned? As an oil state, Nigeria much resembled Angola in its corruption and destitution. Lagos and Kinshasa were larger versions of Luanda. The rural areas on my route were blighted: idle youths, ailing villagers, beggars, rappers. The lessons I had learned so far were that an itinerary of urban squalor is unrewarding; travel is difficult, and sometimes impossible; a foreign traveler represents wealth, an opportunity for the thief or "social bandit"; and the repetition of squalor is ultimately so futile in its frightfulness as to be banal in the retelling. I imagined my onward journey to be no more than spirited slumming, the usual ordeal of rank smells and bad food, but without a redeeming feature, a toxic tour through the bowels of West Africa, along the Côte d'Ordure.

It takes a certain specialist's dedication to travel in squalid cities and fetid slums, among the utterly dependent poor, who have lost nearly all their traditions and most of their habitat. You need first of all the skill and the temperament of a proctologist. Such a person, deft in rectal exams, is as essential to medicine as any other specialist, yet it is only the resolute few who opt to examine the condition of the human body by staring solemnly—fitted out like spelunkers, with scopes and tubes and gloves—up its fundament and trawling through its intestines, making the grand colonic tour. Some travel has its parallels, and some travelers might fit the description as rectal specialists of topography, joylessly wandering the guts and entrails of the earth and reporting on their decrepitude. I am not one of them.

Forty years ago, when I planned my *Great Railway Bazaar* trip, I had considered taking the train from Turkey into Iraq, traveling south from Mosul to Baghdad and onward to Basra, where I would cross into Iran. "What's Basra like?" I asked a friend who'd been there. "It's not the asshole of the world," he said, "it's eighty miles up it." So I went to Iran by a different route, and I have spent my traveling life avoiding such places. What had I learned? That proctology pretty much describes the experience of traveling from one African city to another, especially the horror cities of urbanized West Africa.

But the scientific inclination is not enough. Some artfulness is required. To chronicle this anguish, you need to be a traveler with a taste for ruins, someone who takes pleasure in them, as Giambattista Piranesi (1720–1778) did in eighteenth-century Rome. He was the inspired artist whose wayward brilliance lay in depicting the cracked remains of an ancient civilization, meticulous etchings of ruination, down to the last decayed detail. His dark etchings of crumbled, toppled-over, and scattered Rome were sold as souvenirs for visitors to the city. Travelers at the time, making the Grand Tour—English aristocrats, and writers such as Smollett and Goethe—seized on them, because Piranesi had found a way of bringing a vision of lost glory, even of splendor, to these scenes of antique devastation.

That was what was needed, proctologist and Piranesi, science and art — a strong stomach and a fascination with decay, and disorder, and hopelessness, and township anarchy.

There is something constricting and claustrophobic about the traveler's being limited to cloacal ruins and urban dead ends. I had become a traveler to be free to wander, and on some of my most difficult trips I had felt liberated by the space and light. I have seldom been a traveler in cities. I have generally avoided them — all cities, not just in Africa, but also in Asia and Latin America. I am by nature a city hater, finding urban life nasty, hidden, and hard to penetrate. To me, even the greatest cities are places of loneliness and confinement where people are strangers to each other.

Why would I wish to travel through blight and disorder only to report on the same ugliness and misery? The blight is not peculiar to Africa. The squalid slum in Luanda is not only identical to the squalid slum in Cape Town and Jo'burg and Nairobi; they all greatly resemble, in their desperation, their counterparts in the rest of the world. A squatter camp in California is in every detail a duplication of a squatter camp in Africa, and worthy of close examination by a traveling writer for that reason. But I am not that writer, neither so committed to discomfort nor so noble-hearted.

The earth is becoming intensely citified. "The megacity will be at the heart of twenty-first-century geography," Robert D. Kaplan writes in *The Revenge of Geography*. But the world I grew up in was not a world of big cities, and I began my traveling life hoping to find differences in landscapes and people, not repeated versions of the metropolitan experience. I don't mock the effort. I am not equal to the task. The traveler in cities needs to understand cities better than I do and not be disgusted by their chronic deficits; that traveler needs to care more, to be more expert in some areas, more innocent in others, more hopeful. Anyway, the successful city dweller is gifted in coping with the horrors, the stalkers, the foul smells, the loud music, the casual rudeness, the foxy habits of taxi drivers, the absence of trees, the menacing faces, the noise, the squawk of voices — many of them screams; the rumble and whine that is unceasing — the night drone too, along with the nighttime light; the physicality of it all, especially the closeness of the crowds, the lack of elbow room, the daily experience of bumping against other people, which is a constant violation of your space and your body, the physical rubbing against strangers that amounts to frottage, known colloquially in New York as "subway grinding."

That life is not for me, either to travel in or write about. It has nothing to do with my age. Now Africa is a continent of huge, unsustainable cities, and the majority of Africans are themselves city dwellers, having forfeited their poor villages for much poorer slums. It is impossible to travel overland in Africa by public transport — as I did from Cairo to Cape Town, and now from Cape Town to Luanda — and not make a circuit of the cities, awful places where there is nothing to learn except what you knew already from the worst neighborhoods of your own country.

One remedy for the revulsion in such travel is that of the French aphorist Nicolas Chamfort, who wrote, "Swallow a toad in the morning and you will encounter nothing more disgusting the rest of the day." I have spent a life of travel sleeping in strange beds and dining on sinister food, and I have only mildly objected, because it is in the nature of travel to be uncomfortable, if not scared silly. But insult is another matter, and gratuitous insult is objectionable for being unrewarding. You can stay home and be insulted; you don't need to go ten thousand miles to be jeered at. There is no revelation in being yelled at, heckled, cursed, or pestered, as began to happen with greater frequency on my trip. I think this harassment is the fate of many women traveling alone in male-dominated countries — most countries, that is — and I sympathize with women, usually burdened with a child or a backpack, for having to endure it.

It is undignified and tedious for anyone to have to battle his way onto a dirty bus. Yet I pitched in and found that pushing and being shoved and biffed by impatient oafs is not the worst of it. If, at the end of the journey, after nine or ten hours of travel on the miserable bus, with its piss stops and children with the squitters and chickens dying in baskets and shouting passengers and its inept driver — finally needing to elbow your way off the bus — if, then, the traveler sees nothing new, it is a pointless journey too, and no one would want to read about it. I found more and more, in these cheated places with diminished resources, that I had to fight for a seat, and I became less and less willing to do so. The single woman, the older traveler, the weak-looking or undersized stranger, the loner, the wanderer at night — all are taken for easy prey, and bullied or fleeced. The only lesson is: *caveat viator,* traveler beware, and perhaps ask again, "What am I doing here?"

My answer did not amount to a manifesto for staying home but rather an essay on other directions, since there are so many places on earth worthy of a traveler's effort and more likely to evoke a traveler's bliss. I am not too old for this, I am more patient than ever, but I am temperamentally unsuited to chronicling the gutter life of the African slum that necessitates my swallowing a toad every morning. There is nothing to write about it that I have not written already, and at length. Such places are transit camps filled with people who have been abandoned by their fattened and corrupt governments. Such places might, as Kalunga Lima predicted, one day explode in a blaze of fury, the spontaneous combustion of enraged, cheated people. I know enough of the score-settling and fickleness of uprisings to avoid them.

But I have no idea what will happen to these sprawling cities and slum areas. My feeling has always been that the truth is prophetic, and if I write accurately about the present, seeing things as they are, aspects of the future will be suggested. I was somewhat heartened by the progress made in ten years in the townships of Cape Town, how the shantytowns and squatter camps had been upgraded to habitable settlements. This was largely due to the efforts of sympathetic and innovative well-wishers, both South African and foreign agencies: the installation of water and electricity, the improvement of houses and roads, the novelty of indoor plumbing, the building of schools.

I was enlightened. So this is how a city grows, how cities — something of a rarity in the early life of the populated world — have grown through history. It is impossible to say when the first city appeared on earth, and it is probably true, as the historian J. M. Roberts wrote, that "more than any other institution the city has provided the critical mass which produces civilization and that it has fostered innovation better than any other environment so far." Africa is a showcase of cities in their messy infancy — dangerous, unhealthy, corrupt, lawless, improvisational, and still growing. Modernity is conspicuous in Africa nearly always as blight, the disfigurement of cities and landscapes, a great and overwhelming ugliness.

Yet the upgrading of a shantytown to a place of tidy huts is not the end of the story. There is no end. I knew that when, after my visits to Khayelitsha and Guguletu, I saw the new, exhausted, and wide-eyed arrivals from the provinces. In an unregulated country, mismanaged and badly governed, there is no limit to the growth of a slum. Every improved slum area attracts a new shantytown, every new shantytown attracts a squatter camp, every squatter camp attracts more people leaving their traditional homelands for an uncertain life in the city, among the multitudes of unemployed. There is a point beyond which squalor cannot sink any lower, or get any worse, and that is the point these African cities have reached. People live in them in a spirit of renunciation. An African city of this sort is an agglomeration of desperate people, a static mob that feels safer in its dense numbers.

"You didn't see the wealthy areas!" I will be told. "You didn't see the great houses!" But I did see them. I peeped through the perimeter walls and saw the sentry boxes, the private clubs, and the gated communities. I was welcomed in some of them, ate and drank in their delightful rooms—"Do have some more kudu carpaccio" —and I found that really these were tiny enclaves, mere precious islands in a sea of wreckage.

My horror interest in the futureless, dystopian, world-gone-wrong, *Mad Max* Africa of child soldiers, street gangs, reeking slums, refuse heaps, utter despair, misplaced belief, new-age cargo cults, and bungled rescue attempts—this horror interest is rooted in detachment. It is unworthy, no more than idle, slightly sickening curiosity over modernity in its most odious form, the sort that technology worsens by making people lazier and greedier, tantalizing them with visions of the unattainable, driving many of them to be refugees and bludgers in Europe and America. We have bestowed on Africa just enough of the disposable junk of the modern world to create in African cities a junkyard replica of the West, a mirror image of our own failures—but no better than that. Writing about it, choosing the urban landscape and urban misery as a subject, is something for an obituarist. Such a vision, or a visit, represents everything in travel I have always wished to escape.

I am not an Afro-pessimist, though. Apart from the obvious unchecked proliferation of people and the inevitable disappearance or extinction of wild animals, it is not certain what Africa's future will be. But what is happening in Africa now is also happening with greater subtlety in the rest of the world: the diminution of resources, the vanishing of work, the growth of urban areas. The difference is that Africa's population is growing much faster than that of any other continent. There are estimated to be a billion Africans now. Within four decades it will be two billion people—most of them living in cities, in countries without industry, without sufficient food or water or energy, countries that are poorly governed and insecure. It is projected that in a few years Nigeria will grow to a population of three hundred million, in an area the size of Arizona and New Mexico. Donor aid can take some credit for what little infrastructure exists. But donor aid and self-interested foreign governments and "rogue aid" from China and North Korea—money proffered with no questions about human rights—all these are largely responsible for the persistence of bad governments, too.

The murderous, self-elected, megalomaniacal head of state with the morals of a fruit fly, with his decades in power, along with his vain, flitting shopaholic wife, his hangers-on, and his goon squad, is an obscene feature of African life that is not likely to disappear. When I complained to a bureaucrat from Burkina Faso (because that country, too, was on my proposed route) about the persistence of tyrants, she raised her voice and said in a froggy accent, "It is the *réalité!*"—because her own country was governed by a long-standing (twenty-five years and counting) clinger to office. It is not a reality at all, but a fantasy of power promoted by the tyrant.

Most politicians believe their own lies, but the foreign-aid givers make them worse. Take the corrupting forms of foreign aid away and popular desperation might become productive, rebellion leading to elections that might improve matters in the long term. A better alternative to the endless gift-giving is investment. Yet investment is more trouble than the grandstanding presentation of donor aid, requiring more accountability, more humility, more patience, and greater risks—and, of course, less colorful mythologizing of the effort, the photo ops with destitute children.

Colonialism oppressed and subverted Africans and remade them as scavengers, pleaders, and servants—and turned some of them into rebels. The colonial-mimicry of post-independence Africa has been a continuation of this—more scavengers, more pleaders and panhandlers. And the consequence of each new civil war or outbreak of religious strife or warlordism is that there is more willful damage to repair—more land mines left behind, more burned-out villages, more amputees, refugees, and orphans.

There will always be lions and elephants and impalas in Africa, because there will always be one sort of game park or another. If many animals are eaten or their habitats destroyed—or if, like the rhino, the wild dog, the quagga, and the giant sable antelope, they face extinction — there will be private reserves and fenced-off game farms where other large animals can be viewed. This is the case today in South Africa, where for a price you are guaranteed an African experience, even if it is no more than the commercial thrill of a glorified theme park that offers the illusion of what Africa once was — if not an Eden filled with animals and people living in relative harmony, then a still-forested land of market towns and viable cities and mud-walled villages, with its soul intact.

But the giraffe on the game farm and the ridable elephant on the bush concession are not for me either. Once you have seen animals in the wild, it is impossible to enjoy the sight of them behind an enclosure, no matter how vast the enclosure. "What's the difference between this and a zoo?" Trevor shrewdly inquired in Etosha, in Namibia, as we sat behind the fence at Okaukuejo with the hundreds of German tourists watching the floodlit eland drinking at the waterhole. And Trevor knew: We had seen all of this before. Nothing to report.

Time is a factor in travel, one of the most crucial, though it didn't matter when I first started traveling as a youth, and later as a middle-aged man: I believed I had all the time in the world then. My travel was open-ended. "I'm not sure when I'll be back," I used to say to my family. I vanished into countries and was so far out of touch I seemed to evaporate. I had no idea where I was going, but it was a joy to be on the move, and I kept finding places where I wanted to live — a great incentive in travel, the sense that I would discover a new home.

I recall traveling through Afghanistan and down the Khyber Pass to the lovely town of Peshawar, thinking: I could live here! How wrong I was. Peshawar became a city of refugees, fanatics, mujahideen, suicide bombers, and a bazaar of the Central Asian drug and arms trade. But I was tempted to drop out in other places in the world—dropping out seemed to be one of the temptations in travel, that I would remain in Bali or Costa Rica or Thailand and never come back. I had not yet discovered what Camus wrote in his *Notebooks, 1942–1951:* "When a man has learned—and not on paper—how to remain alone with his suffering, how to overcome his longing to flee, the illusion that others may share, then he has little left to learn."

Suffering has no value, but you have to suffer in order to know that. I never found it easy to travel, yet the difficulty in it made it satisfying because it seemed in that way to resemble the act of writing—a groping in the dark, wandering into the unknown, coming to understand the condition of strangeness. In travel, as Philip Larkin says in his poem "The Importance of Elsewhere," strangeness makes sense. Yet the more I traveled, the greater my homing instinct. As I grow older, the consolations of home take on a deeper meaning.

Although I lived for more than six continuous years in Africa, and kept returning, I resisted the temptation to stay for an extended period. I never met anyone who said, as the Dutch missionaries in long-ago Malawi often did, "I plan to be buried here." I once played with the idea of founding a school in the Malawi bush, until I realized that it was not for me to patronize Africans by running a school for them, but for Africans themselves to take on that responsibility. There are still outsiders who are prospectors, adventurers, and entrepreneurs in Africa, and I know some of them, but none are in it for the long haul, and all have an exit strategy. It concentrates the mind to be in a place where you know you have no future.

Time means so much more to me now than it did. These days, keenly aware of wasted time, I hear the clock ticking more insistently. I hate the idea of travel as déjà vu. Show me something new, something different, something changed, something wonderful, something weird! There has to be revelation in spending long periods of time in travel, otherwise it is more waste. Another effect of the deaths of Nathan and Rui da Câmara and Kalunga was this very insight. Was I where I wanted to be, doing what I loved? The answer was sometimes Yes, sometimes Where am I? But more often it was What am I doing here?

Because all cities are possessed by an incapacity to be known, and so must be invented or imagined, these were questions I asked in cities. I never questioned being on safari in the *zona verde*. The bush was Africa's salvation, and mine. Camus exhorted himself in his *Notebooks:* "Write the story of a contemporary cured of his heartbreaks solely by long contemplation of a landscape."

It is the natural landscape that I have always yearned for — and human figures in that landscape. I cannot stand the thought of traveling from city to city, and cities were mainly what awaited me on the last leg of this ultimate safari. Long contemplation of a landscape was once the very definition of a trip through Africa. No longer.

Nor was my old passion to get away at any cost still driving me. "Starting in a hollow log of wood — some thousand miles up a river, with only an infinitesimal prospect of returning — I ask myself, 'Why?'" So Richard Burton wrote in the Congo, in a letter to a friend. He answered himself, as I once did in my way, "And the only echo is 'damned fool! . . . The Devil drives.'" But Burton was forty-two at the time. I was once a forty-two-year-old hearty in a dugout canoe on a river to nowhere. When he was nearer my age (Burton died in Trieste, at sixty-nine) he was more cautious, no longer a risk taker, but gouty and bronchitic, and happiest at home, indulged by his wife, his days spent fossicking among the books of erotica in his library.

"A question is commonly put to explorers: 'Why could you not go further when you had already succeeded in going so far?'" Francis Galton wrote this in the preface to his *Narrative of an Explorer in Tropical South Africa*, because he headed home somewhat abruptly.

"And the answer to this is, that several independent circumstances concur in stopping a man after he has been travelling for a certain time and distance."

Galton then reviews these circumstances: the refitting of the expedition, finding more money, learning another language, studying customs, finding helpful information, making new plans. "But [the traveler's] energies are reduced, and his means become inadequate to the task, and therefore no alternative is left him but to return [home] while it is still possible for him to do so. It is therefore not to be expected that any large part of the vast unexplored region before us will yield its secrets to a single traveller, but, rather, that they will become known step by step through various successive discoveries . . . It is probable that for years to come there will still remain ample room in Africa for men inclined for adventure to carry out in them, if nowhere else, the metier of explorers."

That was also how I felt. Let someone else (proctologist, Piranesi, foolhardy wanderer, someone with time to kill) continue where I left off, and the rest of Africa might yield its secrets to this traveler. In my rigorous experiences with space and time I had just one guinea pig to torture — myself. And now, self-reprieved, back in Cape Town, revisiting some of the places I'd seen earlier, ending my trip, I was happy.

On my last day I woke as usual, meditated a little, took my gout pills, and wrote some notes over breakfast. Then I gathered my clothes, everything except what I stood up in. I was sick of the clothes I had worn every day of my trip. I made a bundle of them, with my silly hat on top, took the train to Khayelitsha, and, randomly stopping a woman at a market stall, asked her if she wanted them. She wasn't surprised at the sudden offer, a perfect stranger hoisting an armload of old clothes at her. She reacted as if this sort of thing happened all the time and accepted them gratefully, saying, "These will fit my husband." With a kindly smile she advised me to be careful in the township, to keep my hand on my wallet, and to leave as quickly as possible.

Not the end of travel, or of reckless essaying—there is no end to those for me—but the end of this trip and this sort of travel, marinated in politics and urban wreckage, where the only possible narrative I see (and am unwilling to write) is an anatomy of melancholy. *There is a world elsewhere.*

What am I doing here? I knew at last. I am preparing to leave. On the red clay roads of the African bush among poor and overlooked people, I often thought of the poor in America, living in just the same way, precariously, on the red roads of the Deep South, on low farms, poor pelting villages, sheepcotes, and mills—people I knew only from books, as I'd first known Africans—and I felt beckoned home.

+ rich envy town - Hollywood

8 9 50 73 81 252-3 254